Phillip Hodson

Britain's first radio and television agony uncle, Phillip Hodson has been a professional psychotherapist for over 20 years. Author of six books including *365 Ways to Have a Happy Sex Life* (HarperCollins), *Men, An Investigation into the Emotional Male* (BBC), *Growing Pains* (BBC), *What Kids Really Want to Know About Sex* (Robson) and *Wagner* (Weidenfeld), Phillip Hodson has written problem pages for 11 magazines and four UK national newspapers and has been a columnist for *Psychology Today*, *Family Circle*, *She*, *OK Weekly* as well as *First Magazine* in the USA. Widely known on UK television, especially on BBC Daytime and 'Going Live', he additionally presented the much-acclaimed 'Phillip Hodson Hour' on LBC radio for over 15 years, has been a Radio 2 regular for three years and presents his own Sunday evening programme on Talk Radio 1089am. Phillip has made numerous award-winning, management training films on counselling techniques in industry. His first *Cosmo* features appeared in the early 1980s so he's been in a perfect position to give an overview of the changing trends in love, sex and relationships. He was a *Cosmopolitan* Contributing Editor until last year. Phillip has a private psychotherapy practice and lives in North London and Gloucestershire with counsellor and best-selling author Anne Hooper.

Jacky Fleming is a best-selling cartoonist. Her books, *Be a Bloody Train Driver*, *Never Give Up*, *Falling in Love* and *Hello Boys* are published by Penguin.

COSMOPOLITAN
GUIDE TO LOVE, SEX & RELATIONSHIPS

Phillip Hodson

HEADLINE

First published in 1997
by HEADLINE BOOK PUBLISHING

10 9 8 7 6 5 4 3 2 1

ISBN 0 7472 7780 X

Typeset by Avon Dataset Ltd, Bidford-on-Avon, Warks

Printed and bound in Great Britain by
Mackays of Chatham PLC, Chatham, Kent

HEADLINE BOOK PUBLISHING
A division of Hodder Headline PLC
338 Euston Road
London NW1 3BH

To my three sons
Barnaby, Joel and Alexander
in case they have daughters

Contents

Foreword

Ever since its launch in the early seventies, *Cosmopolitan* has been both the vanguard and barometer of bright young women everywhere. Sensing the mood of the moment, the magazine has unflinchingly reflected women's interests and concerns. This has been particularly true when it comes to relationships. No other magazine has understood so well the dynamics and complexities of our dealings with people – our desires and longings, our insecurities and needs, our challenges and triumphs.

Cosmopolitan understands women and their relationships with men. Over the past decade, both women's and men's lives have changed enormously, but throughout these changes, *Cosmopolitan* has been the young woman's stalwart friend, guiding, advising and celebrating with her through the complexities of modern living.

Twenty-five years on, *Cosmopolitan*'s understanding of relationships and how they work remain as astute as ever. And as we move towards the millennium, I know *Cosmopolitan* will continue to lead the way, encouraging and supporting young women well into the twenty-first century.

Mandi Norwood

Acknowledgements

I want to thank Emma Dally of the National Magazine Company for her continued and enthusiastic support; Mandi Norwood and staff for their encouragement; Lindsay Symons for her careful editing; Linda Thompson for proof-reading; Kesta Desmond and Joel Levy without whom the typescript would have been a lot shorter; Justine Mark for her questions; Jacky Fleming for her perfect cartoons and Anne Hooper for her love and friendship and many answers. Thanks to my clients for teaching me what I did not know. And to *Cosmo*, down the years, for getting women to stand up and be counted. The mistakes in the book are mine. My only excuse is that they've taken many years to make.

Introduction

The Cosmopolitan Guide to Love, Sex & Relationships marks the 25th birthday of a magazine famous for changing the way women have regarded their emotional and sexual lives. Since the Seventies, 'Cosmo' has offered a sensible platform for a brand of practical feminism. This was never the doctrinaire gospel of 'having it all' but rather an encouraging vision of the possibilities available to this generation of women for the very first time. A young woman today can become an airline pilot with two children, enjoy a commitment to politics and fun while remaining both female and feminine. All it takes is energy, planning and grit   plus the right magazine subscription.

Freedom from female stereotypes is only part of 'Cosmo's' philosophy. Down the years, all the editors have taken an open-minded stand on sex and love. As a result, the dragon of unthinking Puritanism was slain long ago. 'Cosmo' expected people to become explicit, to ask for what they wanted with honesty and courage.

Overall, this is a remarkably exciting and challenging moment to be young and female. One of the book's important considerations is that equal friendships now exist between the sexes, again for the very first time. Men don't always expect women to come across sexually; or to marry early. The average age of first marriage has been pushed up to 27. Modern women would be offended to be mistaken for mere sexual pickings.

Even so, today's 20-somethings live in sexually difficult times. Love may be freer but this is the age of recession, soap opera and AIDS. Some young people started going steady at 10. A decade ago, they would have waited till they were 16. Girls of 11 want to know how to French kiss. Boys of 12 want to 'get off with their girlfriends'. A magazine such as 'Cosmo' has to pick up the pieces of this early social pressure. The

Cosmopolitan Guide attempts to finish the jigsaw, putting in place the most detailed sexual insights and explanations, not from the mundane standpoint of biology and plumbing but in terms of the fascinating psychological interplay of love and sex with relationships.

To take six examples:

- Why do some of us always fall in love with the wrong people?
- How can you tell if your relationship *isn't* working?
- Why is fear an aphrodisiac when anxiety is not?
- How can you endlessly reinvent the act of love to achieve the continuous orgasm – called 'status orgasmus'?
- Is it true that sex has become *less* sexy since the advent of the Pill?
- What's the best way to blow a man's mind?

Answers – inside.

Yes, these are sexually difficult times. But then again the times always are! I am bound to be asked that hoary old question: why write another sex book? Well, apart from insisting that this is much more than a manual and my personal approach is different, I think each generation needs to discover love and sex for itself, to make the traditional mistakes, to find contemporary solutions, to establish individual moral and sexual lifestyles and to select from past knowledge and current wisdom the ideas which they personally find most useful. History in this sense is *always* being rewritten. I wish my readers joy in the journey.

For the last 25 years, *Cosmopolitan* has been the young woman's vade mecum, guiding her footsteps through every phase of her discovery of the enticing worlds of work and love. 'Cosmo girls' are clever, active, thinking, idealistic, well-read, self-made as well as sensual. The monthly edition is eagerly awaited by 'Cosmo's' millions of loyal readers worldwide, and unlike other women's magazines enjoys an ongoing life throughout the month, treated more like a book than a journal and read continuously until the next 'Cosmo' hits the streets.

But sometimes twelve times a year is not enough.

Chapter One

What's Love Got to Do With It?

Health warning

Love can give you as much pain as pleasure. People die for love, killing themselves and others. Love causes mental and physical illness. *Love's middle name is trouble.* The price of what we want – having our love returned – includes drudgery, deception and the risks of unwanted pregnancy.

Love was originally invented by nature to make us have babies. It's a sort of biological computer programme. There's no Microsoft label, however, just our genes tripping our hormones, telling us to change from 11-year-olds fascinated by horses into 15-year-olds desperate for sex: Love is a curse and a redemption. We suffer for it but cannot live without it. So this first chapter is about survival.

DIFFERENT TYPES OF LOVE

When falling in love, people talk as if they'd been shot by a magic bullet. People also speak about falling in love as if the consequences were uniformly predictable. While for some it means proposing marriage, for others it means having first sex, or better sex, or no sex, or a baby, or terminating the relationship altogether because it's too intense. Cupid rules? I think not. Love has a hundred different faces. There are endless ways to say 'I love you'. But pronounce the magic words and most people are none the wiser.

For Gail love means 'I will be faithful.' For Raymond, it means 'I'm having a good time.' For Sue, it means 'I'll kill you if you ever leave me.' For George, it means 'I hope she'll take her clothes off soon.' For Jayne, it means 'I think this is the

I'm in LOVE

reciprocal and inspiring
or lopsided and desperate?

most amusing man I've ever met.' For Dick, it means 'Two
people have become one.' For Margaret, it means that she's
found yet *another* friend who's going to treat her differently
this time. For Jonathan, it means 'Thank you for having me.'
For Christine, it means next to nothing.

By turns romantic, companionate, playful, erotic, possessive,
unconditional, dispassionate, sometimes pathological, love
is . . . just another four-letter word. Can you give a one-sentence
definition? Can you define love at all? Is it 'Never having to
say you're sorry' or 'Always having to say you're sorry'?
Unfortunately, love comes weighted down with a whole freight
train of confusion and self-delusion. We all want the world to
accept *our* definition of love and it's not going to.

This chapter aims to let you sort out the baggage big and
small, get a handle on what's happening emotionally and think
your way to better romantic decisions before there's a crash.
Let's start with two frequently asked questions:

He: 'Do you love me?'
She: 'What is love?'

The nature of love
Some people believe there's no difference between liking and
loving. In other words, love is the same as liking someone a
lot. This assumes a high degree of involvement, contact and

2

intimacy. While there is support for this view – more than you might suppose – most people think it fails to capture the 'specialness' of being in love.

Psychologist Robert Sternberg thinks it's more complicated by far. He's invented the 'Triangular theory of love'. Whether or not his theory is 'true', it provides a useful way of getting at what people mean in detail. Sternberg's Triangle is made up of the following basic elements: Intimacy, Passion and Commitment.

THE THREE COMPONENTS OF LOVE

A. INTIMACY: This is a combination of emotional warmth and openness, and a free and open flow of communication. It involves sharing, valuing your partner, knowing he values you, and all the acts that make you feel close. But there is nothing necessarily sexual about intimacy – it can also be the friendship and trust you have with a platonic friend. In other words it functions on an emotional level without the physical fire of passion.

B. PASSION: This includes sexual passion – the overwhelming desire you feel every time he walks into the room, the trembling knees, the urge you have to spend the entire weekend in bed, the lust that gets you to perform intimate acts in public places without giving a damn. It also means the passionate feelings inspired by the way your self-esteem is enhanced if he finds *you* irresistible. And it includes the subtler ways in which he turns you on – perhaps by giving in so you can boss him around or perhaps by being masterful; even by being 100% 'super-cool'. All sorts of factors conspire to produce the intense and sexual feelings that are uppermost in our minds when talking about being 'head over heels in love' with someone.

C. COMMITMENT: Sternberg calls this 'decision/ commitment', referring both to the initial decision that you are actually 'in love' with someone (a big step that some people never get over) *and* the process of offering a longer-term guarantee. Of course, these two are not the same thing, and it is in the gap between them that many relationships founder. Commitment is all about maintaining love and the relationship, about deciding to put in the work, and make the sacrifices and compromises that will be necessary.

The type of love you enjoy depends on how much of each key component you have, and the similarity of your 'triangle' to your partner's shows what sort of a match you are for one another. Sternberg says the worst scenarios are those when only one component is present. This gives birth to some of the classic doomed loves that you may have been through your- self or seen your friends dive into despite warnings, or history offers as a caution.

Just good friends?

When you only have one of the three components, your relationship is unlikely to get moving very far. If intimacy alone is present, it can't really be called love at all, just liking. Karen, a 24-year-old sales executive, had exactly this experience while at university:

'Ed had been a friend of mine for ages – since the first year – and we'd always told each other everything. In many ways he was my Best Friend. In the final year we shared a house and became even closer – too close as it turned out. I was horrified when he told me that he was in love with me, and had been for years. When I thought about it later, I realised that I *did* love him; but only platonically. I loved *being* with him, and talking to him, but there was never anything physical about it. I guess I was a bit dim not to see that things weren't the same for him, but as far as I was concerned, we were just

4

friends, and we could never have been anything more.'

Ian found the same problem with Lizzie: 'We played in the same college band. I enjoyed Lizzie's company and I suppose I also enjoyed the attention she gave me, always popping round and taking an interest in me and my family. It was really nice being admired. But I didn't ever think about her sexually or romantically. It wasn't that I didn't fancy her – it had never crossed my mind (silly me) to ask whether she could be interested. She struck me as just a friend, like mates at school. When she came out with it – that she wanted to sleep with me and experiment with things like oral sex – I just cringed. I didn't know where to put myself. Should I let her have me out of compassion? Should I tell her I thought she was like my kid sister and crush her confidence? I was too immature to hold the proper conversation, to explain to her how we'd got our wires crossed and what sort of potential short circuit this might produce. Instead, I let her dangle. Till one day she got so mad with frustration, blew her fuse, smashed my windows and all the landlord's furniture. We never could communicate.'

Lust but not trust

Probably more common than 'Just good friends?' is the opposite syndrome – when your brain surrenders to your libido. 'We absolutely couldn't keep our hands off each other,' says Katie, a 27-year-old teacher. 'The fact that he was only 19 and we had nothing to talk about didn't come into it . . .' This is what happens when you only have passion – what Sternberg calls *Infatuated Love*: 'I always knew in my head it couldn't last, but it wasn't until the red mist lifted from my eyes that I realised that we were at such different stages of life our affair was meaningless: he was my boy-toy.'

Once the novelty wears off, the lack of depth in the relationship can be a killer. Adolescent crushes and puppy love obsessions probably fall into this category. Of course, you'd have to be pretty dull if you *never* got involved for the wrong reasons: 'I don't regret it,' says Katie. 'How often do you get a sexual high like that? I just wouldn't want to turn it into a habit.'

5

Empty love

What about people who make a lifelong habit out of ritual, who have no passion or intimacy, but get together or married anyway? This sort of *Empty Love* can be the result of desperation; fear that you may not be offered another chance, that 35 is just round the corner and Granny always said you'd be left on the shelf. Sometimes couples simply blind themselves to the reality of their feelings, or lack of feeling for each other, getting into any relationship, however inadequate, with single-minded devotion. It could be argued that arranged marriages fall into this sphere, but as thousands of *still* married Asian couples would attest, commitment can make a good basis on which to construct passion and intimacy.

Hollywood syndrome

Even having *two* of Sternberg's threesome doesn't guarantee bliss. When commitment is coupled with intimacy or passion alone, the results can be good or bad, but probably not great. One such combination is the 'Hollywood syndrome'. This is where a couple have a passionate, whirlwind affair, and decide to tie the knot on the basis of their day-old declarations of undying love. Sternberg calls it *Fatuous Love*, because the commitment has no solid foundations. As many alimony-sore Hollywood mega-stars can ruefully attest, it's probably one of the least likely to last.

Just good friends – for life

Alternatively a love affair can be based on companionship and friendship. This may be more of a slow-burning arrangement, but embers can smoulder deceptively. For 20-somethings the most common first combination is that of intimacy with passion in *Romantic Love*. Most affairs go through this stage, as sexual exploration leads to emotional exchange, and lovers open up each other's minds and bodies. Problems only really arise when one person must 'move on'.

Laura, a 24-year-old lab technician: 'James and I had been going out together for nearly a year, which was a big deal for me. I really loved him, and I wasn't afraid to tell him, but he wanted more. Talk of settling down – of moving in together and mortgages – really turned me off. I wanted to follow an academic career, and I have to be prepared to move around the country, I can't be tied down. Besides, I was only 22, and at that age I found it hard to cope with the idea that James could be my main relationship for life. Eventually he made me choose – make a solid commitment or call it quits. I was devastated – I couldn't understand why it had to be one way or the other – but there was only one decision I could make. It's just sad that it had to end like that.'

The holy grail

Then there's the big one, the full set. I give to you what you give to me – 'I want you because you want me.' Yes; *True Love.* This is where you've got all the passion of a fresh new affair, the intimacy of a brilliant friendship with the commitment of a couple of pioneers building a log cabin in Wyoming. How many people reach this hallowed ground is hard to say. A guestimate would be about a quarter to a third. If you don't meet the lofty criteria, there's no need to despair. Much within your control can change the numbers. Sternberg's own advice is simply to figure out what you're doing wrong, i.e. what your partner wants from you that you're not providing. If you are prepared to meet halfway then a wonderful relationship can still be yours.

Marriage

Regular matrimony is not doing so well. Weighted in theory towards commitment, it seems to perform badly in all three of Sternberg's categories, especially passion. As a result, about 41% of all new marriages are set to end in divorce within five years. This should not be seen by moralists as a cue to condemn 'permissiveness'. For some of the causes of divorce, and the death of love, are to be found in the way we traditionally marry. From love's viewpoint, there seem to be three main objections to marriage at present:

7

● Approximately 20% of young couples cohabit rather than marry, many because they feel the existing framework is too sexist or unromantic.

● A considerable group has trouble taking the terms of the wedding contract seriously. They say that in no other walk of life would you be expected to sign such a vague and ill-considered legal document. Under the terms, love appears to be taken for granted as a domestic service like electricity or gas. By contrast, the psychological evidence suggests that 'love' changes year by year and needs as much tending and feeding as a campfire. Promises to love are comparatively cheap. How could you seriously promise even to be the same person in five years' time? It might be more realistic to pledge the opposite. Moreover, where in the marriage contract does it deal with the really contentious issues like who controls finance and who does the dishes?

● Those with first-hand experience of marriage also include

8

its bitterest critics. Divorcees will often tell you that while they want to form new relationships, remarriage seems superfluous: 'It would only be hypocritical to go through all that again.' 'I no longer believe relationships last for life.' They have less interest in physical co-dwelling, scant desire to have more children and small wish to ask friends and family to celebrate their unions in public.

Sensible women look at the problem this way. They decide if they want to have children or not and only then consider the merits of the family-system within which to raise them. It is obvious that children require their parents to stay together for some 20-odd years. However, if marriage is one of the *causes* of divorce, who's to say that matrimony is the best means of fostering such durability?

FACTS OF LOVE

It also helps to understand other aspects of the psychology of attraction not mentioned by Sternberg. If you want to 'mate' successfully, there appear to be three basic criteria to determine success — parity of attractiveness, proximity/familiarity, and similarity.

First, physical attraction hurls people together like no other force this side of an earthquake. It operates more strongly than intelligence, social skills or personality, not only on the first date but on subsequent ones too. It operates even among children of five or six. The happiest couples are those who are most evenly matched in terms of attractiveness. It seems we tend to weigh a potential partner's attractiveness against the probability that they'd be willing to pair up with us. Put bluntly – less attractive people seek less attractive partners because they expect to be rejected by someone better-looking than themselves. Hence frogs need to know how to avoid princesses and ugly sisters to settle for Pinocchio.

Second, about a third of the population pairs with someone living within a stone's throw – or less than 20 miles – of themselves. People tend to bond with those they see most often – room- or flat-mates, work partners, guys on the same block. This also means there are *more* people who can love us than we may expect. 'Those who believe in miracles when it comes to matters of the heart,' says the textbook cutely, 'may believe there's a perfect mate for each of us waiting to be discovered somewhere in the world. But if this is true the far greater miracle is the frequency with which fate conspires to place the partner within walking distance of our home.'

Third, and most surprising, is the factor of similarity. Over 90% of the married couples in this country are from the same race and mostly of the same religion, same education, sociological class, intelligence, and even physical characteristics like body shape. Even couples who date regularly are found to share the same political values, views on sex and sexual roles. Couples who are the most similar at the outset of their relationship are also the ones most likely to stay together in the long run. Married couples who experience least marital conflict are those with similar personalities – which may even extend to liking the same TV programmes. That's why dating agencies offering accurate personal profiles of you and yours *could* make you happy (see Chapter Three).

LOVE BYTES

1. Does 'absence make the heart grow fonder' or is 'out of sight out of mind'? It appears to depend on whether you are an introvert or extrovert. The former take nearly twice as long as the latter to recover from broken or 'geographically challenged' romances.

2. Do you drown in your lover's eyes? Yes. Couples who love each other a lot make more eye contact than they do with friends.

3. What's the prime characteristic of being in love? Authorities disagree. Some say 'joy'. Others 'despair'. Some say 'satisfaction'. Others 'frustration'.

4. Fact: people whose parents are divorced or dead

have a far more romantic view of love than those with parents still living.

5. Girls tend to have their first infatuation at 13 and fall in love at 17. Boys are half a year behind in both respects. However, *after* the age of 20, women fall in love far less easily than men and out of love with less difficulty. Adult men are both more vulnerable to love and more compulsive about seeking it.

6. When both men and women were asked to nominate the part of the male anatomy most admired by females, the men plumped for 'muscular chest and shoulders' followed by 'huge penis'. The women overwhelmingly selected 'small and sexy buttocks'. Only 2% of women thought the penis was worth a mention.

7. Over 60% of both sexes have been 'severely depressed at some time over love' and more than 25% have 'contemplated suicide' as a result.

8. Women more frequently break off affairs than men. The most cited reason is: 'His involvement with somebody else'.

9. If love is chemical, its technical name should be 'copulins', the pungent secretions produced during ovulation.

10. Even rats are more like humans than feels comfortable. Granted unlimited access to each other's bodies, rodents lose interest in rutting. Offer them a new partner and they resume frantic mounting activity. Researchers call this dependence of libido on novelty the 'Columbus effect'.

Love as attachment

It appears that the way we are treated by our mothers (or mother figures) in childhood can also determine our romantic style as adults. There seem to be three broad connections:

A. About 60% of infants have mothers who are reliable and trustworthy. On reaching adolescence, their children can easily fall in love and readily trust their partners.

B. 19% of infants suffer interrupted childcare or inconsistent parenting making them both clingy and 'angry-resistant'. As adults, they have a powerful desire to merge *into* their partner, craving constant reassurance, coupled with the fear that they will never be loved sufficiently.

C. 21% of children do not make lasting maternal bonds and all their lives tend to avoid external offers of contact. Such individuals tend to hold the most cynical views about love and trust as well.

LOVE'S DYNAMICS

We must love our parents!

Because you are too young to know any better, the first people you tend to fall in love with are your parents. The qualities you will therefore admire in others are chosen by circumstances and based on family traits and traditions. Where love is concerned, a child has to tolerate and accept whatever emotions she receives. If parents are inadequate, they cannot usually be 'fired' and certainly not by the whim of the child. So even if your parents are unpleasant or abusive these emotional traits infiltrate and colour your personal understanding of the word 'love'.

How a love 'template' is formed

With super parents, love may come to mean wonderful things like 'empathy'; with bad parents, horrible things like 'antipathy'. The teenage years will modify this model or template by reinforcing whatever fantasies you have when you enjoy sex. So if your idea of love has been hitched to the belief that you deserve no affection, for instance, and then you have erotic masochistic dreams, upon which you dwell during sexual arousal, it's predictable that as a grown-up you may be attracted to rogues with a taste for mastery.

12

Or, if your father has proved emotionally somewhat inexpressive, you may feel inherently drawn to men of similar attitudes while secretly hungering to reform them as you never could your dad. Unsurprisingly, we sometimes choose our love partners in order to 'carry on the emotional arguments' into another generation. We also make the mistake of thinking our selected partners are totally different from our parents – until we get to know them from the inside and learn otherwise. Like Mr and Mrs Archer (see below), there's nearly always a degree of common emotional style between lasting mates.

Living life out of sequence

Often, a woman with an overbearing parent may seek to escape the family home by making an early marriage. In order to do this, she must first find a man powerful enough to stand up to Momma and Poppa. Once this has been achieved, she then has to deal with an over-bearing husband. What she's probably missed out on, meanwhile, is her adolescence – a time for self-educa-tion and exploratory romances. It frequently happens in these circumstances that a 30-something woman with two children turns round, gets divorced, enters college and embarks on a series of affairs with con-siderably younger men. She is living her emotional life out of sequence; teenage years *after* adulthood. Her ideas of love don't really develop independently until both these phases are complete. I should warn you that by then she may well be 50 years of age!

MYTHS OF LOVE

Love features in such a dazzling array of clichés and sayings there's no wonder in the past couple of hundred years we've become perplexed. Falling in love promises so much, but can disappoint just as strongly. Myths about love span the whole spectrum, from love at first sight, to falling head over heels, to losing your head, to loving to death, to living happily ever after, to loving forever (even beyond the grave).

1. True or false: opposites attract
The evidence (above) shows this to be complete nonsense. Of course, everyone knows a long-standing couple who survive despite having 'chalk and cheese' temperaments. Or we've come across a pair who rubbed each other up the wrong way at the outset but fell into bed and stayed there for several weeks. Appearances can be deceptive. Mr and Mrs Jeffrey Archer, for example, claim to be 'absolute opposites' – she the pernickety scientist, he the romantic novelist. But scratch the surface and you will find two practical optimists, full of unshakeable confidence. Apart from these and similar exceptions, it's clear that you need more in common than joint lust if you expect to enjoy a lasting partnership.

2. True or false: love at first sight can and does happen
Here's one that may actually be true. Experts call this fascinating phenomenon the *coup de foudre*, or 'lightning bolt'. Apparently it really is possible to lock eyes with a stranger across a crowded room and fall head over heels in love *instantly*. You may also get married and spend the rest of your days together feeling more or less as strongly.

There's no solid explanation, but love at first sight probably happens when two people meet who match each other's mental ideal – the 'template' that we all carry round in our heads – of our perfect partner. We probably form this ideal from the most powerful or familiar characteristics displayed by our parents, coupled with the significant qualities they lacked which we remain desperately hungry to experience. If this is combined with 'readiness' to have a major emotional adventure, the fireworks will go off. How often this happens, and more importantly how long the relationships last, is something we can only guess at.

Obsessional love: de Clarembeau's Syndrome

Love at first sight can cause mayhem when Person A falls in love with unsuspecting Person B. Informed of the passion, the beloved may not wish to reciprocate. If the lover then turns out to be a 'stalker' suffering from some obsessive-compulsive fixation, the person loved may come to detest the one pursuing.

It may cast a light on our own 'crushes' to consider examples of such misplaced love in relation to the famous. Robert Hoskins stalked the singer Madonna; John Hinckley believed actress Jodie Foster was sending him messages through the ether and orthopaedic surgeon Klaus Wagner tailed Princess Diana through Harrods' food halls and round and round the ponds of Kensington.

Why do they do it? Most stalkers are men, but Dr Paul Mullen, a British forensic psychiatrist, has even studied eight cases where women were stalked by other women. Often the motive is sexual; occasionally the desire is to find an 'ideal friend' or 'new family', especially if the sufferer has come from an unhappy background. 'One stalker just wanted his victim to listen; he wrestled her to the ground, sat on her chest and read a love poem to her', reports the *Independent* newspaper.

A third of victims didn't know their shadows. One third were former lovers who couldn't believe or accept that they had been rejected. Another third had met at work and the association may have been prompted by mistaking professional for personal concern. This was certainly the case with Lucy who interpreted the friendly 'How can I help you?' from her Blackheath GP as 'I will love you forever'. She besieged his London address for 17 months, constantly ringing the doorbell and insulting his wife, 'her rival' who had 'poisoned his mind against her'.

Lucy would be included in the minority of shadows who suffer from erotomania or 'de Clarembeau's Syndrome'. This is a mental disorder which manifests as a morbid and delusional preoccupation with a person whom they 'love', and whose behaviour to them is always interpreted as love. Sex is offered constantly regardless of circumstances. Lucy raised her skirt

15

whenever the doctor passed, revealing no knickers and a large hole in her tights 'prepared specially for him'.

And lovesickness

Obsessional love at Lucy's level of intensity is obviously no common disorder but each of us is capable of a version of it – lovesickness. The psychologist Dorothy Tennov has renamed this 'limerence'. In her research, she found that where love goes unrequited, the sufferer may take up to two years to recover – more if they constantly come into contact with the person they pine for. Meanwhile, they are far more likely to experience all kinds of ill health and stress disorders, eating problems, depression and an increased risk of both homicide and suicide. So it's quite true that this 'limerent' form of love can kill. If your ex is suffering from lovesickness, you may think you should see him 'out of pity'. My advice is don't – in case you make the problem far worse.

3. True or false: love is blind

This is a tricky one. For many people it is all too true – for a while. We fall in love and exhibit the symptoms of mood disorder, including the failure to judge our partner's conduct rationally. We think the object of our affections is the most wonderful person alive. We assume they have all the virtues on the planet while we're unfit to kiss the ground on which they walk. We may be completely unaware of their short-comings, or we may simply choose to ignore all of them.

Either way, we fool ourselves. Nobody can be that wonderful and even Mother Theresa must have faults. When we know full well that our partner's irritating habit of humming classical music during sex, or their blatant disregard for the sanctity of our bank account are *not* the actions of a model human being, we may still kid ourselves these traits are endearing in the initial stages of infatuation. As a relationship matures, things are likely to change. Michelle, a 28-year-old anaesthetist:

'Nowadays I go crazy, but when we first went out together I thought his quirks were what made him so loveable. You know, the way he screamed at the sight of a spider, his mania for comics or his constant use of 'funny' voices. At the time, I actually encouraged him! Today these make me want to do him an injury.'

Obviously not everyone has a nightmare like Michelle's, or there'd be few couples left to write about, but there's no doubt that everyone who falls in love is to some degree or other wearing blinkers. Experts call it 'projecting'. We imagine what we want to see – then find it in the other person. The problem comes when the purple haze of infatuation wears off, removing the blinkers at the same time. Suddenly we can appreciate the other person as they actually are – a human being with faults and weaknesses, some of them uncomfortably like our own. 'I remember the day it hit me,' says Michelle. 'One of my friends asked me if I didn't find his constant references to Beavis and Butthead childish. Suddenly I realised that I did – that I'd scream if he mimicked Beavis and Butthead

one day you'll wake up and see him as he really is – where you saw an Adonis you'll see a selfish child, where you saw a prince you'll see a FROG...

17

ever again. A veil had dropped from my eyes.'

We're all in danger of making these sorts of mistakes, so what steps can we take to protect ourselves? Ideally we should be more realistic and level-headed, ready to face up to potentially difficult issues rather than just sticking our heads in the sand. Failing this, we should simply be prepared – inevitably there will be a honeymoon period, and inevitably it will wear off. If we know that this potential pitfall is lurking in the future then hopefully we won't be knocked for six by the shock of cold, hard reality intruding on our fantasies. What's more, we'll be able to enjoy the honeymoon period to the hilt – making sure we take no life-important decisions while still under the intoxicating, mood-bending effects of lovesickness.

A DEFINITION OF LOVE

Perhaps we can now manage a definition? Love strikes when we think we suddenly recognise in another person that missing 'unconditional parent' (or other half) who alone can understand, accept and comfort us. The language of love is full of tell-tale phrases like: 'There's something about you . . .'; 'you're the only one for me . . .'; 'it's your eyes, your look, your smell . . .'; 'it's as if I've known you for years'; 'it's like coming home at last'. Now, all these qualities are pre-existent – by definition we cannot 'recognise' something which is unfamiliar. So 'love' must be based on past emotional experiences, probably selected from early family life.

---

4. True or false: all is fair in love and war

One of the most potent and perplexing myths of all – the view that love acts like a magic wand, that it sweeps everyday, humdrum considerations to one side, that in some way it can justify anything. Seen like this, love is a supernatural force that moves in mysterious ways none of which is under our control. Equally, we should never have to make any effort to fall in love, to resist love, to maintain a loving relationship;

18

nor do we bear responsibility for the consequences of our love – since all's fair in love and war.

Most of us probably believe in these assumptions to a lesser or greater degree even though they are clearly false. For instance, Sally, a 25-year-old secretary, thought that falling in love would change everything else in her life, solving 'all her problems':

'I was having a really tough time at work, and had just gone through a string of bad relationships. I fell out with my sister and had a huge row with my mum. I knew that I was in serious trouble, that I needed something to change, and when I met Barry it all seemed to slot into place. He and I clicked instantly, and it didn't take long for me to decide that I was in love. The only problem was that Barry was going out with my best friend Geraldine at the time, but that didn't seem important to me. I said to myself that Barry and I were in love – we couldn't help ourselves – and there was no way I was going to let anyone else steal my happiness.'

Unfortunately, estranging her best friend was just the beginning of Sally's woes:

'When Barry and I moved in together I thought that all my worries were over. I knew he and I both had stormy temperaments, but our fighting hadn't really bothered me. If you love someone heart and soul that sort of thing just doesn't matter. But now that we were together all the time I discovered that I'd simply added the stress of constant domestic arguments to my problems at work and I hadn't got my best friend to talk to about it. Barry and I have worked things out. But Geraldine has never spoken to me since.'

It took a fairly traumatic experience to open Sally's eyes to the fact that often as not love *adds* to your problems rather than solves anything. Perhaps her example is an extreme one, for as she freely admits: 'My mum made me a terrible sucker for that sort of "Ken and Barbie" myth.' Most of us would claim that we would never behave so badly. Yet at love's heart is the desire to be Number One, to feel Queen for the Day. Annette Lawson's research into why married women have affairs echoes this idea.

19

She asserts: 'From time to time, we all need to star in our own story. Most of us lead humdrum, difficult lives. The antidote is to promote ourselves to become the leading player in the domestic drama. Many people who commit adultery sometimes with disastrous consequences causing immense pain to all including themselves, say "The excitement made it worthwhile – I'd still do it over again".'

5. True or false: love can take care of itself

Experts see the role of romance in a mature relationship as being the framework on which the construction hangs. But keeping romance supported takes time and trouble. It is all too easy to slip out of actively being *in* love, and simply to assume that you and your partner can leave love to take care of itself. In practice, however, if the relationship is to move forward, your love has to grow, and for this to happen you and your partner need to be actively protective of it. It's what people try to explain when they talk about 'working on their relationship'. All it really means is adapting to the changing face of love through time:

Helen, 26, PA: 'Ben and I fell into a comfortable routine fairly quickly after we became an item, and for a couple of months it suited us both well. We had different groups of friends and a lot of different interests, and we were very relaxed about letting each other be independent. After a while, though, I realised that we were in danger of taking things too much for granted – that simply saying "I love you" and going our separate ways every morning wouldn't hack it. Ben didn't seem to understand, and kept bleating about "just carrying on as normal" but I put my foot down and said that from now on he'd have to make time for me. I said I needed him to ask me about myself, share my anxieties about work, talk about my plans and look at things from my point of view too – if only for a quarter of an hour a day. Fortunately, he heard me and agreed to make the effort. Now I'm a lot happier and I think our relationship has more future.'

SO DOES FALLING IN LOVE MEAN YOU SHOULD SETTLE DOWN?

Moving relationships forward is all very well, but a couple may have widely differing views about their destination. As I said earlier, one of the archaic, but nonetheless persistent assumptions is that an automatic sequence of events follows on from Cupid hitting his target. Classically this means marriage, but even if you eschew the formalities of a white wedding or an exchange of surnames, chances are that one of you is thinking about kids, insurances and a joint mortgage; in short the whole shooting match.

If both of you are thinking this way then you could be living happily ever after but of course there's no guarantee this will be the case. Dissent may arise from having different long-term goals (he wants kids, she wants a career), or being stuck at the Romantic Love stage – intimacy and passion can be present in spades, but one partner is short on commitment. Whatever the reason, you are jumping the gun if you really do believe that love and marriage are inseparable.

What's more, the consequences of making such a broad assumption could be dire. Alexandra married John only after agreeing 'never to have children'. John's father had died when he was eight and he associated childhood with grief. There was no interest on his part in reawakening these painful emotions. Alex naturally assumed that he would 'come round' and after four years, she let herself get pregnant. Alas, she didn't realise with what discipline John could control his feelings. As soon as she told him the news, he left – that very night, even though his entire family thought he was behaving abominably. And he went on to sue her for divorce.

Alex's pain was merely redoubled when the reluctant John remarried and decided to become a parent with new wife Judy. By now he felt able to cope with his earlier anxieties – if only as a result of surviving the depression of divorce which forced him to grapple with his underlying unhappiness!

Chandra, a 26-year-old City analyst, also made an expensive assumption about love: 'Ghopal's parents were fairly

21

traditional, and I knew that some of it had rubbed off on him. They weren't best pleased when he told them he had no interest in an arranged marriage, but were slightly mollified when he hooked up with me, as my family hailed from the same part of Pakistan as he did. Ghopal and I fell in love, and I thought I knew him quite well, and that he knew me.

'But I got a shock when I found out that Ghopal and his family had started to make full-scale wedding plans. I couldn't believe it. It wasn't so much that he hadn't bothered to consult me, he hadn't even bothered to propose! After a year and a half together he had no idea what I was like nor how I would react. They got a shock themselves too. I told them to forget it, and I quite enjoyed the looks on their faces. Fortunately it didn't ruin Ghopal and me even though we really had to start again from scratch.'

WHEN LOVE FAILS WE TURN TO POWER

Power enters the love equation early on. If we don't receive unconditional love in childhood, we get deeply angry at this affront to our omnipotence fantasies. These juvenile expectations may damagingly persist into the adult years. Not convinced? Well, have you ever been known to say 'He's *got* to love me?' Or have you thought to yourself: 'How dare he chuck me *before* I'd finished with him!'

Such fantasies are utterly disabling should we encounter emotional abuse. If your family never gave you much confidence your lover may capitalise on this by exploiting you or even hitting you. At once you have a credulity problem: you cannot believe this is happening to you. He was supposed to bring your story to a happy conclusion and now he's making you live in the same old miserable plot. You scream for justice. You discover deep in your soul you've been waiting for the world to apologise for years. It's got to; this man *must* put things right. And in order for him to apologise, you

22

have to stay around to listen. Meanwhile, he hits you again. *On average, battered wives are beaten 35 times before they leave their brutal husbands.* In other words, dependency increases if the only person you think can make you happy refuses to satisfy your desires. Gail, 36, one of my clients, a beautiful and gifted marketing analyst, was regularly beaten up by her semi-literate Glaswegian boyfriend until she realised she could make *herself* happy – and with the aid of two police officers had him chucked out of her life.

CAN LOVE LAST FOR LIFE?

What happens if you make it through the myth-strewn obstacle

Martha, may I just say that I find you PARTICULARLY attractive in your gardening outfit

course of love's young dream? What will the long-term future hold? In other words, can love last forever?

Statistics provide comfort. To return to the much-quoted figure that 'over one third of all new marriages will end in divorce within five years' you must be left with *two* thirds of all new marriages not terminating in divorce, at least for half a decade, and perhaps this means that people do go on loving each other 'enough' over time? In fact, some 50% of all couples can expect to celebrate their silver wedding and one in nine will turn up for their golden jubilee. Long-term love is possible since plenty of couples can testify to these decades of accept-able, even blissful togetherness and millions of people are experiencing aspects of it at this moment.

What isn't going to last is love that takes the other person for granted; or believes relationships don't need attention; or fails to appreciate the paradox that all stable unions are built on change because people grow up or old at different rates (see Chapter Eleven, 'A Brief History of Change'). Love *can* endure for life, but not without a lot of effort, communication, understanding, and above all, adaptability.

If your love is going to travel the distance, the likelihood is that both you and it will have changed out of all recognition by the time you arrive.

Finding the space to love

What were once upon a time innocent diversions from the business of getting a husband – work, friendships, travel, family – nowadays tend to compete with romance *to the death.* 'Cosmo' readers scarcely need reminding that juggling, although a supreme skill, is difficult to master. Keeping an ever-increasing number of balls in the air can make your head spin. How exactly do you fit a lover into all this hurry?

From celibacy to commitment

You might think that your life is mixing together happily, and that falling in love and entering a relationship will simply be the icing on the cake. Yet even the best-matched couples are bound to come up against problems they never expected. Some of them are obvious: will you get on with his friends? Will he get on with your friends? Are you working to the same sort of 'life timetable'? What will it be like to move in with him?

But there are plenty of issues that you will only be able to identify with hindsight. To take a simple example, have you thought about just how much time a relationship consumes? Having a lover could involve as big a reassessment of your priorities as having a baby.

Previously you only had to carve the cake of your week into, say, five slices: staying late on Monday and Tuesday to finish that project at work, going to the gym and doing some shopping on Wednesday, having a night in to put your feet up (but spending it catching up on all that housework) on Thursday, spending Friday and Saturday nights clubbing with mates, and Sunday at home for a family lunch.

Now factor in your boyfriend. Suddenly you've got someone with whom you want to spend most evenings, and who'll be hurt if you go out without him. He might understand that you had to stay late at work two nights, and he might even come along with you to the supermarket on Wednesdays. If you're lucky he likes your friends, and you'll all go clubbing together on Friday. But on Saturday he wants to spend the whole day with just you, on Sunday he wants you to stay in bed until late afternoon vegging out and having sex and on Thursday he's taking you to dinner.

Already you've had to drop two-and-a-half slices of your week. Supposing you still want to go to the cinema, or he wants to go to the theatre, or you want to take up a sport, or try something different, or your parents complain you're neglecting them, or your friends don't like him! Something's got to give.

Or perhaps not. If you can accept that in order to have your cake and eat it you only need to slice it differently, you can probably work things out. But don't kid yourself this will be painless. It will require a greater level of organisation and maybe more cash (if the supermarket delivers, if the laundry does the ironing, etc.). Few lovers are prepared to tag along with everything you *used* to do so be ready to make compromises too.

THE LIFE CYCLE OF LOVE

It's completely normal for two people who fall in love to have daily or sometimes hourly sexual caresses. Ethologists like Desmond Morris suggest this is a bonding activity. When two strangers link their lives, they know next to nothing about each other. In order to overcome anxiety, sex supplies a short cut to intimacy. First, you can get physically close to someone – skin to skin. Second, you can test their goodwill. Sex is a cooperative business which quickly unmasks selfishness. However, if the theory is true, it's also perfectly natural for sex to settle *back* into comparatively infrequent routines when two people feel they *do* know each other. If they then have children, the research indicates the quality of their relationship declines further and sex may be rendered even less regular. Love mirrors this sexual patterning so that during the lifetime of a single relationship, two people would naturally find themselves less close when careers or businesses were being established or threatened, when children sap their energies and during identity crises like the big 30, 40 or 50.

Loving your career

If there is one major difference between your life today and what it would have been like as recently as 1950, it's the career dimension. The revival of Jane Austen on film and television illustrates this point graphically. Surely nothing highlights the incredible sea-change in women's lives as strongly as the sight of Emma Thompson and Kate Winslet's *entire existence* revolving around the arrival of a potential suitor for tea at the cottage? Perhaps you'd wait in the whole of Saturday for some thoughtless guy to telephone but you wouldn't do it twice.

With women now making up more than 50% of the work-force, it's obvious that financial freedom is high on your priority list. Of course, pursuing a career shouldn't be a stumbling block for those in search of romance – men, after all, have managed it for centuries. But with the career dice still loaded against women, those who are serious about their jobs require equal measures of gritty determination, ambition and plain old-fashioned hard work.

So how can you fit a man into your in-tray? Jo, 25, market-ing consultant, says you must wait till you're established: 'I sort of got sucked into being a workaholic career girl. When I moved up to Edinburgh I didn't even know if I wanted a full-time job. But then I got into marketing, and found that I was good at it and that I could climb the corporate ladder quicker than I'd ever imagined. As my pay's increased, so has my workload, and I have to stay later and later. My friends under-stand – lots of them are in high pressure professions – but none of the blokes I meet seem to agree with my priorities. But you can't really compromise in marketing, and I've seen too many women fall by the wayside, using relationships and having children as excuses for not being able to compete. There are some really big bucks out there, and I'll think more about settling down when I've got them.'

For someone like Jo, who has a very clear picture in her mind of what is important to her, and where her priorities lie, the career/relationship dichotomy seems acceptable. Melanie, 26, who works in a similar industry to Jo, has more difficulty with it: 'I was very driven for the first few years. I think I also used work as a substitute for the relationship I felt I was missing out on. Then by the time I met Mike I was really into my job. At first I spent a lot of time with him but work suffered and my boss pressured me to stay later and catch up. That swung me the other way so I neglected Mike instead. Eventually things blew up and I effectively chose my job over my relationship, which ended soon after. It seemed like the right choice at the time. In the last six months, though, I've come to hate my boss and blame him for being so uncompromising, and I'm angry at myself for not being able to reconcile these conflicting desires. Next time I'm going to try a damn sight harder.'

Work can affect your relationships in more subtle ways than direct conflict between career and love: many couples have plenty of time to spend together but use too much of it fighting because they bring work stress home. Too much stress can kill and as the management consultant said: 'To live for your work may seem admirable. To die for it seems both unnecessary and uneconomic.' Circumvent misunderstandings at the most basic level by ensuring your partner knows all about your job, and equally important, that you know about his.

'Sally drove me crazy by making no effort to understand or find out about my work,' fumes Dennis, a 28-year-old systems' engineer. 'I'm very far from being work-obsessed. Yet sometimes in my line you absolutely have to keep going non-stop for several days in a row. I always tried to explain, and to make it up afterwards. Sally simply insisted I was insensitive and a chauvinist and doing it out of spite. It was nonsense, but she wouldn't listen to me.'

It is also very important not to let people pressure you unfairly. Again, communication is the key. If your boss acts as if you have no life outside of work, don't just play along until you crack. Try to reason with him or her. Equally, make sure your partner understands that you don't work at weekends just for the hell of it, that you would much rather be playing with him, and above all, that you are not taking anyone for granted. When you have a night off to spend with him try and make it a special one (see Chapter Six: 'Great Sex').

Also, be realistic when it comes to allotting your time. Don't say you'll be home in 'about half an hour' if you know it's going to be the full 60 minutes. In fact, it's better to overestimate the delay in these circumstances. Should you get home sooner, you'll gain credit. If it takes an hour, you've lost nothing. But if you are habitually late, people naturally assume you don't care. If you are going to be unavoidably held up make sure you phone and explain exactly why. If you do have to stand him up, remember that your partner needs to be reassured and valued as much as you do, and a few well-chosen words of apology and explanation are essential however stressed you feel.

Generally, keep a mental note of just how much time you spend wrapped up in your job. Maintaining love in a relationship is in fact a job all by itself. Ask whether it feels right for you to put more effort into your career than your relationship? As we keep seeing, it's a myth that you don't have to 'work' at love!

At the same time, if your career really is of major importance, don't let yourself be bullied by family, friends or lovers into making compromises that feel completely uncomfortable. Unless you at least try to fulfil your ambitions you will not be content with yourself, and your relationships will almost certainly suffer too.

Hilary, a barrister, with many years' experience of the conflict, explains why: 'When I was 23 I was one of only a few women who managed to get a training place, a "pupillage". It was a struggle to overcome the sexist prejudices of the day yet I felt I had a real calling. When I fell in love everyone assumed that I would give up my career and start being a housewife. I experienced such enormous pressure from my boyfriend, my parents and even my girlfriends that eventually I caved in. My marriage lasted for four years. I knew all the while I'd made a terrible mistake. Twenty years on, I've got a new husband, two children *and* a career. The only way I manage to make it all work is by being true to *me*. Of course I make constant compromises and sacrifices, but I always, always make sure that I believe in what I'm doing.'

THE CHEMISTRY OF LOVE

So far we've heard how difficult it is to find the right sort of love, to build and maintain it, and to integrate it into your life. Cupid's job probably seems a lot harder than he ever thought possible. But in many ways we've only heard one side of the story. For while we are acting out our very own soap operas in the conscious world, there is a whole other realm of bubbling hormones, wafting pheromones, surging endorphins and intoxicating neurotransmitters which play out their own microscopic dramas. The burgeoning fields of behavioural psychology and biochemistry have linked up in recent years to open this mysterious world to human inspection. If you are an incurable old romantic, what they've revealed makes for extremely uncomfortable reading. According to the rat doctors, we are almost total slaves to the base forces of biology. Personal choice has little to do with where our animal instincts take us.

The scent of a woman

Chemistry kicks in right at the very beginning. It seems that all the stuff you read about pheromones is true. Studies show that men are most attracted to a woman when she is ovulating – in other words when she is at the peak of her fertility. Apparently men have developed a mechanism that allows them to literally sniff out when a woman is most ripe for getting with child (a move which made good evolutionary sense for our cave-dwelling ancestors, as it does for all primates). Noses can detect the sensual secrets of pheromones which are themselves triggered off by critical levels of female sex hormone,

above all oestrogen. This, of course, is present at its highest levels during ovulation. From then on it's sex all the way.

Adrenaline rush

Lured like a moth to the flame by the heady scent of phero-mones, the amorous male is further aroused by the visual stimuli that the female offers at the time of ovulation. These include dilated pupils and a general 'glow', and are the work of an intriguing chemical known as PEA, of which more in a moment. Already hot with lust, the man's fires are stoked still further by the release of a blast of adrenaline (which makes him giddy).

More hormones spark. His testosterone levels rise, making him aggressive and frisky, while her elevated oestrogen increases potential receptivity to his advances. Brain neurotransmitters get in on the action. Levels of serotonin drop, relaxing inhibitions and generally improving mood, while dopamine hits the bloodstream, intensifying sexual desire. It's at this stage that PEA, merely a bit player before, takes centre stage.

The chemistry of infatuation

PEA, which stands for phenylethylamine, appears to be chemistry's version of Cupid. Its effects account for many of the classic sensations of falling in love, including butterflies in the tummy, breathlessness, rapid pulse, dry mouth, low appetite, excitement and general euphoria, and the radiant glow of infatuation. It comes as no surprise to learn that PEA is related to the amphetamines. PEA also occurs naturally in chocolate and roses, hint, hint!

Of course the incredible elation that PEA gives us is desirable, but in some people sets up an almost narcotic addiction. Sufferers are effectively love junkies – they have a chemical addiction to PEA, which they express by recklessly falling in love with all-comers, and the moving on as soon as the high wears off. Next time you wonder why your friend has thrown herself headlong into yet another ridiculously unsuitable relationship, remember she could be a slave to her

31

PEA and not just selecting 'losers' because her self-esteem was damaged in the cradle.

The opiate of love

It's just conceivable that falling in love is mostly induced by chemicals. The infatuating effects of PEA eventually disappear in all of us: we become tolerant and unresponsive to PEA over about two years – the lifespan generally attributed to the infatuated stage of love. Superseding the effects of PEA are the brain's natural opiates – endorphins. These start to seep through the brain, spreading feelings of calm, warmth and security. In short, the perfect ingredients for encouraging the development of a deep, loving relationship. But endorphins in their turn have a natural shelf-life, which turns o to be only about seven years, coinciding remarkably enough with the well-known Seven Year Itch, a period when many couples break up and repeat the cycle with someone new.

However, you are not *compelled* to be a slave to your neuro-transmitters. Nor can it be shown that they control *all* your reactions. A loving relationship itself can be rescued by choice. If you decide not to take each other for granted you can recover the intimacy and commitment and also the passion you used to have, even the biochemistry. When you reawaken loving feelings, you also reproduce the appropriate hormones. The secret lies in adaptability to change; in being willing to see your partner in a new light. Once he resembles a changed version of his old self, your biochemical love compounds can come back on line with all their original force.

Becoming resistant to endorphins may be part of the reason your love life is flagging but the chances are that psychological and interpersonal factors can cancel this out. Indeed, this is true at all stages. Biochemists tend to overlook the human element. Monkeys may need ovulation to get interested in sex but people can mate every day of the year – whenever they *feel* like it.

'The greatest lover in nature is the boar, statistically

speaking; he ejects eighty-five billion sperms at every copulation; even a stallion can only rise to thirteen billions or so. So where does man rank, with his measly dribble of a hundred and twenty-five millions? But man knows love, whereas the boar and the stallion hardly look at their mates, once they've done the trick.' *The Rebel Angels*, Robertson Davies, 1986.

ALL YOU NEED IS LOVE?

It should be obvious by now that this is perhaps the biggest myth of all. Love is too wide a concept, composed of too many subtle paradoxes. We've all been deceived by the word 'love' into hearing what we want to hear. Love is a lazy shorthand, a catch-all phrase that reduces a much bigger set of issues to clichés. In the end this damages and destroys love itself – it confuses more than it clarifies.

Every stage in building a working relationship throws up different problems, and requires different skills and solutions. Finding a partner, matching your needs to theirs, negotiating a way to live together are all parts of love *management*. And at each step you will need more than love – it could be said that love is a *necessary* but not a *sufficient* condition for any lasting relationship.

Alas, women, when in love, tend to be the greater romantics. They take in with their mother's milk the idea that sex is best with someone very special, someone whom they love. The ideas of sex and love become irrevocably intertwined. And often women assume that the situation is the same for men.

It is therefore vital to understand that not only is this not true about many men but it's also not true of all women. There's an old Byronic saying: 'Men want a lot of sex with a lot of different women; women want a lot of sex with the man they love.' This is indeed frequently the case but there are exceptions. Though many women believe that love and sex are identical, it can come as a giant surprise to find your-self having an absolutely amazing sex life while not being

33

remotely in love with the person on the other end.

Women also suffer from the double standard of believing that while they ought to be faithful (because that's what nice women do) men naturally act differently. There is a learning moment, therefore, when someone who thought herself perfectly happy with the man of her dreams finds herself powerfully attracted to A. N. Other. There is also new evidence (from Drs Baker and Berris of Manchester University) to suggest that, biologically speaking, women have *never* really been monogamous. Sexual desire works in mysterious ways and it is perfectly possible for women to *desire* and *love* more than one partner. This makes a further case for not confusing love and sex.

It is equally wise to acknowledge when love fades. As I've said, you may be left with no sexual desire or alternatively sex may still work well in spite of your change of heart. There are no hard and fast rules about this but I've counselled many women who are stuck in a rut with a man for whom they no longer feel affection but who is a marvellous lover. If you have no children, you will widen your options by eventually separating despite the good sex. Women can comfort themselves nowadays by realising that it's quite accepted that they are capable of leading full lives (including sex) without living with a male. When you dig down to the bottom of desire the most basic feelings are the need for security versus the need for respect and appreciation.

Love is all very well. We should both enjoy and praise it. Love may arrive inconveniently and sometimes immorally. It's still your decision whether to enjoy it. But notice that love occurs more frequently in youth than later. There is a bio-chemical conspiracy afoot which wise women see through. Nature wants you to make babies – and love is her advertising agency. So don't be duped by the packaging. First, read this next chapter and consider the benefits of remaining resolutely single . . .

Chapter Two

The Single Life – Part One: The Plusses

'Single people are chastised by the married for all manner of grievous deficiencies: ready-made food; indolence; selfish lotus-eating; the pursuit of money; deserved loneliness,' says journalist Catherine Pepinster. 'Yet in a world of so much married misery, no wonder people opt for the single life.' Or as singer Ray Charles put it: 'I don't have any trouble livin' with Ray Charles. I like him. I mean, he's a nice man. We get along fine, me and him.'

Dr David Weeks, the author of *Eccentrics*, has been studying loneliness for 17 years. His research has culminated in one overwhelming insight: 'The best single criterion for mental good health is to make constructive use of solitude.' According to Mintel, the market research group, single people do precisely that. 'The under-55 single person is healthier than the happily married person. He or she is more socially and environmentally aware, has more leisure time, and a better social life with a stronger community spirit.'

Today, for 'single' then we should read 'singular', a word revelling in positives: 'unique', 'proper', 'wonderful', 'pre-eminently good'. A century ago, a woman 'left on the shelf' was unattractive. If you were still single at 30, you'd failed your God, family and biology. You could expect to enjoy intimacy only as the long-term carer of some aged relatives. As one Victorian, Miss Emily Downing, observed: 'The daughters of professional men cannot but feel themselves a burden and a drag on the hard-won earnings of their fathers; they are a constant source of anxiety and, should they *not* get married, there is every probability of their being, sooner or later, obliged to enter the battle of life utterly unprepared and unfitted for the fight.'

Few singles today suffer such social and sexual death. On the contrary, single is sheer bliss. You call the shots, exercise freedom, choose your pleasures and enjoy to the hilt the power of your own company.

There are more single people in the world than ever. Over the last ten years, the number of single young women (aged 16–34) has risen in Britain by nearly one million. There are now 3.8 million of them. What's more, as part of the peace dividend (men no longer dying in wars), there are far more single men. In fact, between the ages of 20 and 34 men now outnumber women by about 800,000 and not all of them are celibate or gay in case you were thinking of going shopping.

Young men and women are also getting married later and deferring parenthood, with new mothers often deciding against having another baby. People also have children within a bewildering variety of households.

All sorts of singles

So today we have singles with babies and singles who've been through the hell of divorce and feel vaccinated against family togetherness – 'I will never touch marriage again.' There are singles who've never committed to a partnership and singles who invent their own sexual arrangement with another person. There are singles who are semi-attached and singles who are semi-detached.

Nowadays, single is just another norm. The concept of spinster or old maid no longer exists. Singles are both choosing and choosy, discriminators in a world of imperfect traditions. Getting married is ridiculously easy, there are practically no legal precautions. You can even purchase a marriage package to Las Vegas, St Lucia or Lake Tahoe where the preacher's bill is fixed by your travel agent.

Singles are definitely *not* what you get when you subtract the social norms from the rest. Singles think it through. They are those who decide *not* to cohabit, *not* to wed, *not* to share their lives for the time being thank you with somebody else's untidiness, boring relatives and dubious taste in music.

Strong role models

Singles are tough customers and consumers, a force to be reckoned with in and out of the workplace. Singles are significant in social geography. Fifteen years ago, the only women who appeared in adverts on TV were bimbos and sad 'grannies'. The popular career option was nursing. Now you can't turn on the screen without seeing another strong, independent, well-groomed single woman who is getting divorced, driving like Damon Hill or terminating the employment of a male underdog. Advertisers have twigged that what women want is more than tampons, soap and custard creams. They want sex, money and power too.

Market research shows that in real terms young single women earn twice as much now as they did 25 years ago on which they have an extraordinarily good time. They may not always buy the most healthy foods or serious products. The average grocery bill includes a mind-boggling quantity of crisps, cola, ice cream and chocolate bars. An impressive 10% of you are vegetarian. But the overall spending picture reveals a happy-go-lucky person, not over-bothered by other people's opinions, resourceful, kind, more gung-ho than her continental sisters.

Twenty-something desirability

Of course, even singles can experience the odd wincing moments of ennui. It might be nice to put your feet on the small of somebody's back at 11 p.m. at night. There are times when we'd all like to have somebody bring us breakfast in bed or hire a nanny. But even the grumblers could probably do something about their position if they wanted, because an unmarried 20-something woman is currently at the pinnacle of her desirability.

Single in other words is high status in the revolution of women's self-esteem and social advance. But we're not just talking about women. The single revolution has also been good for men. Look who's talking about his inner self (a bit)? Look who's learning to cook (if not clear up)? Look who's discovered the washing machine programme is a doddle compared to the mysteries of the Internet? No, it's not just about women. Men can also get sex now without selling themselves into Holy Wedlock, or wash a shirt without putting their heterosexuality through the mangle.

We should show more appreciation for this welcome reduction in social pressure. Fundamental joy of joys, it's no longer compulsory to have a child. At least one in five women now in their twenties and thirties will have no children. (Statisticians who have identified the trend suggest that women are opting for careers and further education rather than children for the simple reason they now *can* choose them). Parenthood is not destiny. Family life becomes optional. If you *would* like to be a mother, all you need is commitment, equipment and cash. What's more, 'Women who choose to delay having babies till their 30s are often healthier, from a higher socio-economic background and less at risk of producing damaged offspring than was previously thought' (Professor David James, Obstetrician). There is no backdated social message which goes 'Fall in Love at 18; Get Engaged; Light the Blue Touch Paper; and Retire to Domestic Servitude'. In the past, we *had* to choose marriage to service the division of labour between men's paid employment and women's taken-for-granted drudgery.

So, singles today are no longer looking desperately for any old mate. On the contrary, what they most hope to encounter is a soulmate, one who can truly provide what William Blake called those 'lineaments of gratified desire'. In our inventive new society, this can mean an intense friendship of any category or description.

Soulmates are *not* people you fear or cling to from personal insecurity, or appease in case they cut the 'housekeeping' budget, or go to bed with in case they fancy someone else, or take for granted because you can never imagine a day in your life on your own or in an empty room. Soulmates are friends who can accept the untrammelled you – that time you shoplifted, when you had dirty sex, incorrect fantasies, faced death, did something silly abroad.

Soulmates are the ones you might take on holiday, that otherwise singles' scene par excellence. Here too there's been a revolution. More single women than ever are going abroad for a break – it's up by 21% over 10 years. 2wentys and Club 18–30 are the companies specialising specifically in singles' holidays, but singles' holidays are no longer the love-ins they once were. Despite medical advice, getting a tan remains the principal reason why single women go abroad. One recent 2wentys survey of women revealed it's far and away the most popular daytime activity, with 'finding romance' bottom of their list for going away. Modern singles are no longer desperate to fly off and mix their genes.

Parents have also become aware of this new order of things. Some were always enlightened and jokily advised, 'Daughter, never get married.' But even those who have lived and almost died by the matrimonial vow are no longer so convinced that marriage is the only route for their children. About 150,000 divorces a year are potent evidence that all is not well in the Nuptial Movement. No one can insist that morally you should get married, especially those with bad marriages.

What's more, they don't want to. According to Julian Saunders of the advertising agency Ogilvy and Mather, the

Go on Jessica, take me with you! Nobody will know I'm your mother...

increased confidence of today's single women is largely down to parental encouragement. 'Twenty-five years ago equality and liberation were new-fangled ideas which mums wouldn't support. Now, older women in their 40s and 50s positively *want* their girls to enjoy the opportunities they missed out on . . . Time and again our research showed single women coming across as unusually tough and independent, able to send up men with the same vigour men send up each other. It's been a radical shift in the way daughters are educated.' So farewell you old romantic stereotypes – 'Man's love is of man's life a thing apart, 'Tis woman's whole existence.' The Nineties offers no market for Byronic quips.

The right to choose

The single outlook also embraces a concept for which pioneers have been prepared to die – 'the right to be free'. Free to define our own lives, choose our social roles, invent our family limits, make a working contribution. We might even ask why we're on the planet. Begetting children and spending cash may satisfy traditionalists but for others existence must mean more than the struggle to cook and inter-marry.

It's not that singles are against marriage. What they don't respect are inadequate marriages when single can be so heady. Why copy other people's mistakes when you already enjoy a viable alternative? The desperate truth is that too many people commit to coupledom before they've discovered their true singledom. This in turn puts excessive pressure on a relationship since no mature partner could volunteer to be your full-time parent. Unless you feel whole in yourself, have grown up and 'left home', until you can live within your own mental and emotional resources, the truth is you've little to offer another besides your deficiencies.

I don't mean this unkindly and the situation may not have been of your own choosing. For instance, as explained in Chapter One ('Living Life out of Sequence'), if you grew up with a bullying and overbearing father, it would be understandable for you to seek out a strong male mate able to stand up to your powerful parent. The only trouble is you discover when it's all too late that you've simply swapped one dominant male for another. You never got to sow your wild oats or discover the power of single.

Then again, you may have grown up with a neurotic mum who couldn't promote the joys of solitude since *that* was her existential nightmare. Mum's second nature then becomes your first and it's exquisitely hard to learn at 20 the lessons you might have waltzed through at 12 with a different teacher. Do you still sleep with the light on, beg the telephone to ring to break the silence, cling to bad friends and lovers when you know you ought to break up? You, too, haven't managed to taste the power of single.

Yet this world lies waiting at our feet. Never before in human history have men and women tasted such potential autonomy. You don't have to cook and clean, serve others' sexual desires, propagate, affiliate or placate if you don't want. The world is our oyster if we can only develop the skills of asking and choosing. The pearl beyond price is preserving our freedom whatever the context.

Put it another way, there's a new model army of singles equipping themselves for the best social future with the perfect retort for any bigot mouthing Victorian platitudes about old maids: 'A single female of 20- or 30-something? Why, sir, that's a liberated woman!'

On the other hand . . . if you do want a partner today, turn at once to Chapter Three.

Chapter Three

First Impressions and Finding a Partner

A smiling divorcee approaches a lone male in a bar. 'So what do you do?' 'I've just come out of prison.' 'So what did you do?' 'I murdered my wife.' 'So you're single?'

There are 11 million single adults in Britain. You'd think with that level of supply, it would be easy enough to meet a mate. A halfway decent line of chat in pub or club should bring success. But for many, especially those with long working hours, the traditional pattern of dating has obvious disadvantages. If you never have the time to go to a pub or club, it's easy to get left behind altogether.

Technology is also influencing the way we date now. Caution and paranoia contribute. Sometimes, a computer can find that non-smoking, athletic commodity dealer with the passion for Plato more surely than nature. If you're worried about sexually transmitted disease or insolvent partners, it may be desirable to use a screen to sift possible options. Appearances are sometimes not enough. If you've been betrayed in love you'd like to minimise the chances of more hurt. Many of us seem to trust the bits and bytes of a computer programme where previously we trusted our hearts. We want to know people who have addresses and PIN numbers.

But before delving into computer and other solutions, what's so difficult about the traditional method of picking a partner by reading their body language?

MAKING A GOOD FIRST IMPRESSION ON SOMEONE

1. Reading others
For a start, you have just four minutes to make a good first

impression. According to psychologists, both parties will make assumptions in that time which are likely to persist for several weeks before being revised. Of course, wise humans have for

centuries been cautious with strangers. In the worst case, those who were not your kin might treat you as food. Accordingly, the smile plays a central role in any new encounter to this day.

For primitive people, the smile was originally a warning sign – 'I'm baring my teeth in case you get too close – I can bite.' Gradually, it became identified as a 'pacifier' – 'Look, I'll be friendly if you will.' That's why the first rule in making a good first impression is to smile with some sort of conviction – *any* sort of conviction.

In addition, you need to be able to read the other person's initial body statements to see whether it's a good idea to pursue an encounter. If we don't read body language correctly, we can get into an awful lot of trouble.

Secondly, body language is the best clue to other people's real inclinations. It's been calculated that 93% of all human communication is non-verbal. This is relatively simple to understand when you think that the brain, our conscious computer, can only give close attention to one activity at a time. So when we're speaking, we may not be noticing what our feet or fingers are saying. Sometimes, they will be very out of step with our words.

A good environment to observe the split is on an aeroplane. People pretend to be cool, calm and collected but surveys show that 80% of those travelling by air perform ten times more displacement activities (fiddling with hair, drumming fingers, scratching and picking) than those who go by train.

We also know the pupil of the human eye is looking for sexual opportunities by tracking all the bodies it meets along life's merry way and checking them out for impressive features. Men and women focus on salient points – eyes, nose and mouth – and also abdomens. As you may be aware, heterosexual women look at rear abdomens on men rather more than heterosexual men look at the same places on women.

The earliest alphabet of body language was compiled by the Victorian philosopher William James but we can all think of our favourite personal examples:

There are 'approachers', and I'm one of them. I've learned

with my therapy clients that it's a good idea to lean slightly forward in an open posture as if willing to listen with an accepting mind. There are also pushy 'approachers', people who like oil tankers can scarcely be steered and are almost impossible to bring to a stop. (I once met Baroness Thatcher. That kind of an approacher.)

There are 'withdrawers' – those who give the impression of being shy or bored. One paradox of body language, as we shall see in Chapter Nine, is that shy people suffering social anxiety often look hostile because their features get frozen. Wallflowers can end up repelling the very bees they wish to attract. As a rule of thumb, therefore, try to copy Walt Disney's Bashful. He's far more endearing although uptight because in his nervous anxiety he usually remembers to *smile* as well.

Then there are 'expanders' – people like Jeffrey Archer, Basil Fawlty – confident, dominant, military types who take a pride in their erectness. Or 'contractors', those submissive/depressed/disappointed individuals who quickly crumple under life's pressures.

Posture is endlessly fascinating and a prime signal you can easily change. Get Mr Bean to stand up straight and he's a new man, almost a General; get a General to slouch and he's reduced to the ranks. Choice of posture reflects your underlying state of mind in many ways, at least the following four:

a. It obviously tells us a lot about your physical somatic condition: how well nourished you are, whether there are wasting illnesses, mobility and flexibility impairments, skin conditions, nervous ailments or if you've had serious physical accidents. It also shows whether you tend to favour a particular muscle group, or have played professional football and can't for love or money buy a pair of trousers to fit your thighs.

b. More importantly, it tells us the history of how you hold yourself, what your body's habitual memories have been – from confident to cowering – and perhaps provides some insight into 'why' they should be this way. As one physiologist put it: 'The living form of each human being is the physical expression of the mind and spirit which animate it.' We know that healthy children have a delightful physical flexibility but even by the ages of nine or 10 'have learned unnatural ways of holding themselves'. Young teenagers frequently need to get help with 'depressed posture' from teachers of the Alexander Technique.

c. It provides additional clues as to the 'current' state of a potential partner's psyche or mood which may be modifying the body's typical posture; but a word of caution is necessary here. Some people really do cross their legs because they want to go to the loo not because they feel sexually defensive or have rape anxieties. They are defending their bladders not their virginity.

d. It is also a matter of whether your body language can lie – not everyone has the talent to act convincingly on stage or, for example, appear innocent in the witness box when accused of a crime, or when trying to get a sick note from the doctor. The genius of great acting capitalises on this by using the whole body to tell the lie, so to speak. Which reminds me of the delightful story told by the neurologist Dr Oliver Sacks about a group of speech-disordered children who for some peculiar reason remained geniuses at reading body language. He found them falling about in convulsions at a televised talk by ex-American President Ronald Reagan because there was no congruence between his eyes and his smile – they could tell how passionately he didn't believe a word of what he was saying.

2. Presenting yourself

When you catch the eye of someone you'd like to impress, what signs do you habitually send out? We've all met the bureaucrat who hides behind his desk. My response is always, 'If I'd really wanted to meet a good desk, I'd have gone to a furniture shop.' So how can you maximise your attractiveness?

In my own work, I make it a matter of discipline to give another person my full attention. In a social encounter, it's not a great idea to yawn, or tap your foot or peel your nails, or stare out of the window. It's even better to ignore the car alarm in the street. Eye contact is important but beware of overdoing it – staring makes you look dangerous or mad (see also Chapter Nine on 'Shyness').

The greatest success in first encounters comes when you learn – almost by instinct – to mirror the mood and posture of the person you're meeting. The goal is to achieve enough 'affinity' of body language to help communication. So if they are standing four square to attention, stand up too. If they are at ease, put your limbs in a similar position. The exception arises if they are very nervous. Then I find it's far better to seem well composed, and give an unconscious message of 'You're not making me nervous, nor putting me off, even if I guess that's how you are feeling now.' As they say in therapy-speak: 'The person with the most behavioural flexibility will ultimately control the exchange.'

More body language clues

Besides posture, there are also five groups of body splits you can learn to use when assessing and selecting potential partners. These are known as the 'Dytchwald' categories after the first doctor who described them:

1. The first split is right body/left body. About 80–90% of the population is right-handed. If you put your hand up to ask a question, it will probably be your right. We nearly all have a dominant side to our body – as can be shown in so many ways. Most people wink with their right eyes, clap with the right hand on top of the left or link fingers with the left little finger on the bottom. Very right-sided people (full of military precision but lacking imagination and dominated by the left-hand side of the brain) may well prove pushy, thrusting, 'controlling' personalities. Is that what you seek in a lover? It's said that right-side favourers are more verbal, rational, analytic, symbolic and digital. Don't take my word for it – check it out with your next encounter. Left-side favourers are thought to be the opposite. So there may be personality clues

at the outset from which 'side' a person tends to present to the world, although remember genes also play a part in the shape and strength of things like arms and legs and history can stir the pot.

The actor Peter Lawford, for instance, who married into the Kennedy clan and was best friends with Frank Sinatra, was a very 'right-handed' chap until he put his arm through a French window severing an artery and causing permanent nerve and muscle damage. This made him acutely self-conscious – in all his films, if you look hard, you can see him surreptitiously trying to hide his right arm with his left hand! It also cost him a promising tennis career.

2. The second split is top/bottom. Often we're two people vertically – the bottom half may betray our sexual longings, or as Shakespeare put it: 'But to the girdle do the Gods inherit, beneath is all the fiends'.' Cases could include Elvis the Pelvis, or movie stars like Cyd Charisse who famously possessed 'endless' legs, or the broad-hipped Kim Basinger. Their top halves don't quite have an identical impact although someone like Marilyn Monroe had complementary halves – both capable of causing trouble. More commonly, the bottom half tends to weigh us down, especially in Anglo-Saxon cultures.

A Harley Street plastic surgeon once said to me that in this country we tend to produce 'the pear-shaped woman with the tree trunk legs'. She often has a different self on top – almost a ballerina – but her fertile, child-bearing, grounded, earth-person weighs her down. From the feet to the waist she's emotional; from the tummy upwards she's a real toughie. Well, so much for the sage of Harley Street. Certainly, I was fascinated to notice that the chap making the analysis had a barrel chest, no bum and mincing legs.

3. The third split between front and back is often one of the most revealing. When was the last time you saw your back? Answer – you never really have. Quote: 'I couldn't identify him, m'lud, I only caught a back view.' It's our fronts by which

we are habitually identified. We almost end up putting everything into our front and hiding the rest. You can liken this impersonal 'back' to the less conscious part of your mind. The back is a dump – the screen behind which we conceal our true feelings and a massive storehouse for tension. We say things like 'I'm going to put all that behind me' – quite, although you can't; and 'Put your back into it, girl' and 'Where's your backbone?'

In other words we tend to stiffen the back from neck to ankle using it as an added support when we 'put a front on things'. What we properly need to do is release negative feelings. So when a new person swims into your view, take a good look at the front but keep asking yourself what lies behind the screen and what interesting secrets are hidden. For instance, do they flinch when you touch them from the rear? Or can they trust you to approach their defenceless side?

4. The fourth split is literally between head and body. Occasionally, politicians are described as 'Dead from the neck down' or like 'desiccated calculating machines'. We've nearly all got one male relative who could be described as a 'computer zombie'. You will also read about children who have forgotten how to use their limbs except to switch on a video console, who are less fit than their ageing parents, and cannot outrun a 40-year-old. All I'll observe is that we were given a whole body by the good First Computer in the sky and if we only use a third of it we invite system breakdown. Most people look after their faces. They use make-up and groom their hair. The head is a public icon, there to be seen, its expressions to be read. Bodies, it seems, may be hidden in clothing and subject to scandalous abuse, an area of private squalor.

As a result, bodies are all-revealing. I wonder, for instance, what tycoon Sir John Harvey Jones or MP Kenneth Clarke feel on seeing their vast pot bellies on television? Pride, anxiety, psychic denial? It has nothing to do with faulty camera-work. Both are malnourished and ill-exercised. Perhaps I am *sticking my neck out* here – some people always do and run the risk of *getting their heads chopped off.* Others have protruding jaws to *take it on the chin.* Others grind their teeth and squash their necks in anxiety – maybe because life is just a *pain in the neck.* Others shake and jiggle their heads to stem unpleasant thoughts – you cannot think easily while your head is moving. That's why we cup our heads in exams and Rodin's *The Thinker* gives his brain all the immobilising arm support a model can muster. (If you don't believe me, try waggling your head and subtracting 971 from 647 at the same time – you can't.) Others walk about with *head laid low* in submission – all it needs is for the executioner to arrive.

5. The fifth and final split in Dytchwald's system is between torso and limbs. For example, I tend to talk with my hands – almost as if they are not attached to my body and I find it extremely difficult to express myself if they are held at my sides. Highly excited doers are forever tapping, fidgeting and engaging in displacement activities – taking fluff off cardigans, drumming their fingers, nibbling nails. On the other hand or hands, very closed-up people have a great deal of difficulty in using their limbs expressively, and a social skills' trainer might profitably be called to get them weaving. Others keep their hands in their pockets which either indicates they are cold, have a difficult itch, belong to the Royal Family or tend to be personally secretive. Others put their hand to their hips to draw sexual attention to themselves, or sell dresses on a catwalk by the same means – although in men it will always look effeminate. Walking is another funny area, as *Monty Python's Ministry of Silly Walks* made immortally clear. There's strutting arrogance and goose-stepping dominance but also a therapeutic opportunity: those who learn 'correct' deportment and grace actually move through life with increased confidence. Many of us constantly lay hands on our faces – sometimes to touch our noses because we're lying, sometimes to stroke our ears to suggest someone else is lying and sometimes to scratch our heads to think up a good excuse for being caught out lying. The head is a reference map of many topographical truths.

51

The face itself is the key area. Did someone yawn? Stop it in the back there, this section is nearly done. You may be tired but it's also known that waves of fatigue wash over us when we're faced with difficult learning or challenge or a situation we'd like to evade – would someone dare yawn in your bed?

In the face, the eyes are said by psychologists to be the greatest giveaways: if you want to find out, look in a mirror and see which direction your eyes drift when you think about the following:

a. Imagine a picture of fried pink potato chips.
b. Remember what your breakfast looked like this morning.
c. Try to imagine the cry of a codfish being caught.
d. Imagine the feel of being suspended by your hair.
e. Remember the cry of a baby.

Different colours, pictures, anguished sounds, tastes, sensory ordeals and pains all make our eyes look up or down, to left and right depending on how we're trying to think. Sexually, your eyes reveal your personal preferences. If you are hetero-sexual and a member of the evangelical church of purity, your pupils will still dilate with interest should you be shown a picture of a naked blonde of the opposite sex with large pectorals even as the words 'He must be banned' come to your lips.

Similarly, you may turn your head away from a persistent admirer at a dinner party but woe betide you if your leading foot is still pointing in his or her direction. It could mean you don't quite know what you really want. If matters progress and lead to a kiss, don't worry if you catch him with eyes wide open. Some 97% of women close their eyes while kissing but only 30% of men do (the anxious creatures). You could take comfort from the fact that each kiss also burns three calories. Kiss him 100 times and you can shed half a kilo.

DATING PSYCHOLOGY

If these are the unconscious, non-verbal cues we can exploit to get a date, what should we actually say when the smiling has got a man to make his move? It was suggested by Ellen Fein and Sherrie Schneider in their book *The Rules* (1996) that if women wanted men to chase them till they were caught they should play a little harder to get. Their main prescriptions included: 'never accept a date without three days' notice' and 'don't have sex on the first date ever'. However, when intimacy does occur you should 'always put his needs first'. It's a kind of New York manual (and probable movie) showing women how to manipulate men into monogamy. But could it work?

Undoubtedly, those with low self-esteem who fling themselves at men, showering them with presents and instant sex, are likely to meet bastards who'll take them for all they've got. The Duchess of York, for instance, has been known to shower a potential beau with gifts – one was a gypsy painter – and the man has been known to say thanks and immediately disappear with another. Sarah Ferguson is one who could profitably play 'harder' to get.

As could Sally who had been fancying Charles at work for more than a year when one day she bumped into him on the office back stairs (the lift was broken) and he asked her out to supper. She couldn't contain her delight. Nor when he took her walking in the park afterwards, could she stop his hands moving round her bottom into full, intimate touching. She simply stood by an oak tree and let him feel freely.

It was of course what she wanted but in the circumstances – and not knowing enough about him or his romantic situation – it was hardly wise. He naturally pressured her to go to his flat – she did. They began to make love. She was even foolish enough to dispense with the condom which he said was making it feel awkward for him. But this wasn't half as awkward as she felt when his girlfriend suddenly turned up and banged on the door saying, 'I know you've got someone in there, you rat.' Humiliation ensued. Charles actually packed her off home in a taxi and took his girlfriend to bed instead!

Clearly, 'the rules' might have disposed of Charles. But any such universal dating system is ultimately bound to founder since we're not all in Sally's situation with Sally's particular needs.

For instance, Lina, 26, a single journalist, tried 'the rules' in her encounter with James. As instructed, she didn't ring him back when he asked her out, thinking this would make her seem 'pretty hot stuff'. He only found it rude and stopped calling. For those who regard dating as a sort of war game culminating in the 'capture' of the beloved, such manoeuvres may seem a good idea. For men who expect reasonable interactions between grown-ups, leading to amity and lovemaking, they are absurd. As they must be for women who expect men to deliver the sexual goods to them.

Maggie, 25, single author, would be the first to agree. She met Francis one day at a conference, fell in love at first sight and gladly took him to bed the same day: 'I'm not promiscuous but I know when my bowels are erupting with desire. I also trust my brain to identify a counterpart who shares my interests, with a sense of humour like mine. When he also speaks in a seductive baritone, I don't even care if it's a mistake. Voices get me – I know I shall never love a badly spoken man. I've been living with Francis now for nearly five years. If I'd followed 'the rules', I would probably have lost my soulmate.'

ARE THEY INTERESTED?

1. Eye contact is crucial to falling in love. If you want a potential lover, you should stare into their eyes *a lot*. See Chapter One ('Love Bytes').

2. Pupils also enlarge when you are aroused by someone. People with large pupils are also seen to be more attractive, which is why candlelight adds to allure.

3. Making eyes at someone also involves the muscles surrounding the eyes. Raising eyebrows can mean 'approach me'. Smiling with the eyes by screwing

them up slightly suggests 'come hither'.

4. The 'modesty flirtation signal' is controversially described by some social scientists as 'characteristically female'. Ritualised hiding of the face behind the hands first appears in early childhood and even in children who are blind. In mature women, dropping the eyes to the ground then looking up or making bold eye contact then glancing away as though embarrassed is said to mean 'get me'.

5. Touching someone's hand or arm when you meet is a proven way to increase the chance that they will remember you – according to studies at supermarket check-outs.

6. Giving someone the slow 'up and down' is a more blatant version of the 'eye smile'.

7. So is opening the eyes very wide.

8. So is blinking a little or a lot.

9. So is 'smiling with the mouth open'.

10. So is letting the togue show, usually the top pressed to the upper lip. It suggests you are considering the other person's bedability.

JOIN THE PROFESSIONALS?

But rules are superfluous anyway if in these workaholic Nineties your private life is practically abolished by the demands of your job. How does the new dating cope under these special circumstances?

You could say romance isn't dead – it's just been privatised like everything else. Boy meets girl. Girl meets boy. They pay their agency subscription and live happily ever after. That's the theory. Arranged marriages were the norm for centuries; our society is choosing to rearrange some aspects of courtship. The look across the crowded room, the allure of kismet has been replaced by a data file. And given the work schedule pressures, this trend will only continue.

'Who's got the time to go to the loo these days, let alone

find a lover!' laments the working women in the six o'clock meeting who *still* hasn't had her breakfast. And she knows the same meeting will regather in 12 hours' time. And company policy penalises fraternisation or sisterhood on the job. And when she leaves the building, her mating opportunities consist of – one newspaper seller, three commuter males in dirty macs, the next-door neighbour high on Madonna records and the Domino Pizza boy for whom half-an-hour is a long time.

Work-guru Professor Charles Handy says it's not going to get any better: 'The average American now works 164 more hours per year than 20 years ago. That's the equivalent of an extra month. Organisations have realised there are 168 hours in the working week, not 40. In five years' time there'll be half as many people in successful businesses being paid twice as much to produce three times more. The future is about profit and performance, pay and productivity.'

On which note consider the plight of Manhattan man. This one – Owen – happens to be an international marketing director but could just as easily saw bones, pull teeth or write columns. He's 35, receding, rich, distrustful, divorced with a daughter, set in his ways, tired of one-night stands, wary of matrimony, yearning for friendship, paranoid about smoking, passionate about playing chess, and on a schedule that means you cannot hope to have a drink with him before 9 p.m. for at least the next two months. Where's a guy like this going to 'find' a girlfriend who wants to keep things simple and relocate in Manhattan? More to the point, why should Owen *not* get what he wants? Life, he says, is too short. So he pays a well-known dating agency $6,000 a year to meet his precise romantic requirements.

And so does Louisa, a psychology graduate in London (single, 32). She pays a similar amount to a British introduction service because she believes it will work. She's read all the books on Interpersonal Attraction and Social Attitudes and she *knows* what's likely to make a relationship succeed, 'And it ain't thinking that Mr Perfect speaks Portuguese and is waiting to be discovered on some moonlit beach in Brazil.'

So if it's no longer remotely naff to use a dating service – in fact, if it's now intensely fashionable judging by the pages of adverts in newspapers and magazines – where do you start? There are matchmakers for the disabled, rural toffs, gays and lesbians, men seeking plump partners, Asians for British husbands, vegetarians only, 'Green' persons, incurable romantics, the Astrologically challenged, Americans, accountants and even 'obnoxious individuals' – 'Are you covered in boils and do you work on a sewage farm?' A recent edition of London's *Time Out* lists no less than 34 separate agencies.

The choice is bewildering, so how can you tell whether an agency is right for you? The top ten questions to ask are:

● Has it been in operation for at least two years?
● Do they have a good local reputation? Ask around.
● Do they have an active social programme? How often?
● Do they offer a refund-guarantee?
● Do they have organised and accessible offices?
● Can they indicate success rates?
● Do they give value for money? Size of database is crucial – if the agency has less than 2,000 clients, your chances are limited.
● Do they meet all potential members personally?
● Is there a members' code of conduct and do they belong to the Association of British Introduction Agencies?
● Do they protect your confidentiality or pass your number to anyone?

With notable exceptions, most agencies seem trustworthy. In the words of the *Independent* newspaper: 'We have featured dozens of agencies up, down and middle market, catering for everyone from skiers, Christians to Muslims, Irish people to Australians, and many more, and one thing is clear: the introduction business is as reputable as any, probably more than most.' They did quote against an outfit called Together, which managed to send a top London male barrister a succession of calamitous introductions (most of the women wanted to start a family – he didn't) for which they charged him more than £1,000 and then quibbled about a refund. There has also been at least one spectacular bankruptcy.

Personal confession time. I did go along to be interviewed by one of the upmarket agencies and was extremely impressed by what they told me about myself. My one-hour profile analysis concluded: 'Mr Hodson is influential, persuasive, confident, friendly, a self-starter, decisive, mobile, active, alert, persistent, strong-willed, very independent and sometimes defiant.' I would respond, wouldn't I? More to the point, I attended one of their parties at the Riverside studios in Hammersmith, West London, and met – well, people I liked: the head of Personnel at the store which is never knowingly undersold; a concert musician; an ex-Olympic gold medallist; a computer software programmer; one of the marketing managers for Walt Disney USA and absolutely no MPs.

As for costs, why do we spend more servicing our cars than our inner cores? I paid an estate agent my left leg to sell my house and gave my right leg to bury Papa. A tumble drier costs £350, a dishwasher £600 and a new Volvo £20,000+. Put it this way – if you met the person of your dreams, would you query the bill?

COMPUTER DATING – FOOD FOR THOUGHT

● One agency billed as 'exclusive to farmers, professionals and the gentry' managed to send a country landowner out on a date with his much-disliked ex-wife.

● Plump Partners advertises for 'men and women who don't like hearing the bones rattle'. Most clients are cuddlesome and come complete with love handles. Recruits are sorted by weight not age: under 10 stone; 10–15 stone; 15–20 stone and over 20 stone. So if you're size 24 and feeling frisky . . .

● Prolink was started by Paul George to 'counter the

I don't believe this – I ask for a real heavyweight, someone unsquashable, and what do I get, a TWIGLET . . .

prejudice against accountants'. He claims John Cleese is to blame: 'You're an appallingly dull fellow, unimaginative, timid, lacking in initiative, spineless, easily dominated, no sense of humour, tedious company and irredeemably drab. In most professions, these would be considerable drawbacks. In Chartered Accountancy, they are a positive boon.'

● An agency called Together excited over 70 complaints to Westminster Trading Standards' Officers. The *Independent* newspaper ran a headline: 'Together? I'd rather be on my own.'

● Venus Introductions base their matchmaking on astrological compatibility. After a few months in business, they only had 50 clients so there was some danger of Aries getting stuck with Pisces which must be bad karma . . .

20 WAYS TO KEEP A PARTNER

Having found a lover, is there some magic programme you can follow to perfect your partnership? Of course not, but here are 20 top tips to increase your chances:

1. Being able to say sorry – the next day.
2. Being able to wait for the other person to say sorry – the next day.
3. Having genuine common interests, similar quirks, complementary vices and virtues.
4. Wanting the other's good opinion.
5. Enjoying mutual silence/time off.
6. Giving permission to say the unpopular/voice anxieties.
7. Giving verbal encouragement always.
8. Reading the other's moods.
9. Taking second place often enough.
10. Being given first place often enough.
11. Learning each other's skills – work/domestic – so each is the other's back-up.
12. From Day One, sorting out money issues.
13. Making criticism constructive/using assertion skills – 'I'd prefer this . . . I won't tolerate that.'
14. Touching – especially when things are difficult.
15. Planning and having fun.
16. Being open-minded about new ideas or adaptable to change (age/outlook/capacity/habit) at roughly the same rate or ratio.
17. Dragging a problem out by the teeth when necessary to move it on.
18. Respecting the other's family – within reasonable limits.
19. Forgiving.
20. Learning how to enjoy domestic life – since we all end up in an armchair eventually.

Chapter Four

Learning About Sex

Question. Does the following passage from a sexually explicit novel called *The Midnight Partners* (HarperCollins) ring any bells? The author is of course a man:

> 'I entered Blythe. I have never ever forgotten the exquisite feeling of her vagina slowly separating around my hard penis for the first time. The shortest and longest of journeys. When I had fully entered her I was as completely at peace as I had ever been, truly linked with another person, and happy. The sensation was glorious. Knowing as little as I did – as most of us did – I just pumped and heaved and kept my lips glued to hers until I came. Selfish, male-oriented, lust-driven, sure. Maybe that's the definition of being seventeen. It doesn't matter. To this day it was one of the sweetest, most powerful and most loving moments of my life. I gave what I could. All I had.
>
> 'Of course, Blythe didn't orgasm. That was totally out of our league. I wish I could have made her happier sexually. I don't even know if she really enjoyed it . . .'

Isn't that what often happens when two young people make love for the first time? Or even the second to the tenth? They experience sex as designed by the gods to help the first caveman impregnate the first cavewoman. Fred Flintstone either jumps his partner or flips her into the missionary position, enters rapidly, pumps lustily, ejaculates blissfully, feels a little 'moved' then goes off to play with his pet dinosaur or bow and arrow. His partner, meanwhile, lies there wondering what all the fuss has been about.

I have to believe this is a totally unacceptable model of sex for the start of a new millennium. My question remains – does it ring any bells? If so, let's hope this chapter can improve things.

Sophisticated 'Cosmo' readers already know the facts of sexual plumbing. I'd be staggered if you hadn't also discovered the joys of masturbation. But what you may not know is how to persuade the Fred Flintstones of this world to give you satisfaction. In order to do this, you first need to be an expert on your own requirements, remembering that women can have many more orgasms than men and sexual intercourse *without modification* is poorly designed to produce them.

THE PHYSIOLOGY OF ORGASM

They say that orgasm isn't the pinnacle of sex – the journey can be as much fun as the arrival. But you rarely find people *unable* to have orgasms agreeing. So what is this luxury that the sexually rich take so much for granted?

An orgasm has been described as a body spasm akin to a sneeze. Tickle the right nerve and you must come. It is actually a physiological reflex which occurs when the correct sequence of thoughts and touches becomes synchronised with your personal arousal pattern.

It may be an all-over body response, confined just to the pelvis, felt only in the vagina and anus or solely focused on the clitoris. It will feel different on different occasions. Some women talk of overlapping excitement in the breasts or even their ears which they describe as a mini-orgasm. Sex researchers would probably define these sensations as those of extreme excitement which can sometimes be confused with climax. But since all these experiences are subjective, who's to say it's not the real thing?

Perhaps one of the most ignored features of climax is that as the responses begin, your brain temporarily loses control and you are transported into a timeless state. But the main part of the orgasm consists of rhythmic contractions measured at 0.8 second intervals (the same as in a man) mediated via the clitoris. The biological purpose of the orgasm was only recently discovered – the contractions increase the chances of pregnancy by dipping the cervix into the pool of semen deposited by the male. This makes a pregnancy happily more likely with a supportive lover than a rapist but still favours male premature ejaculation.

THE SEXUAL RESPONSE CYCLE

According to Dr Helen Singer Kaplan, sexual response is a drama in three acts: Desire, Arousal and Orgasm. What matters here is Kaplan's view that you can experience *any* of the stages separately. In other words, although a complete sexual experience would include all three, it is possible to feel great desire but be held back by anxiety from experiencing arousal. Or you can get the desire, grow highly aroused but fail to climax. Or you may feel no desire or sensations of arousal but then surprise yourself, not to mention your partner, by coming without warning. These are *all* common patterns.

For those with sexual problems this gives a clear idea of where things may be going wrong. It explains for the first time the case of a woman who can masturbate to orgasm with a vibrator but along the way gains little sense of excitement. At climax, she only detects the basic muscular contractions – the so-called 'anaesthetised' orgasm. Dr Kaplan believes those who miss out on the desire and arousal stages are probably suffering from high levels of sexual anxiety. To feel excited and experience a more intense sensation during climax, they would obviously need to trace this anxiety to its source.

However, there is another, quite different line of sex research on this issue. New hormonal research indicates that a proportion of women have their sexual response thwarted by chemical malfunction.

Female hormone cycles are finely tuned. How much of each hormone travels around your system is strongly affected by all the others. If one goes wrong, so do many of the rest.

63

Researchers now consider the hormone testosterone to be mainly responsible for our sex drive. Besides oestrogen and progestogen, women do produce testosterone although not in the same quantities as men. The majority of testosterone in women is regulated by a substance called binding-globulin which makes most of the testosterone sexually ineffectual.

The small amount left becomes sexually free-ranging throughout the body. But a slight malfunction of one or several other hormones can be responsible for greater amounts of binding-globulin turning up in the bloodstream. This additional amount of binding-globulin wants to be 'fed' so it chemically seizes the free-ranging testosterone and absorbs it. Result – there is less testosterone available and little urge for sex.

A simple sounding solution is to rebalance the system, by taking testosterone pills. This not only increases the sex drive but actually makes the genitals more sensitive, more responsive and allows the experience of orgasm to be much deeper. What the testosterone won't do however is make you turn on to someone that deep down you don't fancy. Swallow too much, on the other hand, and you could grow a beard.

If you get hormonally depressed, there's also something to be said for taking anti-depressants. The use of these is interesting. They are prescribed on the grounds that depression, amongst other things, dampens the sex urge. In order to be sexual again, the depression needs to be alleviated. But be warned. Some of the newer type of anti-depressants actually make it *more* difficult to climax, so make sure the doctor fully understands what he or she is prescribing.

But let's go back to what actually happens during Kaplan's stages of desire, arousal and orgasm.

DESIRE

Sex researchers have recently wanted to reclassify desire:

a. If you feel virtually compelled to seek a sexual partner, you're having a party in your pants and are practically on the prowl, that is considered to be the result of sexual *drive*.

b. If on the other hand you only feel desire for a *specific* partner such as your boyfriend, that is considered to be psychological *desire*.

One of the changes in sexuality that women sometimes experience as time moves on is that although they feel desire for a love object, they no longer get driven by their hormones to 'put out' messages of interest and availability to this person.

For younger women the opposite may be true. Their libidinous impulses are intensely provoked by the menstrual cycle. For instance, researchers in Vienna have discovered that twice as many women wear extremely scanty clothing in dance clubs when ovulating than when dancing at any other time of the month!

Lack of . . .

People lacking in desire also tend to fall into two categories. The first includes those who behave as if their sexual circuits had been cut. Should an interested and willing partner come along they don't grasp the opportunity. If they start a relationship, such people rapidly lose interest in sex – even supposing there was much in the first place. Possible causes are a lack of the necessary brain activity (i.e. neurological fault) or very early and profound psychological disturbance.

The commoner second category covers those women whose lack of desire is *selective*. Either they feel desire and enjoy sex only with certain people or in certain circumstances, or they never actually want to instigate sex but, when stimulated by a partner, are capable of responding. In this second category, the inability to feel desire affects both men and women and is demonstrated by a subsequently low sex drive. Most persistent problems of desire, as I've said, are probably triggered by psychological anxiety.

For some thwarted lovers, the lightbulb of sexual pleasure is directly connected to the warning bulb of erotic alarm. This upsets the whole sequence of events from Desire through

Arousal to Orgasm. The inner message rapidly turns into: 'Danger – beware loss of control – shut down the system.' Feelings of pleasure are instantly repressed. With some, the anxiety is so deep that 'shut down' can happen *before* the first flush of interest or any bodily contact has taken place.

Lack of desire will often show itself as a low sex urge because those who do not feel sexy will obviously not want to make love often. People with desire problems, as a group, tend to have more serious relationship difficulties than the rest of us, presumably as a result of their lack of interest in sex.

Getting to the root of any anxiety can be hard. The brain may have good reasons for turning off feelings of desire and attempts to overcome the inhibition may provoke intense sensations of vulnerability or panic. A safe environment – and relationship – are obviously essential before making the attempt. In this context, partners can try to work on the problem between themselves. Below is a summary of the possible psychological paths which could be explored:

■ Traumatic sexual experience as a child or teenager – rape, indecent assault or incestuous experience.

■ Experience of ruptured intimacy – bereavement, divorce, family break-up. Although craving closeness, the individual also feels threatened by it. The key test is often sex, because arousal and orgasm require loss of control, both physical and mental.

■ Intimacy bringing special anxieties – some people unconsciously see their partner as a reincarnated 'parent'. This change may happen after the birth of a baby when the young wife looks at her husband and sees 'father', which may be a turn-off.

■ One partner 'outgrows' the other over a period of years. The acquisition of new confidence can undermine the emotional foundations on which the relationship was first built. As the couple grow in different directions, their sexual feelings lose focus.

■ Constant sexual rejection cools most sexual feelings.

■ Boredom: the staleness of the sex act with the same person, year after year.

■ A past hurt, perceived by only one member of the partnership. For example, the man has an affair when the partner is doing her professional exams. Although both think this is forgiven and forgotten, the sitting of further exams brings back doubt and fears into the woman's mind and she can no longer generate much sexual desire.

■ A sense that lovemaking is a duty. Sex has become a pressurised performance – infertile couples who 'make love to order' are typical victims.

■ A recent shock. Grief which results in depression can wipe out sexual desire as can depression of any kind.

AROUSAL

The first sign of normal arousal is vaginal lubrication. However, the fact that you are lubricating does not mean you are anywhere near to orgasm, which is a myth some young men subscribe to. It is usually the first stage of a *gradual* journey to excitement. As Dr Alex Comfort once quipped: 'Of course women lubricate easily – otherwise they'd squeak when they walk.' The vagina lengthens and distends and the vaginal walls change to a darker hue due to engorgement with blood. This 'vaso-dilation' which in men is responsible for filling and elevating the penis, in women fills and swells the labia and the clitoral shaft.

Subjective sensations at this point can be unbearably exquisite. Bear in mind that women actually possess 'a tactile sensitivity so superior to men's that in some tests there is no overlap between the scores of the two sexes; in these, the least sensitive woman is more sensitive than the most sensitive man' (*Brainsex* by Anne Moir and David Jessel).

During the later part of the arousal phase many muscles become tensed, some of them voluntarily. For example, many women tighten their perineal muscles to heighten stimulation. It is possible to boost excitement artificially by arching your back, pushing your pelvis high into the air, and tensing your buttocks rhythmically.

Different body movements appeal to different women. I remember a story told by my partner who had prescribed the Kegel exercises to a friend. The Kegels primarily consist of tensing and relaxing the vagina by squeezing the vaginal muscles then letting go (see also Chapter Six, 'Great Kegel Sex'). When the friend heard that these exercises were used for strengthening orgasmic response, she was pretty surprised. It wasn't that she was taken aback by the thought of exercising a sexual part of her body; rather, that for years she had been regularly rhythmically contracting her vagina as I've described, *in order to have her climax.*

Another woman confessed to being very anxious about letting herself reach orgasm with her boyfriend, saying: 'My body vibrates when I masturbate. It's how I come. But I'm so ashamed of it I try and stop when I make love to my present boyfriend.' She describes herself as 'shaking from head to foot like a leaf in a fierce breeze' while her free hand danced involuntarily around her hips. Her climax resembled a minor fit. Another story of my partner's tells of a woman who lifted her hips right off the ground during masturbation almost as if she were limbo dancing in order to intensify pelvic tension.

Another could only climax while standing up and swaying; another needed to squeeze her partner's thigh or (when alone) a sturdy bolster between her thighs; another clenched her Kegels so hard during intercourse, her vagina emitted little fartlets. The air was sucked in during arousal then forced out by her partner's penis – though she didn't give a damn: 'Sweetheart, if they want sex, they must take me as I am.'

At the earlier stage of arousal the nipples usually become erect and the entire breast swells. At the height of excitement, 75% of women develop a sex flush. This is a measles-like rash that spreads rapidly from under the ribcage and all over the breasts, up to the chin and even colours the cheeks. At this point, it is hard to conceal the rampant nature of your wishes.

In the second half of arousal, the outer third of the vagina

closes a little due to the swelling caused by the increase in
blood supply. Masters and Johnson, the famous US sex
researchers, have called this vaginal engorgement the 'orgasmic
platform'. The inner lips of the vulva also undergo striking
colour changes though few women are in a position to observe
their own. For those who have never given birth, the change
is from pink to bright red; for others from red to a deep wine
colour.

The infuriating thing about this second part of arousal is
that your clitoris, nub of delights, seems to go into retreat and
virtually disappears. In fact, it is simply hidden in the folds of
engorged flesh which arise *around* it. This doesn't usually matter
if it's you who is doing the stimulating because you still have a
fair idea of where the good feelings are located. But if it's your
partner, he may have a tough time navigating. A little 'left
hand down a bit' can be distinctly helpful here.

The tissue around the nipples swells with fluid so that the
nipple erection also seems to disappear while the sex flush
spreads to some or all parts of the body.

ORGASM

At the moment of orgasm, breathing is at least thrice as fast as
it would be normally. So one additional way of artificially
assisting climax is by consciously speeding up your breathing
and making each pant shallower. Furthermore, at this time
the heartbeat reaches more than double its usual rate and blood
pressure increases by a third. Most of the body muscles are
tense. If you could see your toes, you would notice they are
curled as if for Chinese foot-binding. No one knows exactly
what it is that triggers the final orgasmic response. Presumably,
the synapses in the brain start to fire almost continuously so
the nervous system says we must get this show on the road.
Climax begins with contractions starting in the orgasmic
platform, in the outer one third of the vagina. This platform
contracts rhythmically as sexual tension is released. The
contractions recur from three to 15 times, decreasing in

frequency and intensity after the first few. Sometimes the uterus contracts simultaneously; sometimes the anus; but, as I've stressed, there is immense variation in women's personal experiences of the result.

Physiologically, orgasm is a release of the muscular tension and engorgement of blood vessels built up during sexual excitement. Subjectively, climax is a boiling over of physical joy. Aesthetically it's what Marie Stopes, the sex guidance pioneer, liked to call 'the Bliss of the Golden Light' (see 'Simultaneous Orgasm' below)

After orgasm, the body returns to its unstimulated state though less rapidly than that of the man. Some women, most frequently those who have not had children, feel an urge to urinate. Many women urinate involuntarily during climax. The best way to cope is to accept that it's a usual part of your sexual response and make provision by lying on a towel during lovemaking, or by simply ignoring it. The quantity is generally tiny and he'll probably assume it's all part of the enigmatic wet patch (for which he often feels responsible).

The G-Spot
(See also Chapter Six, 'How to Get the Most out of Your G-Spot if You're Lucky Enough to Own One'.)

Sex researchers Dr John Perry, a psychologist, and nurse Beverly Whipple described such occasional leakage of urine as a type of ejaculation following intense stimulation of the 'G-Spot', named after its discoverer Dr Grafenberg. The women who took part in their laboratory tests sent out a fine spurt of fluid from their urethra during orgasm. And there is documented evidence of this on film.

What this substance may be, however, is surrounded by controversy. Perry and Whipple insist that it is not urine but a liquid which corresponds to seminal fluid (without the sperm). Other researchers, notably Daniel Goldberg, who has analysed the fluid and insists that it is urine, dismiss the claim. The argument is still not settled.

Moreover, Israeli researcher Dr Zwi Hock has carried out a six-year study of the anterior wall of the genitalia, and found that it is the *entire* area of the front wall of the vagina, rather than one localised 'spot', which is endowed with these special sexual nerve endings.

What matters about this argument is that it tends to resurrect the old Freudian debate about clitoral versus vaginal orgasm. To remind you, Freud considered clitoral orgasm to be somehow 'immature', connected with masturbation, while vaginal orgasm was the hallmark of female maturity. Today, no one would wish to argue about the superiority of one type of climax over another – we now realise that there are *several* sorts of orgasmic response – but the G-Spot argument does mean people are again referring to two types of orgasm, one more 'penetration-dependent' than the other.

Multiple orgasms and 'status orgasmus'

Where women further differ from men in their sexual response cycle is that after they have reached orgasm, some of them, instead of rapidly going through the resolution phase, simply dip back into what Masters and Johnson describe as the plateau phase (the final part of arousal before orgasm), whence they

yep... that's what it says,
' as many as 30 or 40 climaxes' ...

in a YEAR?
in a LIFETIME?

can reach more climaxes – as many as 30 or 40. There is also one particular orgasmic response, noted by Masters and Johnson, which they call 'status orgasmus' in which certain women are able to have rapidly recurrent sets of orgasms with no intermittent plateau phase in between. Riding off into the sunset they are still riding away when the moon rises. Women who experience this may be able to differentiate the peaks or may simply feel they are going through an immensely long drawn-out climax. Only exhaustion calls a halt.

Aids to attaining this disgraceful state would include the following:

■ physical fitness;
■ a man who discovers your best erogenous zones and can stay hard for an hour;
■ a *small* quantity of self-administered chemical disinhibitant, e.g. cognac or amyl nitrite;
■ a vibrator for auxiliary insertion or clitoral service during intercourse;
■ an excellent stock of fantasies.

The clitoris during lovemaking

The clitoris plays a key role during sexual stimulation acting as both receiver and transmitter of sexual feelings. It used to be said that clitoris size is related to the intensity of a woman's orgasm. In other words, the bigger the better. Masters and Johnson in their laboratory experiments have disproved this. It doesn't matter what size your clitoris is, your orgasm will be as good (or as bad) as anyone else's.

Indirect clitoral stimulation

During intercourse, the clitoris rarely becomes stimulated directly by the penis. Anatomically, few of us are so built that these two organs can make contact since they are kept apart by two pubic bones – yours and his. What pleasure you do get comes from the penile or vaginal thrusts exerting a pull on the labia, which helps to titillate and tickle the clitoris.

Here I should mention the role of the clitoral hood. There

has been a lot of 'bad press' given to the so-called 'hooded clitoris' which it was said prevented its owner from enjoying coital caresses. Surgeons have grown rich removing this hood in order that women might experience 'better sexual sensation'. In fact there is only a microscopic percentage of women who actually need such intervention. They are the ones with hoods attached by some kind of lesion to the clitoris who therefore cannot tug back their pubic mound to display the clitoris at all. (A male analogy would be the man who cannot retract his foreskin because it has grown attached to the penis.) But these women are *exceedingly* rare. For the rest, the hooded clitoris is a myth. What these women need is less 'thrusting' and more masturbation. Usually when women can't find their clitoris, it's because they don't know it can be hidden so far inside the pubic folds.

If you'd prefer more direct stimulation of the clitoris, therefore, don't ring your doctor. All you have to do is, firmly but gently, pull back the pubic mound, and the clitoris will roll out from underneath. Then either direct your own or your partner's fingers to the appropriate map reference.

How women masturbate

Every woman masturbates in a way that is uniquely her own. Some women stimulate the whole of their genital area and not the clitoris. Climax takes longer but reputedly causes a stronger and more satisfying result. Some women find that the clitoris becomes painful when it has been over-manipulated. They would perhaps react with more pleasure to very light fingertip circling and twirling on the apex of the clitoris. Very few women manipulate the head of the clitoris directly; most just stimulate one side of the clitoral shaft. For the female orgasm to continue to its full length, stimulation *must* go on till the climax is completed. *It doesn't carry on by itself without continuous touching.* If necessary, train your partner with a breathy but frequently rehearsed 'Don't stop!' as your crisis nears.

The value of masturbation

Besides bringing solace and sleep to the solitary, masturbation represents a valuable phase of sexual learning. It allows you to grow comfortable with your own sexual response. You are then in a far better position to share this with a partner when the opportunity presents. It also helps you detect your *point of passion.* By this I mean a sort of emotional turning point where on one side there is still time to think clearly about such vital pieces of equipment as condoms and door-locks, and on the other, you can never think at all because your attention has raced away to pornotopia.

SIMULTANEOUS ORGASM

It grieves me to say that some sexual hang-ups are created by otherwise well-intentioned, liberal sex educators. For instance, during lovemaking you may enjoy a fine crisis but has the earth ever 'moved' for you? If not, did you think of complaining to the British Institute of Sexology instead of the British Institute of Seismology? The trouble is that sex education in the earlier part of the twentieth century fell into the hands of a group of fervent idealists, nudists and novelists like Dr Marie Stopes and D. H. Lawrence who replaced the old Puritan sexual myths with a new set of mystical ones. Instead of agreeing that sex was sex and a different experience for everyone, they had to lay down the law that sex was ecstasy. Simultaneous orgasm is one of their laws.

Now it may be that your awareness is superior to most but the following passage of vintage Stopes does not describe what takes place in my house:

'The half swooning sense of flux which overtakes the spirit in that eternal moment at the apex of rapture sweeps into its flaming tides the whole essence of the man and woman, and, as it were, the heat of the contact vaporises their consciousness so it fills the whole of the cosmic space. For the moment they are identified with the divine thoughts, the

74

waves of eternal forces, which to the Mystic often appears in terms of a golden light.' (*Married Love*, 1918)

One reason why this writing may fail to shed any light in modern times is that we no longer so enthusiastically share the author's belief in the religion of marriage. For Dr Stopes and her followers, matrimony represented a 'Higher Union' fusing two equal individuals into an 'elevated but exclusive Oneness' yielding a 'wholesale Conjugal Bliss'. Assisted by an abundance of capital letters, the United Couple were supposed to rise to the heights of togetherness on a basis of 'mystical contact with Cosmic Serenity', sexual tenderness and satisfactory orgasms.

Where all this began to go wrong was with the orgasms. If conjugal bliss was the system, simultaneous climax became the tyrant. Just because Marie Stopes was multi-orgasmic and her second husband could defer ejaculation till her final contraction, so all lovers were enjoined to come together or else. The idea is expressed by one of Stopes' disciples, Dr Helena Wright, whom I met in unrepentant old age, in her enormously influential manual *The Sex Factor in Marriage*, first published in 1930. In a chilling chapter entitled 'The Perfect Sex Act', Dr Wright prescribes this:

'As the act proceeds, the intensity of pleasure rises, thought is abandoned, a curious freeing of the spirit, very difficult to describe, takes place. It is as if there were, hidden among the sensations of the body, a spiritual counterpart, a pleasure of the soul, only attained for a few seconds, bringing with it a dazzling glimpse of the Unity which underlies all nature. The rhythm of movement becomes quicker, the breathing deeper, the sensation of pleasure more and more intense, until both the man and the woman together reach a climax . . . no couple should be content until they have learnt how to experience orgasm together.'

On a personal note, I first read this book while in my teens in the Sixties. The effect was that I believed right up until I was 23 that sexual intercourse was an Olympic contest which was supposed to culminate in a dead heat, and it generally did. On the occasions when I was premature or she was slow, I felt like a false starter and she like a tail-end charley.

It was no help that at the same time Penguin Books finally won its battle to publish the unexpurgated edition of *Lady Chatterley's Lover*. From textual evidence, I now believe Lawrence suffered most of his life from premature climax and from the fear that women who reached orgasm *second* had the power to break a man's spirit. The book is no less than the Bible of Simultaneous Orgasm, to borrow the capital letters for a minute and from the outset Lady Constance establishes the theme:

> 'A woman could take a man without giving herself away. Certainly, she could use this sex thing to have power over him. For she only had to hold herself back in sexual intercourse and let him finish and expend himself without herself coming to the crisis; and then she could prolong the connexion and achieve her own orgasm and her crisis and he was merely her tool.'

Never mind that few men can actually stay erect after ejaculation in order for this bizarre act of female one-upwomanship to take place, the theme continues:

> 'He [Michaelis] was a more excited lover that night, with his strange, small boy's frail nakedness. Connie found it impossible to come to her crisis before he had really finished his. And he roused a certain craving passion in her, with his little boy's nakedness and softness; she had to go on after he had finished in the wild tumult and heaving of her loins, while he heroically kept himself up, and present in her, with all his will and self-offering, till she brought about her own crisis with weird little cries.
>
> When at last he drew away from her, he said in a bitter, almost sneering little voice:

76

"You couldn't go off at the same time as a man, could you? You'd have to bring yourself off. You'd have to run the show!"

"What do you mean?" she said.

"You know what I mean. You keep on for hours after I've gone off . . . and I have to hang on with all my teeth till you bring yourself off with your own exertions".'

Of course, Michaelis had to do no such thing. He could quite easily have masturbated his partner to bliss and fallen happily asleep. Instead, he complains:

' "All the darned women are like that . . . Either they don't go off at all, as if they were dead in there . . . or else they wait till a chap's really done, and then they start to bring themselves off, and a chap's got to hang on. I never had a woman yet who went off just at the same moment as I did." '

Shame, but the rest of the novel will be devoted to subduing Lady Constance Chatterley to the masterful will of the gamekeeper Mellors until she learns that the proper way to have orgasms is at the same time as her grass-stained lover. Her 'tormented modern woman's brain' would have no rest until she accepted that 'if she gave herself to the man, it was real. But if she kept herself for herself it was nothing . . .'

Each time Connie makes love, her submission to this idea grows. She finds she can no longer 'harden and grip for her own satisfaction upon him' after Mellors comes. By the time we reach page 139, Mellors is able to exult: 'We came off together that time . . . Most folks live their lives through and through and they never know it.' Connie asks, 'Don't people often come off together?' And he replies, 'A good many of them never. You can see by the raw look of them.'

I've taken the trouble to go into this at length because here's a sexual problem that should never have been invented and I'm determined it should die. Given literary sophistication of this order, it is not surprising that a large percentage of clients still seek help because 'they cannot achieve orgasm together in the proper way'. Some are even more confused, such as the teenager who wrote to me asking if it was true that you couldn't get pregnant unless there was 'mutual orgasm'.

Difficult to blame Lawrence in her case, perhaps, but how about Barbara Cartland ('they were one with the stars'), Judith Krantz ('They came in violent, mindless, wracking shudders'), Jackie Collins ('the come flowed out of him in long satisfying bursts and filled her totally. She gasped and moaned her pleasure') or good old Harold Robbins ('My head seemed to explode with the rush of blood and heat to my brain and at the same moment his orgasm began')? As a matter of fact, the only argument in *favour* of simultaneous climax is quite simply that some people wish to make love that way. It has nothing else to recommend it.

First, as the evidence makes clear, the goal of joint climax positively hurts the premature ejaculator. He needs to be told to forget about intercourse as a target altogether, and concentrate on fondling, caressing, mutual masturbation and familiarisation with his lover. If he can give her oral orgasms, his confidence will increase.

Second, the goal of joint climax ignores the fact that women as I've mentioned may enjoy multiple climaxes. Very few men are similarly endowed. This being so, it makes sense, as Leo Durocher once wrote about the New York Giants, for 'nice guys to finish last'. If a man is in bed with a repeatedly orgasmic partner, then the sensible sequence of events would be to ensure that her first orgasm takes place prior to penetration; her second, third and fourth during penetration, and then he could think about being a nice guy before, during or after her fifth experience – whether inside or outside the vagina.

Third, if his partner finds it difficult to reach climax, or if he knows his erection will only last a few seconds, he owes it to *both* of them to ensure she reaches climax before he does. This again requires investment in foreplay and pleasing skills. He should ask his partner to demonstrate how her body likes to be pleasured. Only she is the expert.

78

Many women prefer clitoral to vaginal stimulation anyway.

Fourth, the goal of simultaneous climax sets up as a dogma that sex is only about orgasms. Other equally mystical but more subtle philosophies such as the Tao have successfully preached the opposite. Certainly, not everyone feels like having a climax every time they get sexual.

Fifth and most tellingly, the doctrine of simultaneous orgasm simply spoils good sex. I'd compare it to two people trying to sit on the same narrow mountaintop at the same time when they are bound to push each other off. The idea of mutual crisis ignores the facts of sexual physiology. Not for nothing has orgasm been called *la petite morte* – the little death. As I've said, when you approach climax your consciousness alters. Sometimes you might even pass out. It only takes a small change in the rhythm of your lovemaking for your partner to lose his or her own climax. How on earth can you be a good lover if you are beginning to abandon motor control and spatial awareness?

Contrary to the old ecstatic myths, we now know that orgasm is not a shared experience. You are never more alone than when you come (*la petite morte* . . .). The ecstasy is in your head and not your partner's. It's a nice idea that if two people come together they somehow fuse into each other, but I'm afraid you have no direct access to another person's circuitry. Intimacy is wonderful and I'd never knock it. But the Myth of the Simultaneous Orgasm is a turn-off.

THE EMOTIONS OF SEX

Sexual enjoyment is also governed by the existence of strong, contrary feelings. When we feel angry we may not feel like making love. I've known couples who have kept their relationship together throughout some violent fights by always ending up in bed together. The activity of lovemaking acts as reassurance. However, unless the root cause of the conflict is addressed (see the Conflict Questionnaire, Chapter Thirteen), it will be difficult to feel much sexual desire. The more likely outcome is that you lose respect for each other and slowly turn off sexually. So trying to talk carefully about disagreements is the best means of preserving your sex life.

And of course there are other times when you just don't feel like sex. You may be tired, or heavy and pregnant, or pre-menstrual, or deeply preoccupied with something else. It's perfectly normal in these circumstances to find yourself saying 'some other night', provided it doesn't become routine. Once you are doing this *every* night your partner will soon retaliate. So take a look at prolonged fatigue and see what else it may be masking.

What *could* it be covering up? The most likely answer is small resentments that have been allowed to fester. Marriage expert Dr Jack Dominian reckons that if you do not talk about such small resentments, they can grow so out of hand the relationship itself may be mortally threatened. Guilt can be a culprit too. Perhaps one of you has been unfaithful? Perhaps there was an abortion as the result of a previous union which also acts as a guilt provoker. Talking through these feelings with someone, even if it's not a partner, is therapeutic.

A great variety of emotions affect sex. One young man, Will, became deeply hurt because he thought his girlfriend Mandy had called him a 'poof'. He had, in fact, misheard her when she said he was 'aloof'. But for days he acted hurt and stand-offish, behaviour which completely mystified her. Finally she forced the truth out of him, denied the offence decisively and reassured him enough to help them carry on.

She discovered two years later, when they broke up, that he had been deeply anxious about his sexual orientation. He was taunted as a 'fairy' at school. His 'mis-hearing' was a kind of Freudian slip based on fears that were indeed real. Mandy's sex life had been damaged by an accidental probing of genuine worries by an imaginary conversation. Will did eventually 'let' himself receive overtures from a male actor whom he greatly respected to find out once and for all where his tendencies lay. He simply could not respond however and retreated in disgust. He was relieved to be confirmed in his heterosexuality but anguished about having offended his friend whom he cared about and also having lost Mandy en route.

Or there's Helen, a 23-year-old woman deeply lacking in self-confidence. From something a previous partner had intimated she feared she was 'no good in bed'. This made her shy and scared to initiate sex or to do anything active for her present partner. It wasn't until he casually said one day what a wonderful vulva she had – not a common subject maybe but he couldn't help mentioning that hers was the most luscious he'd ever kissed – that she felt stronger, more confident and discovered she had a very positive interest in sex indeed.

Sex of course works differently on virtually every occasion it happens. So a woman who is greedy for lovemaking one day may feel differently the next. The same applies to her partner. Men don't have monthly mood cycles but they do have mood swings. Making allowances for a partner's passing emotions is necessary. What is the point of going into a decline because on one night of the year your man has turned you down or doesn't want to come? Far better to find out if he's got worries you can share than turn this into some cosmic failure on your part.

LOSING YOUR VIRGINITY

What about the decision to become sexual with a partner in the first place? For most of you the subject will be historic but it's still possible that *how* you lost your virginity influences your sexual attitudes today.

The case for sex before marriage

I once took a small survey of women in the office where I worked (we were always discussing sex). Of the 13, only one had had a really good first sexual experience and it was pretty clear that she was highly libidinous and able to reach climax without much real assistance.

Anjali said she felt naturally and spontaneously sexual from about the age of 10. At 13 she met a much older man who was a teacher at her school although not *her* teacher, at least not in the academic sense. He rightly or wrongly was attracted, pursuing her with wild excitement. 'We made love and it was wonderful. Because he was older he really knew how to pleasure women. I had the most marvellous experience and climaxed twice. I've never forgotten him and have always been grateful. We saw each other for a while afterwards but I always knew this couldn't last long. He was naturally afraid of others finding out. But it didn't seem to matter – the experience was just so thrilling.' Now this, technically, was sexual abuse. But I have to say that Anjali always enjoyed seemingly easy sexual experiences and in her mid-20s, met the man whom she continues to love and partner to this day.

Jenny, by contrast, at the age of 17, decided quite cold-bloodedly that the time had come. She got herself roaring drunk one night and ended up with a young man whom she had only just met, in a vegetable garden, going down among the brassicas. Not surprisingly, it put her off cabbage for life. It took Jenny another two years and several partners before she met one with whom she could relax and climax.

My colleague Rachel let herself get pressurised into doing the deed. She hadn't really wanted to and knew instinctively that this wasn't the man for her, but he was so insistent she weakly 'gave in'. She regretted it. 'I felt used. And defiled. Looking back it was almost a rape. The guy had no feeling for me, no sensitivity, all he really wanted was relief. I never saw him again.'

Jill reached the ripe old age of 28 before she lost her maidenhead. Jill believed in Christian values about sex and had therefore conserved her body for Mr Right. The trouble was that no one else she met shared the same values. Finally, in a certain amount of desperation, she left the city, moved to the country and attended her rural church. The curate was unmarried, although three years younger. He echoed her views on virginity – to start with. Jill instantly felt that this was the man for her. Casting morals to the winds, she made love fully for the first time. Now things could, of course, have gone wrong.

The curate might have been so shocked by her actions that he opted to disassociate himself. But he perceived Jill's gift of virginity as an act of grace which he accepted happily. They married and lived in reasonable harmony for many years. Jill discovered the virtue of saying yes. More women have problems in the opposite direction – because saying 'yes' means very little if you can never say 'no'.

The ability to say no
No is one of the shortest words in the English language but it's the hardest for many of us to use. The key to finding out if you actually want to say no to a man is to listen, not only to reason, but to your inner voice. Here's a check-list to run through:

THE 10-POINT 'NO' CHECK-LIST

1. Do I trust him?
2. Do I like him?
3. Do I actively dislike him?
4. Do I feel like taking him to bed?
5. If there's distrust, what exactly feels wrong? If the answer isn't clear, it's worth trusting my negative instinct.
6. Do I feel I could love him? Are we similar enough?
7. Does he smell right? Some people smell 'wrong' and it could be his skin and pheromones repel, rather than attract me.
8. Has he responded to my hesitation sympathetically and in such a way as to reassure me?
9. Does he seem to care about me? What's the evidence?
10. Is he more interested in his own sexual needs, rather than mine or me as a person?

While there may be many times when it feels fine to be sexual with someone you do not yet love, or have only just met, it's best to be able to choose confidently. When women can't say no in bed they are stating unconsciously that they can't communicate. They are building their sex lives on incomplete foundations. Even when the relationship is excellent beyond the bedroom, the ban on truth in sex talk can erode the partnership.

'How can I tell John,' asks Lorna, a solicitor, 'that every time he lays a hand on me my heart sinks and my flesh freezes? He's a lovely man and he'd be destroyed if he knew how I felt about his lovemaking.' There's not a lot going on behind John and Lorna's bedroom door. Despite describing her marriage as marvellous, it's not so marvellous that Lorna can openly tackle her problems of sexual boredom, lack of orgasm and lack of communication.

'If I told him that what he does doesn't turn me on, he'd feel so bad that he'd probably stop making love to me altogether and find some other woman for sex. Even if he could take it, I don't see how he could learn to improve.' Lorna is really saying that John is incapable of developing any new sexual techniques, which just isn't true. He feels easily rejected and would not make a solo effort to improve. Yet, if tackled well, his goodwill is immense. Lorna is stating that she herself is so scared he might leave her that she is equally unwilling to instigate change even though the future is otherwise bleak. They are in a sexual checkmate.

What she hasn't yet appreciated is that unless she says no somewhere along the line, her sexually boring relationship is likely to disintegrate anyway. But Lorna, at 28 years old, with confused feelings, no children and only 20 months of marriage behind her, doesn't have so much to lose by confronting the problem, provided of course that she does it in the right way.

SEXUAL ASSERTION

Lorna lacks practice at sexual assertion. She's picked up the ability to be direct at work because she has intelligently learned from the examples of others in the office. But there is nothing in her own family background to help her do the same in relationships. Lorna needs to discover that while half her problem is in finding the courage to say no to unsatisfactory sex, the other half is knowing how to say it gracefully.

Using a female friend, she rehearsed the best way to approach her husband. Lorna acted the husband's part and the friend played Lorna. Some revealing anxieties came to light and after a few duff attempts Lorna worked out the best way to speak up. The role-play dialogue went as follows:

Lorna: 'I have a problem, John. I don't feel I'm as confident about lovemaking as I would like to be. I need some help.' John: 'What kind of help?' Lorna: 'I've started by trying to help myself. I've been reading about women with similar problems and I've been trying to do some exercises. But some of the exercises take two. I'd be very grateful if you would do them with me.'

Lorna has, without making one negative statement, said no to the present state of sex play. She has stated fairly and clearly that she needs help, that the problem is hers. She has reassured John that she doesn't expect him to take total responsibility for what's gone wrong and is already making constructive efforts of her own. Furthermore she has asked him to do something specific to assist.

If John thinks that what she is saying is a slur on his love making abilities, he might say something like: John: 'Do you mean I'm not doing the right things to turn you on?' Lorna can respond: 'What you do is great. But there are some things I could be doing too, and there are things we don't do that we could try.' The reply to Lorna's original request, if John really cares about her, will be something along the lines of: John: 'I'm sorry you feel things aren't working for you. Of course I'd be glad to help. What do you have in mind?'

If, instead, his reaction is defensive, explaining that he's had to work too hard in the office recently, followed by a vague promise that things will get better in the future (an obvious attempt to close the conversation and forget it ever happened) then Lorna should spell out her plan of action and repeat her plea for help.

Lorna and John practised body massage together at home for a period of about 12 weeks until she was able to have a climax through masturbation. The massages allowed them to talk frankly about their needs and both felt afterwards that the relationship had improved. Although, after a while, Lorna no longer felt the need to make a conscious effort to practise plain speaking, it became habit. She managed to tackle a variety of problems far more directly and fearlessly than before – even including the way he drove the car.

Establishing your unique lovemaking pattern

The way any couple makes love is unique. That's because each partner brings a particular body-shape and personality to the union, creating something that can only exist between the two of them. What's more, after six months or so of experimentation, that pattern remains more or less the same for the remainder of their time together. We know this because of fascinating film footage shot by the Glide Foundation in San Francisco. Over the years, Rev. Ted McIlvenna (a Methodist minister) has made a series of films of people making love and demonstrating their coupling patterns. Twenty years on he refilmed couples whom he'd originally documented when they were students. Essentially, they still enjoyed the same moves and routines. This being so, it makes sense to speak up for what you want before falling into a pattern. You've got six months.

Chapter Five

Getting the Most from Your Sex Life

If we enjoy sex today, much of the credit is due to the arrival of the Pill in the 1960s. 'When I first started going out with Geraldine from the Upper Fifth,' says Ian, now in his late 40s, 'our chief concern was to avoid pregnancy. We agreed that although she could have orgasms, I would never come inside her.

'In those days, having a baby out of wedlock usually meant the woman leaving home and throwing herself on the mercy of something called The National Council for the Unmarried Mother and Her Child. Contraception was almost on the ration. Adults could get condoms from chemists or barbers but they were not for sale to schoolchildren, even 17-year-olds ... After a year, our relationship hiccuped when I announced I was no longer prepared to remain a gentleman. Geraldine also wanted to make love normally but what to do? In the nick of time, the Family Planning Association came up with the Pill and all was comparative bliss. Coitus interruptus farewell.'

Today's attitudes to sex and pregnancy are utterly transformed. We now tend to think that a *mature* teenager who gets pregnant does so by choice. After all, she can prevent conception in the first place and take the morning-after pill if there's been a terrible error. Since pregnancy is more voluntary, much of the atmosphere of shame surrounding sex has lifted. Modern women feel entitled to pleasure; those choosing the lifestyle of a single parent are also seen as strong – we know how tough that option can be.

But another, perhaps not so welcome change has followed from the development of the Pill. As intercourse has become 'safer', so young men and women seem to be spending less time getting to know each other's bodies. If anything, sex is probably *less* erotic than it was in the past. To foster desire, there has to be some degree of teasing and tantalisation. So just as fast food teaches nothing of the pleasures of the stomach, so 'McSex' teaches little of the pleasures of the loins. Ian again: 'I must have made love to Geraldine with my fingers about 400 times before we dared risk going further. I could describe to you in the minutest detail every single cell of her vagina in all its various moods.'

I'd take this further. Nineties' sex is not about making babies, it is recreational. Sex is done for pleasure, for play or to create intimacy. But just as we don't use large parts of our brains when thinking so we no longer use most of our sexuality when lovemaking. This chapter is about how to enjoy ourselves *more*. For a start, try answering these questions honestly:

Are you selfish sexually? Is this desirable?

What is good sex for you? Do you think your friends feel the same way?

Is good sex more about different sex positions or erotic fantasies? Or is it about the connections between mind/body/spirit?

Is caring more important than technique? Does good sex come naturally? Has it come naturally to you?

My guess is that you will already find a debate in yourself about the correct answers. So, let's take a look at what *does* make a good lover and how you may become a better one.

WHAT MAKES A GOOD LOVER

'A good lover,' says Hannah, 'is a miracle worker with the fingertips, someone who believes in a great deal of sensual stimulation *long, long* before we get down to intercourse. He's the one with the magic hands and a real understanding of sensuality. He knows where the nerves run round my body, along the sides of my arms and legs. He treats my reactions like a language he needs to learn. He'll discover that the backs of my knees turn me on when lightly brushed with his nails. That the little hairs on my spine can be licked and it's sexier for me if he does that than if he makes a beeline for my cunt. He's the one who can do forearm foreplay in the cinema and actually bring me off so I'm squirming in my seat and snuffling gasps of joy into a carton of popcorn. Sensuality can include intercourse but only at certain points and in certain moods. Sensuality is much more about the way he understands me and seems to know, without being told, just what kind of touch is erotic. So I guess a good lover has to be a mind reader first.'

'A good lover is an active lover,' says Josh. 'I like a woman who is unafraid to make advances, who is happy to seize the initiative and treat me to the special types of stimulation that I really enjoy, oral sex for example. She's someone who can be vigorous and direct at one time, and dreamy and sensual at another. She'll be up for naughtiness one minute (making love out of doors on the spur of the moment) and lying in bed with a book of poems the next. What gets boring about sex is when a couple falls into the same old pattern. I understand there are good reasons for this but I believe it's the duty of good lovers to change things every so often, even if they're only small things.'

'A good lover is a man who is completely masterful,' says Tessa. 'Who knows exactly what to do, who takes charge of the proceedings and is happy for me to follow. I hate the pressure of always having to think of what to do, but I'm delighted to fall in with anything, and I mean anything, that a masterful guy really wants.'

'I like women to be women,' says Richard. 'I guess I'm not very confident and if I think a girl is very experienced, or if she's very active, expecting me to be able to perform like a stallion, I find that terribly off-putting. I like a nice quiet girl who thinks I'm marvellous and who accepts happily everything

I can put out to her. I can get really sexy with women like this and later in the relationship if they want to introduce a few variations of their own, I'll be feeling fine by then.'

'I've only had one good lover,' says Lisa, a student barrister. 'He was the man who introduced me to my body. It's only in the last year that I've known myself. It was almost like a biology lesson. He was purely concentrating on me, teaching me to value myself and my feelings. He gave me oral sex with absolutely no shame and no restrictions – he relished my every sound, taste and smell. Before this lover, there was me and then my body. Then I realised you *are* your body.'

I hope I've made the point that what constitutes a good lover is partly the luck of the draw, partly a matter of individual taste, partly a matter of expertise but *nearly always* when someone decides to take charge. The evidence suggests that lovers divide broadly into the active and the passive, the pleasers and the pleased. If you scream on hearing this and insist that good sex is a shared mix, with one activity simply blending into another, I'd like you to think again. I suggest this is a prime cause of sexual *dis*satisfaction. For example, how many times have you made love with some gorgeous chunk only to feel disappointed because neither you nor he could ask for what you really wanted?

Healthy selfishness
Perhaps the most important quality of good sex, therefore, focuses on selfishness. Women are no longer trained from birth to care for others but there is still a stigma attached to making the following statements:

- 'I want sex now.'
- 'I love masturbating.'
- 'I'm dying for an orgasm.'
- 'Please put your finger in there at the same time as you lick me.'

Now these statements aren't in 'poor taste' or peculiarly

perverted. They simply relate to the normal acts of life and
love as we know them. *They are the sorts of statement you need to
make when being healthily selfish with regards to sex.*

As we saw in Chapter Four, if you think about what actually
happens during the final part of arousal and the whole of
orgasm, there's no room for too much worry about your
partner's needs. If it's going to work well for you, it has to be
a self-absorbed experience. Only *you* can have *your* orgasm.
Afterwards of course you can be as close and cooperative and
loving as you like. Take him to paradise. Indulge his favourite
fantasy. But you are never two people who become one; there
are always *two* people having *two* experiences, albeit at the
same time.

This healthy selfishness also needs to be practical. You
should know your own body. You should know your own
sexual strengths and weaknesses. You should be aware of your
ideal arousal and orgasm patterns and be able to demonstrate
these to a partner. Time spent on private practice, fine tuning
and rehearsal is not time wasted.

And yet it seems easier to groom the cat than look after
your sex life. Every sex therapist in my experience has said
the same. You get people to attend your workshops. You ask
them to set aside an hour each night to do the self-touching
'homework'. And what happens? They devote their creative
ingenuity to inventing excuses: 'I did the ironing in my hour

because I felt this was more important.' 'My boyfriend specially wanted to watch television with me that night.' 'We had this new furniture being delivered so I thought I couldn't.' It's pathetic but instructive. It only serves to underline my point: *the main sex organ most of us need to develop is a stronger ego.*

Balancing the relationship

One way to banish not-quite-good-enough sex is to marry up some of the differences between you and your partner. This obviously applies to *all* of your life together, from the choices of making love with the light on or off, to getting up early or late, to the fact that one of you wants to be a townie while the other prefers living in the country.

But since you are of dissimilar temperaments and opposite sexes you will inevitably have differing sexual rhythms. The good news is that you can learn from these, adding new feelings and ability to your rapidly developing character. Take a basic one – what's your ideal gender role balance? (See also Chapter Thirteen, 'How Bisexual Are You?')

Paul, for example, was intensely curious to know what it felt like to be a woman. Although he had always been traditional in his lovemaking, in his new relationship with someone he believed to be sexually open-minded, he asked to be treated like a 'trad' woman. As a result, Shelley from time to time made up his face, took on the role of initiating sex, running sex, making the moves, creating the feeling that she was in charge and finally threatened him with a dildo for greater realism. She enjoyed this role-reversal thoroughly but ironically, after a couple of sessions, he decided that ongoing passivity wasn't, as it were, for him.

There is a whole frame of mind lovers have to enter when it means altering regular sex practices to accommodate something which doesn't feel instinctive. It involves opening up your mind to new possibilities and not letting yourself be overcome with fear. If you're lucky, this turns out to be indelibly erotic. But the downside arrives when one particular

92

partner begins to dominate with their needs without giving enough thought to the fact that the other person is the only one making the compromises. Listen to the story of Cameron and Susan.

Fetish-fixated

Susan was married to a much older man who had become impotent. She started a love affair with Cameron, a man of her own age, who was excitingly, sexually adventurous. He liked making love in unusual positions, watching their love-making in an overhead mirror or taking Susan out to a massage parlour where the two of them were pleasured side by side. He also liked making love to Susan while she was wearing high-sided boots.

Unfortunately he became fixated on the boots to the point where he couldn't bear to make love without them. (Obviously they represented some psychic 'solution' to his problems which were nothing to do with Sue.) The boots had become a fetish object. While Susan was happy to please her man with this speciality sometimes, she didn't relish every session turning into a footwear parade. She ended up giving Cameron the boot.

Susan was right to do so. Cameron's selfishness was the unhealthy sort. The warmth is taken out of lovemaking where the focus is unilateral. It's a fair bet that a selfish lover is a selfish character through and through and you'd be better off without him.

If special sexual interests are going to be enjoyed – and all the signs from fashion and gender studies suggest they are – then this *must* be by reciprocal agreement. A frustrated female needs to discipline her fetishist male – and vice versa. And, in order to do so, she must feel that she deserves time spent on her, which means she needs to remember from the outset how to be appropriately selfish.

DIFFERENCES WE CAN LEARN TO ENJOY

Appreciate your different mild kinks; try out new tastes in food, drink, erotic films and books. Reconsider your sexual preferences; share fantasies; explore masturbation together; experiment with positions; read Chapter Six on Great Sex very slowly. Discover your different emotional limits (security versus uncertainty, domination versus passivity, shyness versus exploration, childishness versus adulthood). Use funny voices: play with dice, ice cubes; try sex on a really empty stomach (his) and so on . . .

GETTING RID OF INHIBITION

As we all know, inhibitions are learned responses. While we're grateful to those which stop others from murdering us, we're less happy with the out-of-date mental voices telling us to: 'Return home now, do not pass go and never think of anything so wicked again in future.'

Sexual inhibitions are likely to have been learned at a young age, listening to inhibited parents or observing their behaviour. It's those whispered, incidental warnings and reactions that probably do the most damage rather than the overt 'Don't wear black shiny patent leather shoes in case the boys look down and see your knickers in the reflection.' How do we shrug off a repressive way of seeing the world?

1. *Learn to look sexier in appearance in everyday life.* Clothing can often reflect how you feel. What is less appreciated is that if you dress in certain styles, the clothes will *change* your feelings. Sexier outfits and shoes, for instance, can make you walk differently and become aware of your body as desirable. As a result, you will project the feelings towards those you meet.

2. *Relaxation.* Learn simple relaxation exercises so you can survive sexual embarrassments with a refreshing ease. Sit in a chair and deliberately stress then relax each muscle group in turn. If necessary go back to parts that are still tense. Slow down your breathing and pause for a count of four when you have breathed out. Some people find this exercise easier to do lying down. Deliberately run through parts of the exercise, or do it all, when stress levels rise. If he criticises your sexual abilities, for instance, relax before choosing how to share with him your carefully considered response . . .

3. *Learn to be verbally expressive.* Although some women howl easily, others find it difficult to release sexual sounds during lovemaking. Sobs are stifled in pillows; teeth gritted; nasal passages tested to the very limit. This isn't helpful. If God invented everything including sex, noise was part of it. Curbing your joy tends to stifle part of arousal and much of climax. One way of freeing yourself up is practice – not necessarily with your man but by yourself. Next time your hand steals thighwards in a private moment, give voice to a few, rip-roaring groans. Free up those sexual moans Inject sexual words when it feels particularly good. Remember, the neighbours won't be that grateful if you ruin your orgasms and they've known for ages that you've been having sex . . .

The sensual massage
One marvellous method of dissolving inhibitions is called massage. And massage, apart from being gratifying, can enhance your love affair, solve sex problems or simply blow away your sexual cobwebs.

Touch is a primary human experience, one of the first and most primitive methods of establishing trust and security. As a foetus, in your mother's womb, you were aware of smoothly rocking on the amniotic ocean. As you grew and were crammed against the walls of the uterus, you experienced her

95

all-embracing maternal touch from the inside.

After safe passage through the birth canal, you hopefully basked in your mother's stroking, caressing and holding. Baby animals, incidentally, are literally licked into shape by their mothers, so the sensation of her tongue is the first thing they experience in this world. In some cases the careful licking is responsible for actually bringing the animal to life. And careful research studies show that mammals who are raised without touch can end up with brain damage. As Dr Eric Berne has warned: 'If you are not stroked, your spinal cord will shrivel up.'

So how can you share the power of touch with the love of your life? Well somehow or other, you must lure him to bed. Ensure the room is really warm because otherwise you'll both freeze. Put on your little white overall (or whatever) with not a lot underneath and invite him to play this game.

Rub sweetly scented massage oil on to your pre-heated hands. He, by now, has been persuaded to lie on his stomach on warm towels. Remind yourself throughout that the most sensual stroke is a slow one. Say 'Sssh!' to induce an unhurried atmosphere. It may feel leisurely to you but it's pleasant erotic torture for him – which is the effect you want to create.

Massage methods

One obviously sensuous spot is the back of the neck but it's also the place that takes a lot of strain. The muscles there can get tied into knots or bunch up into tension headaches, so go carefully. Begin by moving your fingertips in circles round and round on his skin, pressing firmly into the stress-knots. When the neck feels a little more supple, lighten your touch by degrees until it reaches the point where you're barely touching him, stroking lightly over and over.

Repeat the same up the sides of the neck, the tops of the shoulders, down the sides of the spine to the waist, and all over the back. The simplest massage stroke is circling. To do it properly you swim your hands, or your fingertips, in circles, always away from each other and always outward from the spine. You never massage on bone. You can use the whole palm, a light whole hand or simply fingertips. I suppose the most sensuous stroke is to use the fingernails. Vary your approach from proper strokes to obvious nail-teases. He'll get the message. Spend a lot of time on the back because as we saw in Chapter Three, even more of the tension is hidden in this zone.

Now turn him face-up to complete the chest and upper stomach massage but proceed no further southwards. Place him on his stomach a second time and focus on the backs of his legs and his buttocks. It's here that all your work will really begin to show results.

Start with the legs above the knees, using the same techniques but concentrating on the insides and backs of the thighs just below the buttocks. Using very sensitive manipulation, work along the skin of the thighs with the points of your fingers delving impertinently towards his crevices. You are probably bound to turn him on but don't touch the genitals themselves. Let them suffer. Any wafted supplication may be ignored.

The sensual derriere

When you've finished on the inside thighs, focus on the buttocks. The base of the spine ends here in a sort of Clapham Junction of nerve endings, including the human sex centre. A good buttock massage can therefore electrify all foreign parts. Firm pressure is often needed on the 'glutes' – if he's played sport, it takes strength to make the buttock muscles yield. Far easier is the nail-tease afterwards when you trail your fingers across his ellipses before asking him to turn over again one last time.

By now, his wafted supplication will probably be even more pronounced – be careful how you turn him over. On the other hand, if there's no real evidence of arousal don't be unduly alarmed. Some men only become erect when touched overtly; *all* men occasionally feel bashful. Enquire if you're doing the right thing – or is there something else he has in mind?

Hitting the spot

Finish the front and inside thighs first but still refrain from stroking the genitals. Each man has his special sensual, extra-penile hot spot. It could be on the left side of his back, just above the base of the spine, the inner thighs, the hollows of the buttocks, the hands, the feet, the nipples or near the scrotum. If you haven't discovered it en route, ask about it now and perhaps pleasure this area.

Meanwhile, decide in your own mind whether you want to turn this sensual massage into a deeper encounter or whether you want him to do as much for you before you're willing to yield. Why – there's no compulsion to do anything at all. At this point you could get your hands to make their excuses and leave. That *would* be cruel.

If bent on staying, however, choose your mutual endgames. Penile massage has its devotees, many of them male, one of them probably called your boyfriend. With masses of oil you finally grasp his wand in your hand. Or you do a hand-over-hand stroke rapidly downwards from tip to base of the penis. Or you mimic the 'lemon squeezer' by gripping the penile shaft in one hand while rotating the other cupped palm across the penile head. Alternatively, just remove your remaining clothes and get on with it.

SEXUAL FANTASY

Fantasies don't come in politically correct versions. When you are erotically aroused, you cannot control the images that come into mind beyond adding a little colour here and a few, contrasting details there. Fantasies are always personal – they work for you, but not necessarily for others. So don't be alarmed if your partner says 'You want me to talk about *what*?' when you get your vibrator out. However, if you have few or no fantasies, it is possible to try and enjoy a ready-made scenario.

Fantasy can be used to dispel inhibition, to promote sexual 'growth', to help communicate with a lover or as sheer

---

entertainment. Sexologists today believe that the degree to which a woman fantasises relates directly to the strength of her sex urge. But if women have been conditioned against sexual feelings (as many women have) that urge may be muted. Certainly, guilt can damage the fantasy impulse and many women seeking help with orgasm problems confess they've *never* had any sexual fantasy life.

However, it doesn't mean that the absence of fantasies proves your libido is low. Now does it mean you are non-orgasmic. For there are many documented cases of women who were taught to become orgasmic by first tuning in to erotic films or pictures and afterwards using the memory of these during sex. Hilary's story is a case in point:

Originally, Hilary found it almost impossible to climax. She learned to fantasise by accident while remembering particularly sexy times with her lover and gradually began to enjoy sex a great deal more. For some years her fantasies were of this 'realistic' hue.

When she was 26, she began to act out some more inventive fantasies. She wore black underwear and experimented with hot wax on her lover's buttocks. She found this could be an exciting prelude to easy climax but when she met her next live-in partner (who was an actor) she stopped wanting to act out the fantasies.

'I think I'd worked them out of my system. Which was pretty tough on Adrian. He'd bargained on having this ultra-sexy fetishistic girl who had suited him perfectly. And there I was, changed.'

Adrian, however, was very innovative. And as well as being an actor, he was a playwright. 'So he started telling me stories in bed, fantasies really. He'd begin by telling me something sexual and then the something sexual would be happening to me. Even while we were making love he'd continue with the yarn-spinning. He made me realise there was a whole world of sexual stimulation in my head.'

Hilary is aware that her fantasies grow and expand from one to another. She isn't remotely bothered about the fact that in some of her fantasies she is abused and used by men who in real life, she finds gross and unattractive. She *only* wants to feel like this in her dream life. In reality, she's a strong, forceful character in control of her actions, who, if truly used and abused, would react with violent defiance and dislike. She understands that part of the appeal behind the mental surrender is the daily reality of her independence.

'Once my sex life started off again, with Adrian taking the initiative, I "grew". Almost by accident, we started fooling around with a vibrator I'd had but never used. Before this, I'd always thought my orgasms depended on how I felt at the time and who the person was. Now I know that's wrong.

'My vibrator fantasies are very different from previous scenes with Adrian. The absolutely inescapable intensity of a vibrator climax changes my images. One of them, for example, is about me making a blue movie. There are masses of people involved in this film, all watching from shadowy corners around the set. It opens with me making a deal, fixing the price, going into the business details and so on.

'We start the movie. And once I get really excited I'll do anything. I'm out of control, not in command of my actions any more. And the film men can see that I'll do anything, and they begin making suggestions, more and more outrageous suggestions, and each time, the crazier the things are, the more excited I become. Then I erupt.

'From being a teenager who thought she was frigid and could never enjoy intercourse, I've learned I'm actually highly sexed and fascinated by this subject. I have two or three orgasms daily. I think of myself as coming back from the dead.'

HOW TO INCREASE YOUR SEXUAL OPTIONS

Receive strokes.
Explain to your partner how you want to be touched.
Share feelings.
Ask your partner to share with you.
Be your own lover at least once a week.

Have sex only when you want it.
Find some safe fantasy you can act on alone and do it.
Learn about your body and what you like.
Talk about sex with your partner.
Take care of your body.
Pamper yourself.
Touch yourself all over.
Take a long hot bath for pleasure.
Stroke your body with velvet, feathers, leather, anything harmless.
Touch your partner's body for your own pleasure.
Ask your partner for one thing you want done.
Have a sexual experience with your partner without having intercourse.
Don't perform. Notice that the world and your relationship don't come to an end.
[Taken from: 'Options for personal sexual enrichment' as compiled by the Institute for the Advanced Study of Human Sexuality, San Francisco.]

Menstrual rhythms

I'm still surprised that in this day and age women are so out of tune with their biological sex rhythms. Someone ought to invent a bleeper timed to go off on the days you are mostly likely to be suffering from pre-menstrual symptoms and the days when you are most likely to burst with sexual energy. They'd make a fortune. But if you kept a menstrual diary for a couple of months you could pinpoint physical and emotional changes for yourself. Pre-menstrual tension is an example of this that everyone recognises – a negative example. But there are also positive ones.

It's possible to discover that the first two weeks after a period can be particularly sexy; that during the middle days when you are likely to be ovulating you may feel exhausted and non-sexual; and that of the days leading up to your period the final one can be erotically sensational.

This is just one menstrual pattern. There are several others

101

and the only way to find out what yours consists of is to keep a menstrual diary. Mark the first day of the menstrual month as Day One and write down your physical sensations, note levels of fatigue or energy, times of extreme sensuality and the times when all you want to do is curl up with a good book. If you do this over two or three months you will soon see the pattern emerging.

What's the use of knowing it? For starters you can be easier on yourself if you think you *should* want sex when your menstrual cycle says this is an off-day. You can use your sexual pattern for explanation to a partner. When you discover your most sensual days, it's easier to meet up with your man for uninhibited couplings.

One sex therapist writes in her own menstrual diary:

'Day 25. We made love last night, not on my part from a compulsive need to do so, but because we sort of drifted into it. In fact, to begin with I wasn't even sure if I wanted to. But once we'd begun, I was very glad because I was in one of those marvellous physical states where all my sensations were velvet. Anywhere I was touched, and any touch I put out to him, felt floating and exquisite. Each bit of my flesh was full of tiny air bubbles, all receiving stroking delight. I didn't orgasm in the end, because it would have taken too long. I really could have stayed being stroked and touched all night. It was marvellous. Discovered, in the morning, why I'd felt so sensual. My period began, two days early.'

STRONG FEELINGS

Stress
Sex can't always be amazing and sometimes the culprit will be excess stress. I say 'excess' because a life without any stress at all is actually called death. The original stress may hail from work. Many people bring this home and end up affecting the whole family. One traditional solution might be to go on holiday, get away from it all and just veg out. The reality of

being able to do so successfully depends on a number of factors. Do you have children? Can you afford comfort? Are you capable of adapting to strange places, countries and food? Some people become even more stressed, finally needing a break *at home* in order to recover from the vacation. Don't be surprised if sex is ruined at times like these.

On the other hand, if it's only the two of you making the journey, many of the differences are exciting. Sleeping in a cabin or a couchette can be very sexy. Staying in a country and climate that is totally different is exhilarating. The sheer novelty of being in such a new surrounding turns you on.

Anger
Anger produces a dual effect on its owner. The worst scenario is that you become so angry you want to separate from your partner. A surprisingly common variation is that because you are aroused by anger, you find yourself having an unusually vigorous lovemaking session with the man you love to hate (see Chapter Six, 'Danger – High Voltage'). Anger, however, *is* dangerous. If it continues long enough, it drives you apart. So learning to deal with this savage emotion is wise. Assertion techniques come in useful here. As psychotherapist John Rowan says, context is vital: 'To express rage is healthy and normal, but it has to be expressed in a way that is not oppressive to others.' Rage can be safely vented in shouting and swearing, or when directed against the inanimate but incompetent forces that appear to be in charge of the universe.

Depression
Anger is often brought on by stress. So too is depression. Depression is unfortunately difficult to classify but one of the pervasive symptoms is a loss of interest in sex. The key is to realise that although you may make many well-meaning suggestions for how to lift his depression, the depressed one is often incapable of following any advice. It's all part of being depressed. If you are not brought down yourself, carry on being quietly supportive

but don't expect to be able to change things alone. A further problem in this situation is that it's easy to think things are all your fault. So remember that it is not your depression – it's his. Don't allow it to be pushed on to your shoulders.

Of course you may be the one who is suffering from depression. If so, and if the depression refuses to go away and instead gains ground, you should consider asking for drug or psychotherapy. Unlike tranquillisers, anti-depressants are not addictive and can genuinely help. It's wise of course to seek counselling at the same time because you need to learn about what has upset you in order to gain some control over the future.

Anal pleasure

For those who are revolted by the mere discussion of this subject, please skip this section. For those who are curious, let me say at once that so far as the transmission of HIV is concerned, unguarded anal intercourse is the *most* risky activity you can undertake: condoms are mandatory. It is, of course, also illegal between a man and a woman in the UK with a theoretical maximum punishment of life imprisonment because when Parliament changed the law on sodomy between certain classes of men it deliberately did not change the law for heterosexuals. So for all these reasons, you shouldn't do it.

If despite my warning you are still inclined, the following facts should inform your decision. Both sexes may derive great pleasure and reach climax from anal penetration but from an unskilled practitioner you'll get nothing better than an extremely nasty pain in the bottom.

■ Always observe rules of hygiene.
■ Never put the penis into the vagina after anal sex – wash it first.
■ Use plenty of water-soluble lubricants (oils and petroleum jellies dissolve the latex in condoms).
■ Remember that the lining of this part of the body is not meant to distend much, so the sphincter needs persuasive, very gradual, often digital easing.

■ Anglo-Saxons are probably more fastidious about anal matters than any other sexual subject. It's hundreds of years since our peasant forebears happily put their dung on the garden – so don't expect all your partners to feel as you do.

■ According to the 'National Survey of Sexual Attitudes and Lifestyles' (*Sexual Behaviour in Britain*, Penguin, 1994), nearly 14% of heterosexual men and 13% of heterosexual women reported at least one experience of anal sex. Almost 50% of gay men aged 25–34 have *never* had anal sex.

OVERCOMING IMPOTENCE

What's the difference between frustration and utter frustration? Frustration is the first time your man can't do it the second time. Utter frustration is the second time you find he can't do it the first time.

Case histories

Jessica and Stuart, both in their 20s, painfully in love, planned their consummation to the last detail. As Jess says: 'I'd had the one-night stand thing at college plus four other not very important lovers. This time I wanted the sex to be candles and passion, bought new underwear, undressed slowly and expected fireworks. I was more than a little dismayed when he couldn't manage the tiniest bulge of interest. On the first night he said, "I guess I'm over-excited." On the second night he said, "Oh dear, not again!" On the third night he said, "I don't understand, this has never happened to me before." On the fourth night he said, "It's definitely not you – it's that me *not* getting an erection has now become too important." Did I take it personally? Of course I did. But then I reasoned we were *both* impotent – how could I change it except by backing off? And as soon as I backed off and told him I wanted to forget all about having sex for a while and it didn't matter and could we just cuddle – things began to work. Stuart was able to prove his point.'

Rachel, aged 32, a divorcee living with her boyfriend, says the first time one of her lovers flopped she was completely enraged. 'I felt I wasn't sexy enough or womanly enough. He didn't even offer me reassurance because he didn't know he was impotent. He imagined his erection should be instamatic. If there was a failure it was obviously because I couldn't find the switch. Eventually it emerged he was having a specific problem at work. When that was settled (his boss got transferred) the impotence more or less cured itself. Only then did he connect the two things and realise he'd been under stress but it was too late for me.'

Bernadette, a 40-something parliamentary researcher, claims it's 'Never, never, never' happened to her. Refine the question, however, and you find she's no exception – she just doesn't think you should label the odd 'flaccid episode' with some high-falutin' medical term. 'An occasional letdown is normal and should be ignored, especially on a first date or with an older man. I've learned to roll over and switch to hands if he can manage a halfway erection which allows him to come. If not I whisper, "Do me instead".'

Pippa's 24. Growing up in Los Angeles and Notting Hill she's become, in her own phrase, familiar with male dysfunction. 'I've always preferred older men and they do have more difficulties. In my teenage, what I really wanted to say was "Oh, fuck off, if you can't get it up anyway, why should I bother?" but I didn't. I was always kind and understanding and found that prolonged oral sex helps, especially if you tell the man you won't attempt intercourse again. He just relaxes and disappears into his mind. Most men keep really dirty fantasies in the back of their heads for when they masturbate and you can tell by watching their faces as soon as they start to get into that trip. Then I just point out that – well – things seem to be happening down here and would they care to switch positions?'

Incidence

According to 1993 research, just over 5% of the UK population is permanently impotent. A further 5% of men have trouble once a year. About 15% suffer quarterly – as often as they get an electricity bill. Over five million British men have experienced 'occasional erectile disorder' and at least 8% of men over 16 are unable to achieve or maintain an erection at some stage in any two-week period.

But no man can put his hand on what Sigmund Freud called the 'executive organs of sexuality' and honestly claim there's never been a power cut. I can't. US President Eisenhower couldn't, at least according to his 'aide' and driver Kate Summersby. Novelist Simon Raven can't ('Years of brandy and baccarat have left me impotent'). Even James Bond can't – 'For an hour in that room alone with Le Chiffre the certainty of impotence had been beaten into him and a scar had been left that could only be healed by experience.' Daniel Khanu of Nairobi certainly can't – 'His wife stabbed him to death on 14th October because he was impotent.' Three and a half thousand readers of my newspaper column who sent for my leaflet on impotence in February 1994 can't. This all adds up to a massive leaning tower of personal grief topped with some irony when readers write to people like me about their 'long-standing' problem.

Biology

Here's an insight – if men can't have sex they think they lack what the French call *puissance*. The very label chosen – impotence, meaning lack of power – indicates how their minds work. We see ourselves as pocket dynamos and perpetual motion machines. Yet most of the mechanisms of male sexuality don't respond to conscious acts of will. I can always put my arm in the air but not the other part. Even if you reduce sex to matters of male conquest, the pace is limited. A high proportion of rapists for instance are functionally impotent.

Most of the men who write to me don't understand that a man (unaided) cannot choose to have an erection. He can only choose those circumstances and behaviours which are favourable to the having of one. This is because the moody 'dinosaur' part of the brain is generally in charge of sexual response. In purely biological terms, a healthy male must learn to be passive, to wait for a sexy stimulus to strike home in the right place and the right time and then – provided there is no other fear, threat, danger or preoccupation – his erection will take care of itself. After all, an erection is *only* the pumping of more blood into the hollow spaces of the penis than is allowed at the time to escape. Life would indeed be simpler for men if getting an erection were a muscular action controlled by the will like pointing a finger, but it's not – it's a hydraulic system triggered off by a reflex. This helps keep us human and prevents cramp in a crisis.

Causes
Erectile disorder is strongly linked to diabetes types I and II, hypertension, anxiety, daily drinking of alcohol and consumption of more than 40 units of alcohol per week – 'drink makes men shrink'. Something like 60% of impotence these days is felt to be of physical origin – the result of circulation disorders or nerve-damage. The danger for younger men suffering a momentary loss of psychological confidence is they may find themselves replying to one of those quick-fix ads in the quality papers – 'Impotence – Come to Harley Street!' – and taking radical impotence remedies designed for men battling with the effects of major physical illness.

The mental reaction
Impotence will always have a psychological component even if there's a physical problem like diabetes or poor blood supply to the genitals. When sex goes wrong you feel bad about yourself – and impotence treatments always need to take this fact into account. It's also now known that during periods of anxiety, the production of adrenaline in the body serves to lock the penile valves open. So long as men think negatively about their anxieties, they cannot get an erection.

Relationships

It's important to stress that a 'poor' relationship may be enough to prevent a man from getting an erection. However, the reverse is *not* necessarily true. If he fails to get an erection, this *doesn't* mean he's bored with you nor that he wants to break up. However, a man may be selectively impotent – fine with his mistress or by himself, but incapable of making love to his wife.

The effects of age

Impotence is also age-related, affecting up to a third of men over 45. However, men's refusal to tolerate diminished performance over the years gives rise (so to speak) to a kind of 'false' impotence. Fact: a man of 50 will probably need twice the penile touching and rubbing to stay erect and achieve an orgasm than a man of 30. He may find loss of hardness is a problem, as is loss of ejaculatory power and sensation. Whereas a boy of 17 will probably suffer from unwanted erections and premature ejaculation, the older chap may need a lot of attention from a loving and skilful partner. He may also find one orgasm a day is his limit.

Need for tests

With persistent impotence, the first step is to get a full medical check up to see if there are physical problems. The doctor should know that even if hormone levels appear fine, it is the 'available' level of testosterone which matters and the tests need to be thorough. I'd also repeat that, whatever the cause, impotence nearly always makes the patient feel rotten and this will in turn influence the symptoms.

Treatments

These will depend on the causes. Surgery may be attempted in the case of diseases like Peyronie's (bent penis) or with internal blood or vein leakage. There is also a vast array of hard or semi-hard penile rods and implants, some with external bulb-inflators, which may be fitted by a plastic surgeon.

One of the most interesting developments concerns a range of injectable prostaglandins. Market leader is Caverject from Pharmacia Upjohn which has been granted a full UK Product Licence. This means it's safe and every GP in the land can now offer sufferers 'something for the weekend'. A pill version is likely. Caverject is mixed and syringed directly into the penis by the patient himself. Unlike most drugs, there's a 90%+ guaranteed success rate. However, the more you inject, the longer the erection lasts so overdose may be dangerous. In case you were wondering, the maximum recommended number of weekly drug-induced erections is three. Caverject can also be used to diagnose the *type* of impotence involved. Men usually cross their legs when you describe Caverject in detail – the equivalent experience for women I suppose would be a needle in the clitoris. But such is the misery impotence can bring that most patients seem willing to press the plunger, according to research. The pain is quaintly summarised as a 'tiny prick'.

Various sex aids are offered by medical and supply companies. Genesis Medical for instance produces the Correct-Aid – a rigid external sheath – as well as a range of vacuum erection devices. Their address is Freepost WD 1242, London NW3 4YR. NES Services also supply similar developers, plus the Potenz Condom, the Combi-Ring, Penis Corset, etc. Their address is 26 Cheviot Street, Lincoln LN2 5JD.

Talking therapies are offered by Relate Marriage Guidance and sex therapists generally. They involve what's called 'Masters and Johnson'-style treatment. The couple (singles are rarely taken on) are asked to attend for counselling, given homework to carry out and asked not to attempt intercourse. Instead, in domestic privacy, they're prescribed massage and relaxation exercises culminating in a 'rebuilding' of the joint approach to sex and its performance. Relate/MG is in the phone book, and the British Association for Counselling, which can put you in touch with a sex therapist, can be reached on 017885 78328.

Stop press

Some of the latest research into impotence shows that many men really do have a mainly physical disorder as the valves controlling erection tend to get slack with age. The man can still get aroused quite promptly but to his alarm he finds the erection slowly tends to subside and sag. Surgery is sometimes tried but does not have a very good record. Instead one of the simplest and cheapest remedies is a special surgical rubber band prescribed by a doctor (not one from WH Smith's). It is wider and thicker than an ordinary rubber band, with a moulded groove to avoid putting dangerous pressure on the urethral passage. There are several styles available. The cost is approximately £30.

Besides penetration

Bear in mind that sex can literally involve the whole body and last for hours rather than be fitted into ten coital minutes. Nor is intercourse the *only* way for two people to show their passion or affection. Indeed, some people, though fully potent, *prefer* alternative activities. This could be the best message to Solly, a 42-year-old taxi-driver who, staring mournfully at his 'executive organ of sexuality', moaned: 'We were born together. We grew up together. We got married together. Why, oh why, did you have to die before me?'

Other male sex problems

Early ejaculation

My partner always seizes on the first second of my orgasm as a signal to have his. This is upsetting me, partly because his movements actually distract me from my orgasm and partly because I know I'm capable of more than one. But he never gives me the chance. How can I get him to last longer?

Well, even if you think you've explained all this before, say it again so there's no doubt he knows what you require. Then if he refuses to alter his approach, you can be sure you're receiving either an aggressive or a contemptuous message, and can consider whether you wish to continue in such an unrewarding partnership. If, on the other hand, he can't wait but would like to, the 'squeeze' technique might prove useful. When he's near to orgasm, you interrupt sex to pinch, between your first two fingers and thumbs, the head of his penis just below the penis-crown, applying moderate to strong pressure, counting to three, and his erection should subside. With tender stroking, his erection should return and lovemaking can be resumed. Keep doing this till he gets used to waiting. Alternatively, during intercourse, pull gently on his testicles and scrotum to prevent them rising towards his body – a man finds ejaculation very difficult unless the balls are retracted by muscle reflex like an undercarriage snug against the pelvic base. However, remember that sex and perfection rarely combine. If he cannot last till your fourth and fifth orgasms, do compromise with masturbation.

Delayed ejaculation
I've been going to bed with my boyfriend for five weeks now and he's never been able to climax with me once. Is it me or is it him?

There's nothing biologically wrong with most men experiencing ejaculation difficulties. However, men who cannot come inside a woman may have a combination of technique and attitude problems. For instance, many men learn how to do sex by masturbating. When they bring themselves to orgasm, they may agitate with their hands far more quickly than two people can ever have sex. Hence when they start making love, the sensations seem under-stimulating. The answer to this part of the problem is to increase the eroticism of foreplay, make the guy wait until he's practically on the edge of climax before allowing him to insert his penis. (Make sure you've had fun in the meantime.) If this doesn't help, and you find he has a history of poor female relationships (mother or lover having let him down), then you will have to coax him more gently. Anxiety is preventing him from triggering his ejaculatory

112

reflex. Tell him not to worry, but to show you how he masturbates (all the way) instead. Make it fun. Next time, ask him to masturbate on you. Next time, see if he can do it just inside you – and so on. Sounds a bit boring but you're wrong. This game has great joint potential.

And one female problem

'When I think about it, Amanda's a lousy lover,' confided a marriage counsellor colleague searching for a quick solution between lunch and the afternoon appointments. 'Don't mistake me, she likes to be touched. There's nothing prudish about her. She can't wait to kiss me when we're alone; just closes her eyes and sort of goes. Sometimes I wonder whether she's practising self-hypnosis – heavy breathing, chest heaving, undulating like a dancer. Then she reaches climax. Fully dressed. Just like that.'

Now it may strike you that 'David' as I'll call him is a very lucky devil. As most recent surveys show, men and women spend more time looking for the sexual accelerator than a good set of brakes, but not always. The experienced generation of post-Pill women, high on sexual confidence, lower on patience, are quick to complain if their man stalls. They've read all the books and know their biological capacity at least is superior.

Some high-fliers like Amanda have practically acquired male faults. As a hospital doctor, she's a very busy person who rushes food, drink and travel as well as men. 'Of course if we do have sex properly,' continued David, 'I still feel left out of things. She actually makes me think I'm being cruel. After a few minutes, she's so overcome with emotion she breaks into tears. Then she goes very quiet. If I continue, it's like playing the triangle when the rest of the orchestra's finished.'

I wondered if Amanda would come in for a chat? 'Sorry, chum, she's much too busy' was the predictable response. I told David his problem was like that of anyone troubled by sexual mistiming, man or woman. He could remember that arousal of any kind, nervous or sexual, uses the same pathways from the brain to the spinal column. So if Amanda was wired by rushing through her day she was already halfway to sexual response – just as sales executives addicted to stress can suffer 'hair trigger trouble' when attempting to sleep with their wives or girlfriends.

I could see two solutions. First, in gradual stages, to introduce her to the mysteries of slowing down. He could work out a reward system to give her a treat every time she managed to savour a mouthful of food, or make a drink last ten minutes, or lie next to him on the sofa without letting rip. But the most important remedy was to forget to be a gentleman in bed for a while.

'Drop foreplay,' I suggested. 'Reflect that for her the music's already halfway to paradise so if you want a harmonious ending you really have to get started in the middle.'

THE EIGHT SEXUAL SECRETS MEN DON'T WANT YOU TO KNOW

As you know, it's generally enormous, wonderful and guaranteed to last all night. But will men ever tell women the whole truth about sex? Yes, but only when desperately in love, lust, or lately discovered in a compromising attitude.

For once the cliché is true: men in bed tell their mistresses (and ladies of pleasure) what they want, but their wives (and girlfriends) what they think they ought to hear. The problem for women at large is to improve their skills in doing that crossword-puzzle-on-legs which is a man. What's short and balding and thinks it's Kevin Costner? Or what's strong and silent and needs to be dressed in ribbons and bows? Or what's both Jekyll and Hyde? Yes, you've guessed it. A man.

I don't mean to be cynical when I suggest that in a macho world, men are never likely to be too comfortable with self-disclosure. Actor Dennis Waterman speaks for the silent majority: 'I'm not very good at relationship-type conversations. I find this whole thing of "we must talk about this" doesn't help very much, it wastes time and is often destructive. I'm a bit of a coward and I don't like talking terribly personally. I keep things to myself. If I've got a problem, it's mine. I don't want to change that. I'm over 40 and it's too late to change anything really.' In other words, if Dennis Waterman has a personal problem which he cannot solve all by himself, then it doesn't get dealt with.

As to sex, men are still full of hype, pretence and avoidance, their masculinity rooting for virility (can you do it best? do women fall at your feet?), the whole issue approached more from the point of view of male pomp than sweet intimacy. However, women have to deal with men as they *are* not how they'd like them to be. And to the cynics I'd say there is a real point in trying to help men improve their relationships. Statistics on divorce and health show they need your intimacy even though they won't say so and if it works, they will ultimately be better at loving you back. Check the following for clues to your walking puzzle. All generalisations are fraught – but that's no need to be frightened of them!

1. *Men like sexual control.* Even the bloke who fancies being 'submissive' wants to choose when! For other men, saying 'I Love You' is not a simple expression of delight in wife or partner; it often represents emotional defeat: 'Damn, I've put myself at risk of rejection again.' Men's solution to this problem is to experience sex as a separate entity, which is why they might talk of 'my sex life' as if it happens almost by itself: 'I didn't fancy her but decided to give it a go to keep myself up to scratch . . .' One man wrote to me: 'I can't function if the sexual decisions are ever in the woman's hands' (*Executive Magazine*, April 1982). Advice: forewarned is forearmed. Find out carefully about his favourite ways to be approached. If he does appear wary of closeness, give him time to realise how trustworthy you've always been – in fact, the one who really looks after him. Whatever else, men usually respect loyalty.

2. *Men suffer from penis envy.* Men don't always let on, but they are desperate for women to find them visually . . . impressive. Men believe women are fascinated by what's up front; in fact research quoted in Chapter One ('Love Bytes')

115

shows women are more typically observing men's bottoms. 'He's got some nice jeans that aren't too tight but show off his bum – my favourite part of his body – nicely' (singer Gloria Estefan on husband Emilio). Whatever Freud said, it's not women who want to look like stallions but men who are preoccupied with how their sexual appearance compares with others. As a result, the 'executive organ' gets idealised into a machine, tool or rock of unbelievable durability. In fact, as the writer Gay Talese once observed: 'It is very vulnerable even when made of stone, and the museums of the world are filled with Herculean figures brandishing penises that are chipped, clipped or completely chopped off.' If you want an ultimate perspective on the idea of female envy, share my admiration for the little girl who, upon seeing her first penis, remarked: 'Mother, isn't it a blessing they don't have them on their faces?' Advice: even if it is not your favourite bodily item, never disparage his manly proportions. If you actually are 'impressed', say so, with fervour.

3. *Men hate sexual criticism.* Only male masochists like you to mention the shortcomings of their sexual technique or performance. George and Carol came to see me for counselling after she had complained that he 'went at it like I was a roll of old carpet; he was hopeless'. I asked Carol how she phrased her complaint. 'Just like that,' came the puzzled response. 'He was hopeless so I told him.' Naturally enough, something inside George gave up hope with Carol and I was not surprised that he subsequently became impotent. Advice: if you want him to alter his behaviour in bed, learn to use positive language, not 'I can't stand it when you do X . . .' but 'It's really wonderful when you do Y . . . and I'd love to do some more of it right now, please.' Remember, most of us were lousy lovers when we began.

4. *Men want women to climax.* Whatever they say, most men

take credit if a woman responds orgasmically to them and feel both responsible and miserable if she doesn't. This is true regardless of her history and his level of skill. For instance, Geoff's ego was crushed when Evie didn't respond to his star performance. She explained that what had happened with her uncle when she was a teenager still gave her sexual nightmares. Geoff couldn't begin to see what this had to do with him. As he put it – 'Every other girl told me I was a great lover. Now it suddenly disappears!' Or take the case of Lynne, quoted in the Kramers' book, *Why Men Don't Get Enough Sex* (Virgin): 'We'd been having sex for six years so you'd think he'd get it right by now. If I don't have an orgasm, that injures his pride so I fake it to keep him happy.' Advice: you are the expert on how your body works and no man can make you enjoy yourself unless you decide to let go. Nor can he give you the pleasure you crave unless you find a way to show him. Faking is a big mistake – it only trains a man *not* to satisfy you. If you convey the idea that all is wonderful when it isn't, the poor bloke can only be expected to repeat his mistakes regularly. So, understand he needs to feel appreciated but help him to get it right. Show him how to create moods and fantasies, where to touch and when to be gentle and when to abandon control.

5. *Men like pornography.* Whatever they say, most men will watch pornography because it excites them. Most men will also look at short skirts, indiscreetly revealed bosoms and blatant visual signals from wet lips to wriggling bottoms. In fact, men's eyes zero on the erogenous zones before their brains have time to think. Women do the same, of course, but less openly and often. The real issue here is not sexual politics but consideration for each other's feelings. Diana, for example, simply hated the way husband Brian leered at her girlfriends. She said he didn't just have a roving eye, it was practically revolving. When he started bringing home copies of *Penthouse*, she threw an all-time

wobbly. He was amazed. They survived the episode by agreeing to widen their views and modify their conduct – he would be more discreet; she would be more broad-minded. For Christmas, she bought him Eleanor Bron's *Pillow Book*. He gave her an eternity ring attached to a card which said 'I promise only to smile at strangers'. Advice: men may be basic, but window-shopping isn't a prelude to infidelity.

6. *Men are sexually squeamish.* Some heterosexual men do not like everything about womanliness and cope poorly with the facts of menstruation, sexual odour and childbirth. They may never have been educated to understand these feminine essentials which therefore remain 'mysteries'. My correspondent George B., for example, was shocked to his socks when he discovered that Mrs B. found breast-feeding a turn-on. It took a little persuasion to get him to see that breasts which are functional for a baby can stay 'sexy' for the parents. On the other hand, equally masculine men revel in sexual intimacy, especially a woman's secret scent, or what the French call her '*cassolette*'. Napoleon to Josephine: 'Home in five days. Don't wash . . .' Advice: tastes will always vary. If he has a problem, accept it at the outset but make sure he begins to learn how your body really works from month to month. A lot of male fastidious-ness is really based on ignorance.

7. *Men always have secret fantasies.* Most men have fantasies or near-fetishes of which they are ashamed or about which they feel embarrassed. One reason why men are 'comfor-table' with the idea of prostitution is that bold sexual com-merce removes the awkwardness. Experienced working women expect men to 'have their little peculiarities'. During lovemaking, most men (like some women) will fantasise about others. Freud said that when two people make love, there are at least four people present – the two involved, and the rest imaginary. Advice: remind yourself

118

that fantasy isn't reality – as I've said, we no more get to choose which ones are exciting than we get to choose what we dream when asleep. It isn't a personal insult that someone's sexual imagination roams in bed. On the other hand, how could you use his 'little peculiarity' to your advantage? Perhaps tell him a story while he closes his eyes?

And finally . . .

8. *Men aren't all sex-mad.* It is not true that men will make love with you more often if you offer them sex more frequently. They will only pretend that this will be the case. In fact, just as many men as women have the headaches and just as many men as women withhold sex as a means of punishing or controlling their partners. The secret is this: men sometimes do not want to make love. After the age of 30, men also need more stimulation in order to be able to make love at all. June was extremely surprised, for instance, when the mere presence of her half-clothed body did not drive new boyfriend, 41-year-old Marcus, into a sexual frenzy. Advice: don't be misled by male propaganda that they are ever ready. But if you can tap into item seven (above), half your battle will be over – and the rest is down to deftness of touch and a good relationship.

Despite the problems outlined here, there are many pleasures too. But if we go back to the point I made at the beginning of the chapter, the sexual climate has improved immeasurably on how it was when your parents started out. And the improvement mainly focuses on women. Women now have a freedom to earn, and are capable of achieving a kind of independence that your grandmother would never have dreamed of. It gives choices women have never had before. What I find specially heartening is the progress that has been made in understanding sexual difficulties. Our grandmothers would have found help nowhere. Today the help is not only available; most of the time, it works. Sexually, this is probably the best moment in history for women of the Western world.

Chapter Six

Great Sex (and How to Introduce Your Partner to the Gentle Art of Sexual Surrender)

Great sex can happen at peculiar times. With a soulmate, you naturally hope for hours of ecstasy, but from a lover you have already decided to 'drop' you would not be so optimistic. However, to continue some of the themes explored in Chapter One, there's a paradox at the heart of erotic desire. We don't always get what we expect.

Great love; terrible sex
Sometimes, love gets in the way of good sex. There's that juicy individual you're desperate to impress. That hunk of a chunk. That person you've willed and wiled into your arms. That sex object who fulfils the fantasies you've been taking to bed since you were 14. Alas – he makes you too tense to enjoy an erotic experience.

Or maybe you play a waiting game until you meet 'Mr Right'. You'd like to spend the rest of the week with him – hell, longer. Hitherto you've been very cautious. Now you fling yourself into his bed only to discover that he doesn't actually know how to make love to you. His touch is clumsy. He crushes your lips; mishandles your breasts. The sequence of caresses is wrong for you. Or he grows over-anxious and instead of delivering hours of bliss suffers a premature climax. You were just beginning to find the right mood and now he's retreated into his shell – he's even reaching for his clothes. He's talking about a cup of coffee. So much for love and sex being inseparable!

At this point, you need to stand back and look through a different pair of spectacles. Remember the pressure to perform

121

can sometimes cancel the performance. Maybe the act of waiting too long has spoiled things – you are too used to saying no in your head. Or perhaps you feel so sex-starved, the essentials of foreplay were forgotten.

Gail, a 23-year-old furnishings buyer, had just emerged from the tedium of a bitter divorce. There had been no willing man in her bed for more than 11 months. She was so keen to start an affair with Harry from the supply company that she invited him to her flat on the pretext of collecting some invoices and jumped him as soon as he could be provoked into making an advance.

She undressed and slipped him inside her then demanded he pump faster than his 140 lb frame could go. It only made her hot, cross and bothered. He began to find penile sensation almost painful inside this vagina which to him felt like an over-revved vibrator. Fraught from the start, their sexual relationship never recovered from the conflict between her desire for speedy climax and his personal and biologic need to proceed more sedately.

Great sex; terrible love

Even odder than the failure of love (or lust) to produce satisfaction is the fact that a relationship on the brink of disaster can sometimes yield moments of supreme erotic bliss. Gone is the need to impress; forgotten is the fear of failure. You're left with the skill born of familiarity given an unexpected twist of arousal by the general hostility of parting.

This reaction isn't so difficult to explain. As mentioned before, there is only one system of excitement in the human body and all activities have to share its neural pathways. When two people fight, they press a number of their sexual buttons, producing effects which the human brain finds easy to associate with sexual desire. If you think about it, getting angry looks exactly like getting turned on: trembling limbs, sweaty brow, rapid pulse, gulping breaths. Don't be surprised, therefore, that sometimes a sexual encounter gets transformed into a row, or that people at odds with each other who already feel passionate can suddenly fall into bed.

Danger – high voltage

● Fear causes attraction. It doesn't seem to matter whether the emotionally arousing experience is positive or negative so long as it's shared. Two people who survive a dangerous accident together are more likely to fall in love than two people who go for an uneventful drive, or even separate drives and lust after each other at the traffic lights.

● According to ethologists, people normally seek human contact when feeling afraid and there is a complementary need to offer nurture to those emitting dependency signals.

● Men who are experiencing fear have been shown to talk far more about sex than men who aren't!

● Illicit affairs and 'brief encounters in wartime' appear to be more rewarding than socially sanctioned ones due to the atmosphere of fear in which they are conducted.

However

Why is 'anxious fear' arousing when 'fearful anxiety' is a turn off resulting in loss of sexual ability? Because, according to Dr S. Schachter, there are two types of 'fear'. It seems that the experience of any given emotion must involve separate stages. Stage one includes the physical changes (elevated heart rate, red face, etc.). Stage two is a labelling of the arousal in the mind as a particular emotion – love, anger, fear, hate.

So if fear gets labelled 'love' by Person A, some of the damaging emissions of adrenaline will be curbed and they can enjoy great sex. However, if fear gets labelled 'despair' or 'likely to induce frigidity' by Person B then that's what results. Adrenaline levels prevent the blood from accumulating in the genital area where it's needed. A man will lose his erection. A woman will find it difficult to hold her vagina in the 'tented' or 'climactic' position.

More great sex, terrible love

Some relationships are terrible from the outset but survive simply because the sex is unforgettably addictive. That was the case for Claire, a London secretary, who always adored making love with Ian, a computer programmer. If you asked why she went to live with him she'd say, 'His body.' He had the most sensitive skin and could reach climax just by having his nipples touched. But after sex, she felt bored to death. She could never suppress an awful sense of dread when she knew he was about to tell her something *else* about the Windows 95 Technical Support Line on which he'd worked all day. She began to wish he were female and could have more orgasms just to keep them both distracted. The partnership ended because sex alone cannot bind two people in happy contentment.

But why does sex get us into these pickles in the first place? Most experts suggest the purpose of desire and lust is to keep people together when they might begin to tire of each other. Nature only wants us to breed and it's hard to make babies if you keep rejecting potential partners. I suppose the lesson from this is to consult your judgement when deciding with whom to live or associate. Your loins will only lead you astray!

Great love *and* sex

Of course, great sex does tend to happen when you encounter someone on your right mental and physical, even spiritual, wavelength. Candice had been looking 'literally for years' for a man with the ideal physical shape, smell and skin tone who could not only find her G-Spot but share her love of Art Deco design and doing up old houses.

'I'd always felt slightly superior to men until I encountered Gerald. He was always able to get me to tell him I wanted him. He wasn't fazed the way other men were; if I fluttered my eyelashes he would say, "I see you're fluttering your eyelashes." He knew what I was thinking. Of course I hated him for that but it was wonderful to be able to surrender to pleasure, confident that he wouldn't be selfish. I had total trust in his ability to manage me. When we made love, it lasted for hours. I don't mean he held his erection all that time. We would screw a while, then kiss, then he'd put three fingers inside me, then take me from behind, then we'd have oral sex. Then we'd stop for mineral water and I'd give him my special grin and it would begin all over again. I could not get to the bottom of my desire for this lover – the more I had the more I wanted and for the first time in my life, I didn't care what we go up to. There wasn't a private crevice left in my body. If he'd asked to sleep with his face between my thighs I'd say let's do it.'

A similar experience befell Mary. She was educated in an Irish Catholic convent following adoption. Her parents were embittered at not being able to have children of their own and disappointed because money flowed more easily to others than to them. Mary married as soon as she was legally able to escape the atmosphere of 'Thou Shalt Not' at home. Her marriage was unfulfilling. Not till she started an affair with Graham from the local garage did she enjoy her first orgasm during sex. Suddenly, like a vision, she saw this green light. 'I found myself rethinking sex from top to bottom. Previously it was something I'd sort of put up with. Now I was thinking about it all day long, getting wet just wondering if Graham would ring me. When we met, I was doing things to him I'd no previous experience of and never in a thousand years imagined myself doing – stopping in a lay-by, for instance, and demanding that he let me go down on him. Jesus, I didn't even know how to do it properly – I just knew this was the way I wanted to express my passion to please him and reach out to him. I wanted to get as close to him as I could and express that longing sexually. I guess I would have died if the Garda had come by and we'd ended up in some local newspaper scandal like the woman on television.' Mary didn't live with Graham but she did leave her marriage and make a new independent life for herself and she does think her 'sexual awakening' was instrumental.

Graham also managed to locate Mary's G-Spot partly because of the contorted positions they got into in his car. Strangely, doctors know all about test-tube babies yet can't tell us anything for certain about this region. The trouble is they are unable to map all the sexual nerves in the human body because you can't do scientific dissections on living people – and you can't ask dead ones whether they are having a good time when you touch them intimately.

As I mentioned in Chapter Four, the G-Spot was first written up by a German doctor called Grafenberg. He was a gynaecologist who said a lot of his patients reported a very sexually sensitive zone about two inches or so inside the front wall of the vagina. Not only did this place cause lucky owners to have shattering orgasms, some of them also said they experienced a great surge in their juices as if they were reaching climax like a man. Sex researchers Masters and Johnson claimed to prove that all orgasms needed the clitoral trigger to be touched. Renewed interest in Grafenberg's research then indicated that some women definitely preferred intercourse to masturbation, or at least wanted penetration and pressure on the front wall of the vagina in the G-Spot area.

To find the G-Spot, let me quote the words of my colleague Dr David Delvin: 'Slip a moistened finger gently inside the vagina, and run it slowly up the back of the pubic bone. When you've travelled up with almost half your finger, start pressing quite hard with your finger pad against the firmness of the pubic bone. You may have to move around a little bit until you strike the spot, but with a bit of luck your partner will suddenly say something to you along the lines of "Mmmm . . . that feels interesting." Continue rubbing there, by moving your finger backwards and forwards, and the results should be wonderful for her.'

The feelings can actually be heavenly, almost too over-powering for words. A woman might actually say, 'Just there . . .

don't move . . . oh yessss . . . keep still . . . oh, it's like the world's spinning, it's unbearable, I want it to go on forever.'

During intercourse, the best way to find the G-Spot is either in the missionary position with the man on top, or with the woman on top of the man when he is seated. In the missionary position, place the woman's legs on the man's shoulders, half withdraw the penis with the man pressing downwards, causing the penis tip to press upwards. It is not necessary for the man to continue any in-out movement at all. Just by maintaining this position, his partner can dissolve into pleasure. With the woman on top, she should arch her back away from the man and slightly raise her pelvis till she finds what she wants.

Gillian first discovered the power of her G-Spot with Michael. She was much shorter than him physically and they were actually having missionary sex in the bath when he raised both her legs way over her head and rocked the whole of her body on the very tip of his penis. She said: 'I thought there was something wrong with the electrics and we were about to die because the bathtub had become "live". I was screaming in a mixture of joy and terror. Later we tried the same thing on dry land and it became my favourite position of all – different from clitoral sex; much more shattering afterwards but ever so yummy. I really miss Michael.'

Variation
You could also ask your lover to use two fingers of one hand to stimulate your G-Spot, curling the tips forward to make a pad, while getting the little finger of the same hand to dart backwards and stroke your inner thighs. Meanwhile, using plenty of lubrication he or she could also employ one or two fingers of the other hand to stimulate your clitoris. If sufficiently supple, your lover could even be kissing your lips and breasts at the same time. But the key element is masses of lubrication – love juice and saliva are best.

Great sex could hardly be complete without great oral sex. Christine, a 23-year-old product demonstrator, said: 'I judge my men by two things. Will they go down on me and are they any good at it? If the answer to both questions is yes, then I'm probably in love.'

Enjoying oral sex as a woman is about feeling safe and comfortable with what you're doing. There's nothing more natural than taking pleasure in licking, nibbling and kissing your partner's body, even in private places. People have enjoyed oral sex since history began. For instance, the ancient Indian love manual the *Kama Sutra* describes no less than eight different ways lovers can pleasure each other, including one called 'sucking a mango fruit'.

Obviously hygiene is important but just as you wouldn't want to kiss someone who didn't brush their teeth, why agree to oral sex with a lover who doesn't smell sweet? Washing and bathing can easily be incorporated into the pre-lovemaking build-up if you want to make doubly sure.

How to give . . .

Most oral sex has the giver in control. It's important to look your partner boldly in the eye and say, 'Lie back and enjoy it.' The most comfortable position is for him to lie on his back with you seated facing him, your legs stretched underneath his (more difficult in a car).

There are four essentials in giving your man oral delight.

● First, on a practical note, remove your rings and tie your hair back out of the way.
● Second, think of the penis as no fragile flower. The head is super-sensitive, and so is the foreskin and the underside of the tip, but the rest can tolerate quite strong to sturdy pumping strokes. His manhood is a little bit like a finger with a clitoris stuck on the end!
● Third, always use your hands to stimulate the penis at the

same time as using your lips. This also gives you a buffer on the down stroke.

● Fourth, you must generate plenty of saliva – it's wonderful for him and far easier for you.

In general, oral sex needs to start off very slowly and very tentatively and speeds up over a period of about ten minutes. What you are aiming to do is build up erotic tension and passion which is then discharged – you're not doing the opposite, which is to reduce tension till people lose interest.

For this reason, it is almost always better to go more slowly and lightly than the other person really wants. Eroticism is mostly about teasing and compelling the other person to experience the edge of desire. So I repeat, don't make a beeline for that genital area at once. Nibble down from the chest, linger over the skin of the navel, move purposefully across the hips with hot, passionate lips, aim for the target then swerve at the last minute towards the inner groin, upper thigh and down to the back of the knees (by raising your partner's legs), then move up again and make a second pass. Keep the tension high by promising but not delivering till the other person has to *beg* (and make sure they don't touch themselves with their hands to spoil the fun).

Then, looking him provocatively in the eye:

1. Slowly lower your head and kiss the penile tip. Tease the sides of the shaft with your right-hand fingernails, then form a ring from your fingers and stroke him five or six times.
2. Place your left hand firmly around the base of the penis, using loads of saliva over the penile head, and forming your mouth into the letter 'O'. Make sure your teeth are covered by the inside skin of your lips.
3. Slide your lips down the penile shaft till they meet your left thumb and forefinger. Don't rush, prolong his ecstasy. Move slowly and practise sucking with a variety of pressures as you go.

129

4. As your head comes back up, swirl your tongue across his skin and with your right hand, stroke his balls or inner thighs.
5. To vary the pleasure, place your right-hand thumb and forefinger just below your lips like a second mouth so that hand and mouth move together, both stimulating the shaft.
6. Break off from time to time and remind him to lose his mind in his fantasies. He'll know what you mean. Build up erotic tension and increase your speed as his sighs and cries tell you his delight is intensifying.
7. If at the climax, you want to stay with it – fine. If not, keep a box of tissues handy.

There have been no known cases of HIV transmission through oral sex but herpes can be passed on by kissing of any sort. If you are unsure of your partner's history, a flavoured condom is strongly recommended.

Karen's story may provide further inspiration:

'I knew that Alan was inexperienced and inhibited but he was a really nice man. I also knew that if I made a lunge for his genitals he'd be really disturbed. So I devised a cunning plan. All the sex manuals say use massage to get the whole body sensitised and this leads logically on to 'extras'. Why not try similar tactics with the tongue instead of hands? So I went ahead and gave him a tongue bath. Of course I made sure the room was boiling hot first because I was afraid that he might get cold once I got him naked.

'I just stroked him slowly and sensually with the tip of my tongue. And he liked it. I took a very long time before reaching his genitals and even then I focused on the areas above and below. By the time I reached his penis he was groaning. I touched him lightly in long straight dives up and down. I changed it to twirling my tongue lightly on the head, and then dabbing the very top in quick stabbing motions. He got so turned on then that he kind of grabbed my head and pushed it down on to him. And I got to give him oral sex after all. It was a brilliant success.'

. . . And receive
Karen's method of getting her shy boyfriend to reciprocate was to talk him through it aloud:

'I like a man's tongue to lick me upwards. The most sensation I get is when my clitoris is licked upwards from underneath. There are lots of types of touch that work well – the tip of the tongue is best; the blade of the tongue is OK but not quite so sensational. I also like experiments where he licks up and down one side of the clitoral shaft and then up and down the other. For me to come, the emphasis should always be on the upward strokes with downward strokes just used as a means of returning to base.

'Once I'm a mass of quivering jelly, which doesn't take long, the guy might try covering the whole clitoris in his mouth and gently sucking, or just moving his mouth up and down the clitoris like I might do to a penis. I know from talking to girlfriends that women aren't all the same but I love it when he sucks and at the same time flicks his tongue-tip hard across the tip of my clitoris. It's very important to be able to give feedback and great if he asks for it. The only problem with the whole mouth sucking is that it can be too forceful and can end up anaesthetising me. When ever I say 'Easy!', I mean just lighten the strokes but for goodness sake don't stop.

'The flicking over the clitoris, plus a wonderful twirl of the tongue on the head, or circling the tip gently, are what get me nearest to orgasm. But I've learned not to think of this as leading to orgasm. You feel more sensual if you allow it to be part of a rich experience, and I think anyway I prefer to climax with his penis inside me. But everyone's different. I know some of my friends adore climaxing this way.'

When it comes to a man kissing *you*, remember that he hasn't got a vulva, clitoris or vagina, so he doesn't know how they

131

feel. Most men make three mistakes which you should gently correct by word or gesture. First, they tend to touch the dynamite bud of the clitoris too quickly, thinking it really is as robust as the penis. Second, they don't bother to keep the delicate skin in that region moist. Third, they tend to pump away with their tongues like a piston when what you want is subtle strokes, and then wonder why their neck muscles get cramp.

IS THAT NICE ?

well ... QUITE nice ...
in an irritating
well-intentioned
sort of way

GREAT SEXUAL FOOTWORK

It's not only the head but also the feet that can feature in the Greatest Sex. You can also learn to drive your partner into a sensual frenzy.

Foot sex isn't new. Let me quote a passage from *The Sex Life of the Foot and Shoe* by William A. Rossi, about London's underworld a few years back:

> 'He took me to a sedate home, which I later learned was known as The Palace of Pedic Pleasure. Inside, we were greeted by a matronly woman, the madam. The place was furnished in good though not lavish taste. Several men and women, fully clothed, were sitting around talking and drinking.

'But soon, some of the men, paired with their selected women, disappeared. My friend and I sat and chatted with the madam. Her clientele, she explained, was composed of "sexual sophisticates" . . . What did the Palace of Pedic Pleasure offer them? She said: "Our girls are very special. The most important thing is that their feet must be beautiful – slender, very mobile feet with smooth skin and long, flexible toes. Then we teach the girls how to become experts at pedic love-making . . . All our clients are what you'd call normal men but they have something in common – they enjoy sexual foreplay with the feet. It can take all kinds of forms – having the penis massaged by the girl's feet; or putting the penis between the girl's feet; or sucking the toes of the girl; or using the big toe to insert into the vagina; or holding or kissing the girl's feet while sex takes place – lots and lots of different ways . . . You can find houses like ours the world over." '

There are six clear reasons why foot sex works or the way to a person's sexual desires may be through their feet.

● First, there are many nerve endings in the feet and hands – sometimes more than in other parts of the body more usually associated with sex. Obviously, when cavemen wandered the earth they needed to know what their bare feet were stepping into. So it's possible to send a huge number of signals to the brain about the hot and cold, sharp and blunt, wet and dry experiences your feet are having. Lovers can make the fullest use of these.

● However, we keep our feet pretty well covered up these days and even in the bedroom tend to ignore them. So that's the second reason why they will respond so magically – our feet are unused to being touched and relish the opportunity. Most other parts of the body get attention from time to time but the little crevices between the toes, for instance, are rarely on the receiving end. That's why it tends to tickle when you wash them – it's virtually virgin territory.

● Note – washing is important. Only the most dedicated of foot fetishists is really turned on by badly smelling feet. Clean feet, though, do give off a mixture of sexual scents plus pheromones – the sex chemicals responsible for desire and attraction. These come from the large sweat glands developed at puberty and there are many of them per square foot – as anyone who's ever been on a rave can tell you.

● Fourth, the appearance of feet can be very sexual. Toes look symbolic. If you think about it, they're shaped like miniature sex organs – the big toe more masculine, the little toe with its bud-tip appearance like an excited clitoris. When toes are teased and sucked, couples can fantasise they're performing real oral sex – especially the person receiving. If this is happening to my feet, they think, just imagine how other parts will react?

● Fifth, the feet are connected directly to the genital area by a sort of motorway of nerves running up the legs. Every touch you give has to pass within microseconds through the sexual control centre in the base of the spine and in the groin.

● That's why starting with the feet is subtle – any experienced lover knows that the kisses or licks of pedic love can lead to higher pleasures. You only have to move on to the erogenous zones behind the knees via the outside of the calves before your partner will almost without noticing want to pull your head nearer, and nearer. Chinese sex manuals recommended 18 different positions in which intercourse could be combined with manipulations of the feet. One involved inserting melon seeds and almonds between the toes.

● Sixth, feet are associated with shoes, and for centuries men and women have been drawing attention to their sexuality through footwear. For instance, shiny black boots can be associated with the power of dominance or submission – the high heel being both a weapon and a handicap, because although you might stab a rapist to death with one, you cannot run to save your life. The foot with or without shoes is used to express conquest – placed straight on the chest of your victim.

The best way to make love to a foot is to start by scene-setting – peaceful, with the soft mood music of your choice – then give your partner a foot bath. It can even seem innocent – everyone's feet take strain during the day. With warm water, bathe and stroke each foot in turn, slowly and gently all over. Then with your partner lying down, gently knead the ball of the foot, starting under the big toe and moving across. Use firm, non-tickly strokes. After treating each foot to the same pleasure, begin the kisses by taking the whole of the big toe into your well-moistened mouth and suck sensuously. Nibble and nip with the tips of your teeth. Gradually move your tongue to the space between the big toe and the next one, release the side of your cheek from the big toe and suck the whole of this second toe between your teeth. Repeat with each toe in turn till you arrive at the littlest. Then take all four of the smaller toes into your mouth at once and flick the tongue at random between the crevices. You can experiment by heating your mouth from time to time with a warm drink or by sucking an ice cube so that the sensations vary in excitement. Offer both feet identical attention. Afterwards, with baby oil, massage them sensuously with your hands, your own feet or even your naked buttocks – and move on . . .

GREAT KEGEL SEX

To find the 'Ks', go to the loo and during urination, stop and start the flow several times over. The muscles controlling this process are your Kegels. With practice, you can flex and relax this muscle group anywhere at any time without needing to pee at all. Women who ride horses naturally gain flexural strength and control in the Kegel area.

Once these muscles are honed, they can play a central role during sexual intercourse. If you're skilful, it's actually possible to grip and apply a gentle vacuum to a man's penis so he almost imagines you possess a secret hand which can operate independently of pelvic bodily movements. The sensation for him is both bewildering and ecstatic. Incidentally, it's the same muscle group which tends to get over-developed in places like Thailand so that showgirls can entertain sex tourists. But don't be put off.

GREAT SEX: THE FIVE NIGHTS OF LOVE

Making changes to your sexual routine should ideally be done gradually. An erotic seduction is more effective than a direct demand and the best sex happens spontaneously. Sex isn't a race – you can take days, weeks even, exploring your partner. But for those who *do* want to stir things up and live more on the edge, here's a game two lovers can play that's guaranteed to take the routine out of lovemaking. It ultimately depends on delaying orgasmic sex until the final night . . .

Preliminary
Give up alcohol for at least two weeks beforehand to tone the system. If you want to heighten physical sensation, eat moderately over the same period so your nerves are ever so slightly on edge and ultra-responsive with hunger.

Night one

Body-mapping: the secret gardens of delight
After a roll of the dice to see who goes first we get into the Sexological Exam. The couple sit naked facing each other. The one who starts touches (non-genitally) the other person with a specific stroke and the recipient marks that touch for sensuality on a scale of Plus-3 to Minus-3. The strokes should be varied from super gentle to quite strong. As the body is covered, a mental map of the most sensitive areas and the way they like to respond will be formed.

136

The partners may either take it in turns stroke by stroke, or do all their touching in one go then swap over. The aim should be to learn a secret about the partner's body – to find a four-inch square piece of non-genital flesh which you can drive wild. Or you can confirm your knowledge of your partner's favoured places. Even old-established lovers may have grown careless and sloppy here. The night ends (without sex) in a gentle massage.

Night two

Mind-mapping
1. Fantasies. Each person dresses in their most romantic out-fit (lingerie, silks, satins, etc.) and then you play the fantasy game. It can start simply – which of the following would you most like for a lover? Schwarzenegger? Danny De Vito? Sean Connery in 1960/1990? It can then enter into the technique called 'Guided Fantasy' as the couple build their sensual scenario in words. You might, for instance, start with a room, add some music, put in a four-poster, conjure up room service, add personnel, create dialogue and (restrained) action.

And 2. Psychological Limits. Each person gets to ask five revealing questions and the other person undertakes to reply truthfully. The answers are designed to show or confirm whether your partner is really a risk-taker or a risk-hater, really patient or impulsive, really broad-minded or ultimately reserved. For example, would you ever make love in a lift, car, field, train, plane, office or on a beach? Have you ever done so? Describe. At the end of the evening, the dice is rolled and the winner chooses whether to massage or be massaged. The catch is that the one massaged is also blindfolded while the other replays their favourite fantasy in teasing words. Again, no complete sexual act, though the massage may veer towards what one small boy has called the 'rogerous' zones too.

Night three

Appearance is Sexually Deceptive
The clothes/cosmetics dare. Requires availability of complete make-up kit, also male outfit for the woman. We explore gender inhibitions. The woman gives the man a complete facial, make-up, base, mascara, lipstick – the works. The woman is dressed in a man's suit which more or less fits, plus painted moustache, slicked down hair, etc. She then roleplays treating him like a woman during the course of which dinner will be served and she will aim to seduce him into kissing and petting on the sofa afterwards (but no sex since this is a first date!).

Night four

Power-play
Explore the ABC of Who's in Charge. Not to be confused with the more specific Power Games described below. By a roll of the dice, one person takes the dominant role. The 'Boss' then compiles a set of rules and punishments for any infractions of the rules by the 'Subordinate'. Regulations should fit or suit the temperament of those involved. For example, maybe the 'sub' mustn't speak, or must confess to one embarrassing recent lie and go and sit in the corner for five minutes. If they break the rules, they will be humiliated (or whatever). If they obey beautifully, they will be given a genital massage (short of orgasm). However, halfway through this reward, new conditions will be imposed which must be met, etc. The partners can swap roles during the evening.

Night five
Where we've been leading. Shake of the dice – and the winner (this week) gets the sex of their dreams.

GREAT SEX – POWER GAMES

If you want to experience great physical sex it stands to reason you need to receive some great mental sex. What gets dissolved at orgasm is tension from both body and mind. Therefore, the more obstacles you can place in the path of easy gratification, the more pleasures you can ultimately enjoy.

Physical caresses that go on for ages with subtle, prolonged permutations help prepare you. So do those tormenting thoughts of 'so near and yet so far'. The art of love is the art of timing. You can improve this timing by using the dynamics of unpredictability to bring your partner close to ecstasy. Of course, too much frustration will generate a kind of disappointed tedium. But if you follow these detailed guidelines you'll get your timing absolutely hot spot on. If you want flattery, research suggests that powerful, successful people of either sex are those most likely to enjoy part-time psychological surrender!

Before you start
1. Do not play these sorts of games with anyone you distrust or have only just met. The purpose of the activity is to extend the boundaries of an already close relationship. You are using your private knowledge of your partner to get further into their mind as well as body, so there is no point in even contemplating a casual encounter.
2. Both parties must be willing. It is out of the question to suggest these games to someone who has claustrophobia or suffers nightmares about sexual restraint.
3. Before making the first move, agree an emergency phrase or code to be used if either person wishes to bale out. Sometimes, this will not be a word but a gesture or a specific sound.
4. Do not attempt these games with those who are in poor health.
5. Do not restrict airways or use restraints which prevent the proper circulation of the blood.

Creating the right mood

Every relationship has a 'balance of power'. Different people have different skills and areas of knowledge. Perhaps a woman can speak more authoritatively on matters of tax law and a man on contraception – or it could be the other way round. Different people also have different levels of energy and desire. On some occasions you may feel like urgently initiating sex; on others you may want to be pampered and let your lover take the strain. We all had a special relationship with the first authority figures in our lives – our parents – and the memories they gave us from childhood can colour our deepest sexual wishes and fantasies.

When thinking about broaching the subject of gentle erotic dominance, ask yourself about this balance of power in your partnership. Has the other person ever shown the slightest tinge of interest in erotic control or surrender? Does your instinct tell you to proceed with ultimate caution or could you be pushing at an already half-open door? Clues would include your joint physical behaviour. Have you ever indulged in mild wrestling games together or enjoyed occasional slaps and pats on the bottom as you pass from one room to the next? Is your partner happy to accept forceful touchings and teasing even when sex isn't on the menu? When in bed, does he relish the thrill of prolonged foreplay or generally precipitate speedy orgasm? Is *she* the sort of person who has ever hinted at a desire 'to feel submissive'? Is *he* the sort of guy who has ever shown the faintest desire to fall at the feet of 'domineering women'? All these are the sorts of potential openings to explore if you intend to seize the moment. Nothing ventured, nothing gained. The type of gambit you might try is: 'Funny you should say that. I'd love to take total charge of you tonight. I want to make you weep with pleasure. There's only one difficulty in the way. Will you let me?'

Props you may need
● Be subtle. In the coming weeks, you can lead up to the use of more formal items but the first time, keep everything ultra

simple. A beautiful chiffon scarf can be used to bind hands. Perhaps you will want more than one. Maybe you can wear stockings which, once removed, can be pressed into service as ropes?

● If you want to bind your partner to the bed, think about where the ties will be tethered. Practise in advance to be sure they will hold. You can secure useful hooks into the underside of the bedframe.

● Buy a sleep blindfold. Perhaps start using this routinely when you go to bed 'to curb glare'. This will then be handy on the bedside table when you want to initiate a game.

● Massage gloves faced on one side with velvet and the other with fur can be obtained and are a wonderful secret weapon to use on your partner's flesh as he/she lies naked, restrained and blindfolded before you.

● Other useful accessories include headphones from a Walkman (if you want to close another of your partner's senses), warm oil and (possibly) ice cubes.

Moves you two might make

These are the suggested moves and scripts you might follow on a first attempt to introduce more mood heat into your bedroom. The tone should be gentle and trusting and the voice kept low and seductive till the receiver is 'secured'.

Gaining permission

It's a good idea to begin making love to your partner in the usual way. Ensure they are highly aroused, warm, sexy and full of desire. If they are multiple orgasmic, they can be permitted an early climax by whatever means you both please. Then suggest you be allowed to 'take them to heaven by taking *over*'.

Furthering your suggestion

Build a picture in words of how you enjoy touching and stroking their most secret recesses but don't exactly match words to actions. Stroke *near* but not *on* the places they most want you to touch. The key to success is 'frustration of expectation'. Get them used to you not touching their most sensitive zones then accidentally let one finger wander and trail ever so lightly across the genitals. If you're doing it properly, they should gasp.

Raising the temperature

Now you want to suggest to your partner that it's time for a little extra surrender: 'Would you like to feel unlimited pleasure, to go almost crazy with desire, to feel helpless with passion? You would? Then keep your hands over your head while I get to work.'

The takeover

However, it's very difficult to keep your hands constantly above your head while being frustratingly teased just off centre below the waist so eventually your victim is likely to disobey. Now you suggest a solution. 'Will you do as I ask? Will you put your wrists together and let me tie them so I can really give your skin bliss and make you entirely happy without all these tedious interruptions which neither of us wants? Please? Will you do that for me?' (Hands can also be tied to the bed/bedframe/headboard for complete security – and feet likewise if you both see fit. On a first occasion, remember 'less may be more'. And you also want to have something to look forward to.)

[*Knots*: Use the scout's reef knot – 'left over right and through; right over left and through' because you can always undo this easily by pulling open one of the loose ends and slipping off the remaining loops. Boy/Girl Scout training finally has its uses . . .]

The blindfold

Next, help your partner achieve a mental change of gear by whispering: 'Relax, let yourself go, forget the day, forget where you are, lose yourself, don't think about me, let your mind wander where it will and visit that secret erotic place only you know about and can enter' all the while making your caresses both more persistent and more teasing by slowing down your rhythm even further. Touch the side of the neck with tenderly applied feather-strokes from fingernails. Do the same to the sides of the breasts, inner thighs, buttocks and groins. Make the visits of your fingers to the genitals almost a rarity. Hint in the same subdued voice how it might be more fun for your partner to close their eyes, to see nothing, to float into darkness and focus on their dreams, and suggest they could find this easier if they borrowed your bedside blindfold.

Caution

Since this is a 'first time', be ready to switch the mood back to more conventional lovemaking if your partner requests it. Alternatively, you may now have them at your complete mercy and ready to enjoy a little more psychological pressure: 'Do you like me to touch you there?' you ask, as your fingers momentarily tantalise a nipple, the clitoris or titillate a headstrong penile glans. 'Is it wonderful? Would you like more? Oh dear,' you say, 'it seems to be stopping. Look, it's stopped.' Follow this up with a cruel 'And would you be willing to pay to get it to start again?'

How to pay

This should also be suited to your partner's level of comfort with the overall game. Perhaps you will compel them merely to say 'I beg you to touch me there' or insist they use the word 'Please'. Payment can also be made by tolerating an ice cube pressed to the navel (or any other warm, rosy section of anatomy) or receiving mild slaps on the buttocks, the number to be negotiated. Whatever is decided, remember to keep the price just a tad high – the best caresses should always be stopped *before* the recipient expects them to vanish . . .

Finally

When your partner has reached their 'point of no return', break off from the game and using hands, mouth, or genitals commence rapid and vigorous sex till they climax.

Afterwards

Resume everyday roles, be loving and reassuring, be full of thanks and praise – and suggest you might be willing to be on the receiving end next time, if they dare . . .

THE DYNAMICS OF DOMINATION

' "Do you want a drink?" I asked.

She looked at me deliberately. "You're asking?"

"Yes – I guess."

She deflated slightly. "Then, no . . . thank you."

I don't know why I said it. Maybe there was something wicked in the hot, stained bricks of this place, and I was picking it up by osmosis.

"What if I told you to?"

Suddenly the same light I had seen in other eyes here was in hers. She was waiting for me to tell her what to do. Wanted me to. She was a submissive. I looked over her shoulder. Morty was watching from the bar. He eyed me a question. I shook my head. I can handle this, thanks.

"If you told me to . . ." she began. "If you really *could* . . ."

"Lift up your skirt," I said. I was on shaky ground here. Maybe I was experimenting. I don't know. I was crazy and scared and excited. Mostly scared. I tried to hide my timidity and ride both feelings to somewhere new.

She said "No."

"No?"

"You don't really mean it," she said, and walked away.'

(*The Midnight Partner* by Bart Davis)

144

Case one
Mark, 28, software dealer; Jane, 25, sales executive:
Mark and Jane have been living together for a little over three years and have a one-year-old child called Ellie. Jane experienced post-natal depression and found it difficult to resume interest in sex for months after the birth and while breast-feeding. The breakthrough came on the afternoon Mark ceased to be a complete gentleman and coaxed her into submitting to some pleasure which he warned her was unavoidable . . .

Mark says: 'I was very sensitive to Jane being off sex. I'd read all the books explaining how hormonal changes happen after pregnancy and about the psychology of becoming a new family with extra responsibility. We used to spend ages in bed just lying there cuddling, or she'd finish me off by hand. But I wanted to see if she could respond too. So one evening, when we'd gone to bed early, I asked her to get under the covers which I then tucked tightly in all round. Then I sat astride her chest with my head facing her feet, trapping her arms by her sides. I leaned forward, untucked the bottom end of the cover, and began massaging her soles, nibbling and sucking her toes and getting her to lose herself in a rhythm of dreamy pleasure. Then I slowly worked my way up her body until I could find her clitoris. The position was a little awkward but I kept my legs firmly clamped on her hands and moved my tongue in time to some favourite soul records. She struggled – but I must have found an irresistible spot because suddenly she opened her legs wide and let me do anything I wanted . . .'

Jane: 'I'm not sure I ever want another baby. I adore Ellie now and would gladly die for her if it came to it but at the time she seemed to ruin my sanity and destroy my sexual feelings. I did *not* want to know about intercourse. I've since wondered whether the desire would have returned anyway but when Mark dominated me that night and got me to be 'selfish' I really did start to come back to life. I'd been feeling really *guilty* about not fancying him. It was such a clever switch to make me *unable* to touch him back. I couldn't even see his face – so of course I drifted off into my dreams. My feet adore being stroked and if you've never had a pedicure – don't imagine you're qualified to comment! Purrfect!'

Case two
Alexandre, 36, police officer; Mireille, 29, lecturer:
Alex and Mireille have been seeing each other for seven months. French, competitive, middle class and very go-getting, neither has ever spent much time talking about sex. They got together, fell for each other then into bed enjoying the conventional routines. 'In France, we don't talk so much about these matters. We assume everyone is a wonderful lover simply by virtue of being French,' said Alexandre. But, one evening after a succession of brandies in the front room of the forest cabin his family has owned for three generations, things began to change.

Alexandre has a scar on his cheek which he says is *not* romantic – he fell off his roller skates as a child. But it was one of his first experiences of tolerating pain. The memory recurred when Mireille and he were making love: 'Mireille was giving me the most marvellous caresses on a kind of love seat for two people in the living room. I was very woozy from drink. I even think I snoozed for a couple of moments. When I woke up I found Mireille had secured my hands to some heating pipes high up on the wall. I was lying on my back with my arms spread in a sort of crucifix position.

'Then she stood in front of me, killed the overhead lights so she was just backlit by a tablelamp. All I could see was the outline of this beautiful woman's body but not her face, no details. Then she walked towards me, slid her skirt up over her hips and offered me her sex. She came towards me, very provocatively, and stopped inches from my lips, kneeling across my body. But no matter how hard I strained or how much I hurt my wrists, I couldn't touch her. All I could do was smell that beautiful scent of a woman and I wept with frustration. And she wouldn't relent and refused to let me have her, even though I begged. She even laughed, then masturbated in front of me, then fell asleep herself! Never as a grown man have I been treated like that . . .'

Mireille has learned to be wary of men who make easy promises and has enjoyed running her own life since her previous divorce. 'I wanted to shock Alexandre. He's such a powerful guy deciding who's free to come and go all day long. I suddenly had this hunch that he might enjoy knowing what the loss of freedom is like for all the criminals and illegal immigrants he deals with. I also loved showing him my body and telling him he *only* gets pleasure from it if I *allow* him to. I also loved taking my time because normally he turns me on so quickly I cannot savour the experience. It's not true, of course, that I was very cruel. He's forgetting quite how much he'd had to drink. He also fell asleep again. First thing in the morning I woke him up with oral sex and he was very satisfied. But I notice he now asks me if we can 'play that game' again and I'm planning to become tougher.

Case three
Jenni, 31, fashion designer; Raoul, 32, lawyer:
Jenni and Raoul's happy marriage came under strain because Jenni was tiring of Raoul's very physical approach to sex. For Raoul, intercourse was like a passionate exercise, helping rid his body of everyday tensions. Sylvester Stallionesque. He didn't mind if the marriage carried on in the same routine forever. For Jenni, an artistic person, sex was a means of reaching new moods and exploring her imagination. She had always enjoyed fantasising about her more aggressive side and was attracted to novel erotic ideas partly in response to recent trends in fashion. In bed, she began to want actual control. Raoul was initially confused by her new demands. He didn't understand what was wrong with the old ways since every time they had made love before, Jenni had seemed to climax. Wasn't that the point of it all?

Jenni: 'I sometimes think Raoul has never recovered from discovering that women *can* have sex. He's bowled over by knowing that we have this potential ability to engage in sexual intercourse. It's as if he's still in awe of the vagina. He can't

147

seem to understand that genitals are just genitals *unless* you think of a different way to handle them! I really don't mind if I never have straight intercourse again. But I would kill to be in bed enjoying intercourse with a man who could first tamper with my mind, either by submitting himself to me, placing himself under my control, or else having the magical power to take me over, and make me almost want to hurt myself with desire. Fortunately, Raoul is a learning person and I believe we're going to have a great deal more fun together . . .'

Raoul: 'It took me a lot of grief and self-analysis before I came to realise Jenni meant what she said about our sex life – that it would have to be different from now on, or at least for some of the time. All I heard when she first talked to me was criticism. I come from a culture where men are kings. We open doors for ladies, try to touch them on the bottom as they go past and then pretend nothing has happened. It was a big step to let Jenni tie me up and insult me to my face. But I have to say, although it made me angry at the time, I got completely focused and aroused and when finally *she* let me come, it practically hit the ceiling.'

but I don't want FLOWERS
I want rampant eroticism
and obsessive
uncontrollable
lust

Case four
Carrie, 29, trainer; Steven, 33, politician:
Carrie and Steven have been having an affair for five years.
Carrie grew up in San Francisco where she ran rather wild
from the age of 15 and had one unpleasant experience of being
mugged by a man who sliced her halter top with a knife and
fondled her breasts before taking her purse. This memory
frequently feeds into her sexual fantasies. Later, she had a
relationship with an older man of great wealth who enjoyed
using his money to control those around him. Steven comes
from London, England. Before running across Carrie in
California, he had never known a woman who could stand up
to his sharp tongue and quick mind. For the first two years,
their affair was conducted with more heat than light, always
on the edge, with neither really sure of the other's commitment.
Now they have 'become firm friends' who can still have a red
hot love life even after several years of intimacy. Their other
friends are jealous and would love to know the secret. It can
now be told.

Carrie: 'I tend to divide my life into Before Steven and After
Steven. He's what I've always wanted. He can accept the bits
of my mind which have bothered all my other lovers. In the
past, like a lot of women, I've been attacked physically. There
was also a lot of stress with my dad. As a result, my desires
and memories aren't straightforward. I've got a curious mixture
of the sweet and bitter. When I'm highly aroused, and Steven
is brilliant at tipping me over, I quickly disappear into a world
where people are *not* just oh-so-nice and kind and reasonable.
They're cruel too and it excites me to pieces. I call this mental
place "sexland".'

Steven: 'I don't honestly know whether there's a speck of
native sadism in me or whether Carrie provokes me into
playing a game entirely for her benefit. Whatever the truth, I
get this overwhelming urge to punish or restrain her, to make
her take pleasure even if she doesn't want it, to force the pace,
commence intercourse early (or delay it), to make her endure
caresses that are rude or assaulting but which I ensure are

very pleasant anyway, then to tease her till she begs me to make love again. The bottom line is always the same. I spend a lot of time stoking up her passion so that she has the most explosive orgasms possible. So who's really in charge? Me, the eager-beaver lover, or her, the woman who gets me to approach her body and soul in a totally different and fresh manner each time we meet? Last week, I kissed her for about 15 minutes in the kitchen until her face was red. Then I said I had to go to the bathroom and made sure she waited for another 10 minutes before steaming her up again. She was furious but grateful in equal proportions.'

GREAT SEX CHECK-LIST

No book on sex would be complete without listing ways 'to enhance your sexual relationship'. I'm happy to write these down but please bear in mind they are of little value in the absence of goodwill and a common desire to make things better. And in situations of positive ill will, they could possibly cause harm.

To raise the mercury in your partner's barometer, start by thinking carefully about their preferences. There's no point in greeting them at the front door in nothing but a frilly apron if they 'don't like that kind of thing'. Or if they have a head full of gloom and doom about redundancy – better to respond sensitively to their distress and do a neck massage. On the other hand, if they *do* like that kind of thing, perhaps you'd like to consider where to purchase the apron?

● If you're in a domestic routine, break it, never neglecting the more subtle changes. For instance, slide in on their side of the bed at night so they cannot ignore your body and have to persuade you to move.

● Give your partner a mundane telephone message about the plumber but on the bottom of the paper spill your sexiest perfume and write 'Inhale here – and me at 11'.

● At home, take a good look at the bedroom. Is it really a sensuous space? If not, throw out the television, put a bolt on the door (nice to lock someone in even if there's no one to lock out), find a sheepskin rug (for the bed) or some silk sheets, and leave a bottle of massage oil in a conspicuous position. If the room is ever cold, try to improve the heating till nudity's a pleasure.

● If you only have sex at bedtime, bring bedtime forward either by doctoring the clocks or by kidnapping your lover at 8, locking the door and telling him he is not allowed out till you have crawled over every inch of his skin (or specify the inches you wish to crawl over).

● If you usually leap into bed without any sensual preliminaries, give serious thought to sharing a hot bath, and coating each other with shower gel. Then give your partner the kind of sensitive soaping he hasn't had since he day-dreamed about a two-week vacation in Bangkok.
Or make him submit to the Bangkok massage. Imagine the scene: your lover lies naked on a large towel in a warm room. You anoint him or her with the finest soapsuds from the Body Shop and do the same to your naked self. Then, stomach to stomach, fitting your body over his, you say 'Would you like the Thailand Twist?' When he says yes, you do a sort of breaststroke gently up and down till things get completely out of control.

● Back in the bedroom, consider how to alter the sexual routine. Don't let him continue to make the overtures and first moves if that has become his 'job'. Tell him gently but firmly that he's got to learn to receive as well as give – and then give generously. If he argues, take it in turns to be in charge.

● If sexual attention always seems to focus on the genitals, make a point of kissing and caressing everywhere else. Give at least 10 or 15 minutes to this. Aim to stimulate your partner so much they are literally begging you to go further – before actually consenting. It's the small but different moves that bring variety.

● If your loved one likes his body (and you like yours) put mirrors beside the bed. Visual turn-ons can be captivating and both sexes respond. Here's a very private movie for your eyes alone. You say, 'It's like we have another couple in the bed next to us – your hands teasing my flanks, two bodies swaying, hot kisses on my breasts, your muscles arched in passion, a rhythm of pleasure reflecting our own . . .' PS Do not readily agree to be sexually videoed. Tapes can last longer than relationships and end up being exchanged for cash, shown in strip clubs or screened in the local pub out of revenge.

● Get a dimmer on the bedroom light-switch and/or buy candles. When you can't see someone exactly, your imagination takes over. Low lights raise your senses – imperfections fade; beauty is enhanced; age vanishes. He thinks, 'For a second I see your stocking-tops in the flickering light and my eyes strain to look higher where the dark curves meet.' She thinks, 'Now I can look lower without him knowing.'

● Give your lover a red hot telephone call occasionally, though bear in mind the Post Office Act of 1954 contains certain penalties against obscenity. The phone – as you may realise – puts sweet nothings straight into the brain. Sometimes it's easier to be sexy when you can't touch your lover or see them face to face, so get (legally) dialling – 'Hello, guess what? I'm naked except for my perfume and pretending it's your fingers on my breasts/chest/thighs . . .'

● Tell your lover what you love about him/her every day. What you most like about your lover should include the 'intimate'. Even if it's difficult to say, make the effort. 'It's the softest curve of your bottom' . . . 'It's your smell when you've been exercising' . . . 'It's your aroused nipples under a white shirt/blouse' . . . 'It's the way your jeans strain across your manly figure . . .' Or convey your appreciation of their kindness, consideration and good humour – 'I'm so happy I'm with you.'

● Exchange an intimate sexual fantasy. For example: 'I'm dreaming of you lying face down on my bed with your arms tied in silken ribbons to the bedpost and across your back and buttocks I arrange exotic fruits straight from the fridge – black and white grapes, passionfruit, strawberries, cherries – until you're covered. Then I eat my fill without using my hands . . .'

● Arrange to meet your partner at a pub and pretend to pick him up and let him 'have you' on a first date. Dress in character. Here's a chance to be as over the top as you want. Perhaps you wear those tarty fishnets and very shiny heels, the leather jacket and the Raquel Welch neckline. Or maybe it's the well-dressed look that works for you – the businessgirl pick-up. Or the millionaire and the gigolo – Princess Di meets Richard Gere.

● Tape-record the sounds of lovemaking and listen to them on the next occasion you go to bed. What you hear is the naked truth. Of course you *and* your lover have to agree to this or it's a non-starter. Some people are specially turned on by sounds rather than sights. Eavesdropping on your own groans of pleasure and desire can start you off all over again . . .

● Make love in the living room. 'I want to do it now', is the idea, rather than waiting till a 'respectable' time. Besides, there's a hint of risk and exposure – bodies sliding off the sofa on to the living room rug, clothes pushed aside, hands grasping hips, mouths hungry for kisses, hair in a tangled mess . . . and are the curtains completely closed?

● If you've got the cash, sharpen your wardrobe and not just for street gear. Both men and women could invest in one good set of slightly more provocative underwear. There's no escaping the truth that men like women in silk – silk slacks with silk underwear underneath tends to work. Provoke him into feeling the one through the other. It's not compulsory to make love naked. In fact, it's sexier to retain a few clothes but it depends what the clothes are. For women, anything in black is better than almost anything in white unless you're a virgin or impersonating one. But to work, underwear needs to be *seen.* So don't always sit – how to put this – completely decorously. A glimpse of pure flesh above the stockings, the occasional wisp of hose, is not so downmarket. I remember hearing a senior woman psychoanalyst boast she'd startled her live-in lover in just such a way. Flashes of underwear have been causing havoc with men for centuries, Hollywood notwithstanding.

● Tease your lover's skin with textiles. The skin is the largest, most available organ of the human body, so go for the sensual high spots. She: 'I pull on my black evening gloves and count your goosebumps as I stroke your tummy into a frenzy. Then I take a shaving brush, cut a circle of bristles from the centre, toying with your nipples till you beg me to do it again and again.' And there's still latex, satin, fur and silk for next weekend time.

● Find your partner's secret erogenous zones. You can make love with someone for years and still not know all their bodily secrets. So make time one night to sit naked in private and take turns to touch breast or chest, arm or palm, nose or toes in any way you think the other person wants. Ask 'Do you like that? Did I score?' As hands stray lower and deeper, you find the secret route to their Shangri La.

● Pen a sexy script for two. On really heady nights, don't just share a fantasy, script a new one together. You: 'I'm the glamorous landlady of a private house and you're a beautiful young man who has come to stay the night. I've put a sleeping pill in your midnight drink and now you are completely in my power . . .' Him (betraying his own feelings): 'I'm stripped of my pyjamas, handcuffed and given a wake-up pill. You invite two girlfriends round and . . .'

● Hold the Ceremony of the Secret Garden. Intoxicate your lover's senses in one long sensual banquet: 'He pampers my body in a softly scented bath, sponging between my intimate spaces. He pours champagne into my mouth, spilling some between my breasts as they float coyly in the water. Plates of exotic food appear – a visual feast – and dainties to tempt a Queen are popped one by one into my mouth. At a command from me, when some of my appetites can stand no more, he slowly strips off . . .' You get the idea.

● Survive a sex film with your honour intact. When there's just the two of you, rent the Candida Royalle video *Sensual Escape* and watch without laying a finger on each other. This is difficult. Plot: it all starts at a restaurant with wicked hands roaming under the table. They then adjourn to her apartment for some really great coffee . . . Very simple, watchable, suggestive.

● Asking for the ultimate. Agree to listen to any (repeat any) sensual request your partner makes tonight, without laughing, criticising or flinching. You don't have to do it, but if you consent it might revolutionise your relationship: 'For years, I've wanted to cover your breasts with honey – and *not* worry about the mess on the sheets – then play honey bears together . . .' Or 'I want you to XXXX me desperately.'

GREAT SEX – GIVING A MAN THE MOST PLEASURE

No woman, not even a doctor, can know how it feels to live inside a male skin. Nor the sort of sexual strokes men really crave. My friend Steven is a 31-year-old tape and software producer and he's unhappy. For about five years, he's been having an affair with Lise from Frankfurt. They meet as often as money and planes allow. He confesses: 'The relationship's ridiculous. We don't have time for each other. We're not enormously compatible. She wants to talk about West African art. I want to talk about photography and footie. I feel irritable with her after three or four days of continuous company. But I'm sexually addicted to Lise. In fact, she's spoiled sex for me with anyone else. That woman's so good in bed she's completely ruined my love life.'

Steven's not the only man to say such things. As you grow up and approach your 30s you run the risk of meeting not only your erotic match but your sexual superior. Lise shares her gift with the earthy character played by Susan Sarandon in the movie *White Palace*.

Sarandon tells her upmarket boyfriend (snooty James Spader) that 'I may not have a cute little 23-year-old college-educated tush but in the fucking department you ain't gonna find anyone who can blow your brains out like me, on that I'm crystal.' Spader can only reply: 'I've never wanted any woman as much as I want you' and his 'want' has a very big W.

It's not just in the 'fucking department' that such women appear to have the edge. What happens in the kissing, nibbling, handling and despatching areas is equally vital. Why did Steven fall for Lise? Because on their second date she couldn't keep her hands out of his trousers in the cinema. 'It made me feel simultaneously embarrassed and confident,' he admits. 'On reflection, I loved it.' In *White Palace* Susan Sarandon can't wait to go down on James Spader and nothing is going to stop her – not his hangover, not her hangover, not even the perilous shortage of oxygen under the covers. He's edible and she needs him to know it.

Enthusiastic, upfront desire is one requirement. But what really gets a man addicted is when *she* appreciates how to touch his sexual organs with *authority*. Of course, there'll be dramas playing aloft – men do bring their brains into bed and there's always a fascinating interplay between the fantasy and friction.

However, if you don't start by knowing your genital caresses you'll inevitably ruin the mental sex.

It's essentially a question of degree. For instance, when a man has an erection, blood is pumped into the storage reservoirs of the penile shaft which can therefore sustain high pressure and several hours of pain-free wriggling. In fact, to your surprise, you can grasp the penile shaft and squeeze as firmly as you like without fear of hurting. Bear this in mind the next time he says 'harder and faster' just before coming. A man masturbating will in the final moments apply a fair amount of force and nothing is more frustrating for him at this juncture than manipulation by floppy jelly fingers.

But do not attempt to bend an erection, either at the base or middle when held in your first. It isn't sexy, it feels like someone is trying to break you in two and you could rupture connective tissue and internal blood vessels.

Be equally cautious when it comes to caressing the glans penis, the head of the penis proper, upwards from the coronal ridge. For concentrated nerve-endings, this is the anatomical equivalent of the clitoris, the underside of which could be called Man's External G-Spot. Just as you wouldn't want someone to pretend yours was a sort of Instant Scratch Card, no more does a man want this spot polishing till you can see your face in it – especially after orgasm, when any kind of touch to the glans can prove *intolerable*.

Beneath the glans, there's a ligature called the frenum or frenulum, a sort of rubber band of flesh joining the glans to the undershaft. This responds to the kind of caresses you might like applied to a nipple. What I mean is that while ecstasy may be achieved, sensory overload is also a risk. Touch by fingers, tongue, nose or toes should be lightly measured, conservative rather than radical. Biting is a very bad move. As a matter of information, Roman mistresses applied dried nettles at this point to cause the man a constant itch of desire, thus stinging their partners into added frenzy. (Use young green nettles *only* if you've explored alternative means of ending your relationship, and don't mind being sued.)

The ultimate (internal) Male G-Spot is the Prostate. You won't pronounce this 'prostrate' if you can distinguish a sex position from a love-juice gland. This walnut-sized object, accessible via the anus, lies at the base of the bladder and contributes additional secretions to the seminal fluid. For instance, when a man is erotically teased but prevented from climaxing, there may appear at the tip of his penis a tiny pearl of colourless prostatic liquid.

Even heterosexual males have an anal pleasure zone which feels almost as sensitive as a secondary penis. Centuries of homophobic anxiety have caused men to try to overlook or downplay this erogenous centre but often with poor results. Why do chaps turn up at A & E Departments with embarrassing items lost in their recesses? Because they were trying to add anal pleasure to penile and got carried away. Q: Why does every dodgy massage parlour provide a range of plugs and dildoes to suit? A: Because men know when they are sitting on a good thing.

The prostate mysteriously enlarges with age and is prone to cancer although the new prostate specific antigen (PSA) test (cost: a few pounds) can detect both difficulties, in case he wanted to know.

Palpation by proctologists is a traditional method of checking for abnormalities and can result in functional orgasm without erection. Palpation by a lover (wearing a surgical glove) is a guaranteed method of sending a mortal male to heaven and can be broached either externally or internally.

To stimulate the prostate from the outside, trace the contours of that narrow divide called the perineal gap between testes and anus. This tissue also contains the pelvic floor muscles which contract during climax. Firm digital pressure (rigid middle finger supported by adjacent fingers) at the central mid-point of this gap can help arouse a man, remind him of the forthcoming delights of orgasm or even tip him over the edge once excited. Memo: if you've started him off this way, continue to press *during* orgasm so that his spasms have a continuous resistance against which to flex.

But it's the internal approach to a man's G-Spot that provides most opportunities to spoil his love life forever with anyone else – as Dr K. R. Stubbs describes in his book *The Sensuous Lovers' Guide* (Secret Garden Books, California, 1986):

'When his feelings become more intense, concentrate your right-hand movements on the area just below the pubic bone and above the anal opening. Using the flat of your fingers in a paddle-like shape, put a firm pressure on this cavity. Now make small circles so that his skin moves over the muscles beneath.

'Next make very delicate circles with a fingertip around the anal orifice. If you are finding it difficult to reach, you can ask your lover to bring his right knee upward so you can brace it with your chest.

'Whenever he becomes really turned on, your longest finger (with a smooth short fingernail) begins to enter the anal opening. Until the sphincter muscles become ac-ouctomod to this touch, your lover may find the sensations intense.

'So rather than sliding the finger directly in, begin a gentle rocking motion. Giving small gradual stretches, you invite the muscles to relax. Remember to use plenty of lubricant.

'When your finger is in full length, try a "come here" stroking with the finger pad against the tissues on the upper area at twelve o'clock. Here is the approximate position of the prostate gland. Depending on the length of your finger, you may feel a firmer spongy tissue a little different from those surrounding it.

'If his groans sound deeply happy, don't worry about the exact anatomy . . .'

. . . because you've reached his goal. The man is yours. If your partner has been specially deserving, then the following reward may be granted.

After warm and wonderful sex (during which you alone are permitted to reach orgasm), the man (now a little tired) is asked to lie on his back. You adopt a seated position facing him, with legs extended under his – his thighs wide-spread and loosely wrapped around your waist. His erection should be manipulated by fingertips, fist and lips. Large amounts of appropriate water-based lubricant permit one finger to find the prostate gland as in Dr Stubbs' description above. Then the movement of the internal finger is coordinated with the gentle rocking motions of your head or hands over the penile head and down the shaft as your choice or his wild whimperings may indicate. You are now in sole charge of both male G-Spots, the underside of the penile head and the deep-rooted prostate. Try to catch the precise *slow* syncopated rhythm that will make him putty in your paws. If there is any information about his life or past lovers you feel *he* has ever withheld from you, this is an excellent time to find answers . . .

The male ejaculatory reflex consists of two pleasurably coordinated phases. In the first the prostate suddenly hardens. Your lover approaches his 'point of no return'. (You could, of course, cease moving altogether if still seeking confessions.) The autonomic nervous system gathers fluid from the prostate and testicular tubes, adds sperm from the seminal vesicles and in one delicious spasm (no returns indeed) passes all to a collecting node at the base of the penis. The process is called emission. Your man is now going to come and there is nothing you can do about it – threatening him with death won't change a damn thing. Your one choice is to decide in the next half a second how you want to arrange your body as he finales. Oh *yes*, he'll howl. Later he'll say, 'You got me.' But that's what you probably wanted to hear.

Chapter Seven

When Relationships Go Wrong

How healthy is your relationship?
Some people are fastidious about their relationships and some
are not. Some people treat their relationships like ailing
children, constantly taking their temperatures and checking
for symptoms. Others wouldn't notice if their relationships
developed advanced catatonia, let alone a common cold. Both
approaches are equally dangerous: death by cosseting or death
by neglect.

How do you know whether your relationship is based on
something solid and stable or something shifting and temporary? When you've been betrayed in the past and when you
hear stories of husbands and wives who have been duped by
unfaithful spouses for a decade or more, it's tempting to think
that you *cannot* know. The good news is most of us *can* make a
pretty accurate guess about the stage of our relationships.

The popular barometers of sex, laughter, the delightful anticipation of meeting, and the simple enjoyment of one another's
company are all good measures of love and lust. But beyond
that are the ways that we communicate with each other, how
honest we are and how we handle disagreements. When the
glorious flush of being in love is fading these are things that
really matter.

While it's a bad idea to take the emotional temperature of
your relationship every time you and your partner disagree,
it's important to stay close. This means telling each other how
you feel, asking each other questions – and listening to the
answers – forgetting any hidden agendas and giving each other
space when you need it. Two of the most healthy ingredients
for a relationship are humour and individuality.

RELATIONSHIP SKILLS

Relationships take skill. Some people are naturals, but most of us make it up as we go along, experiencing a mixture of moods and emotions as we enter various stages of a relationship. Being in love is one of the most exhilarating experiences life has to offer, but, equally, the loss of love can be one of the gloomiest. Whether we fall out of love with our partner or they fall out of love with us, periods of grief and reassessment are inevitable. Even when relationships go wrong, we can emerge, more cynical, but more knowledgeable, ready for the next time.

But we don't seem to talk any more

A lot of men would instantly turn round and say 'Of course we talk' but all they mean is that the house isn't silent. They talk all right but it's about the weather, their work, sport, telly, buying a new car or the state of next door's garden. What they may not understand is that such talk is comparatively cheap – the really valuable missing conversations are about the state of your relationship, your feelings, your degree of intimacy and closeness. The sort of things that chaps traditionally avoid talking about.

A relationship that *never* achieves this type of communication is actually beginning to die. Put it the other way round – no relationship can be taken completely for granted. If it's not serviced, taken out and examined from time to time, if you can't feel emotionally connected, then it begins to expire from neglect. Men do have problems in this area partly because they don't want to lose face or power but also because they feel awkward and unsure about how to express these feelings. Some don't even have the vocabulary. You do need to persist and encourage them – to take it slowly and show your tolerance, even when they say things like 'Yes, well I have been a bit fed up with "us" lately,' or 'I didn't like it when you told me off for eating all that chicken casserole.' It may sound like criticism – but at least it's intimate and from the heart.

162

But what if you don't want to talk any more either? Maybe then you've got to accept that the problem is more serious. You may need to recognise you are both avoiding making certain necessary changes to how you live together. A starting point to breaking the ice might go something like, 'I'm getting worried about us. If things carry on like this we're going to end up as total strangers. I'm prepared to sort things out if you are – will you?'

The biggest problem is usually about unfinished business – old bad feelings which for the sake of peace never get put into words but are buried alive where they slowly fester. Perhaps he insulted your mother; perhaps you wouldn't go on holiday to Spain but insisted on Dorset; perhaps he made fun of your stretch marks; perhaps you got back at his sexuality – anything can provoke a prolonged bout of non-speak.

The trouble often originates in the families in which we grew up, especially if your parents put a lot of emphasis on 'avoiding rows' or 'not speaking out of turn'. If this is the case you have a choice: whether to go on doing what the grown-ups once told you to do, or deciding *now* whether you are the grown-up yourself and have the right to speak and the right to be spoken to – even if the temperature rises.

My advice is to go for it. Choose a time and place when you can both give your relationship the attention it deserves – not just after midnight or when he's rushing off to catch a train. If necessary say, 'OK, when can we talk about these things? Give me an appointment,' and make sure it's in both diaries.

The boredom factor

Boredom is a killer. It can strike into the heart of your relationship and make you sluggish and apathetic. Take two people who have been together for years. She knows exactly how he will make love to her. He knows in detail how she hates sex in the morning. She knows his opinion on everything from royalty to pornography. He knows how long it takes her to get ready to go out. She knows how silly he looks when he's pissed. He knows how crabby she gets when tired. Even the most minute details about someone are predictable: the way he holds his cutlery; the way she touches her temple. The cruel irony is that many of these things are endearing before they become infuriating. They become intolerable when no part of the relationship can nourish or refresh.

Boredom is underpinned by the myth that we should expect to find our partner perpetually attractive, interesting, sexy and exciting. When we expect all of this it doesn't happen. If we make the effort, it can happen. On the simplest level, talk to your partner. No one knows everything there is to know about another human being. Even if they did, people change, so you need continually to update your knowledge about someone. Ask questions and listen to the answers.

Relationship counsellors say we've lost the art of listening. 'Most people find listening attentively difficult. Listening is important if you are truly to understand your partner. Listening generously, attentively and uncritically is essential if your partner is going to trust you enough to tell you his or her most intimate secrets,' says one.

Listening not only means not interrupting, it means genuinely taking on board what your partner is saying and if you don't understand, asking him to clarify the situation. You could take up the following suggestion: 'Make a date to talk to your partner for one hour specifically about yourselves and your feelings. Toss a coin to see who begins. Take half-an-hour each to talk about how you feel and what you want in life – as if you are explaining yourself to a stranger.'

Sometimes relationships need a change of scenery. Before you abandon your lover, take him to somewhere neither of you have ever been before. It doesn't matter whether it's south-west China or Brighton beach. You could also try the following:

- Play a practical joke on him.
- Eat ice cream in the bath with him.
- Get drunk together.
- Read him your diary (careful!).
- Do something that he likes and you hate.

- Play Truth or Dare.
- Don't have sex for two weeks and then go away for the weekend.
- Stay up all night and sleep all day.
- Dance together.

Handling disagreements

Disagreements are necessary. When two people enter a relationship two separate sets of beliefs, attitudes, needs and backgrounds collide. With a bit of luck, what happens next is a voyage of discovery. You begin a long learning process – you find out what makes him tick sexually; you find out about his past relationships; you learn about his job, his friends and his social life; you look at old photographs and build up a picture of what he was like when he was younger; he tells you facts about his childhood; you get to meet his parents; you discuss religion, politics and sexuality together; you even learn all the trivial stuff which makes up his character, the foods he likes, the things that make him laugh; the sort of underwear he chooses and what football team he supports.

No matter how laid-back, tolerant and good humoured you are, it is impossible to agree with someone else about everything all of the time. There will inevitably be discussions, arguments and disagreements in your relationships and it is these small – and large – confrontations that teach us how to forge ways of relating to the person we love.

In themselves, disagreements don't matter. What does matter is how we handle them. Another relationship counsellor says that when we continually disagree with our partner we start to resent them. Something quite small like the way your partner never cooks a meal for you can escalate into something huge. At first you may think to yourself that cooking a meal isn't important and you don't mind too much. 'After a while, you can start to criticise your partner as laid-back ... happy-go-lucky. Your thoughts (and maybe words) become more bitter until your partner is seen as a slob ... lazy. You can finally end up believing that your partner "just doesn't

165

care what I want", "does it to wind me up", "obviously doesn't love me".'

Even the best relationships call for compromise. When you find yourself continually disagreeing or arguing with your partner, step back and look at the subject of the argument. First of all, how important is it? Have you both let something trivial get out of hand because you are both stressed at work, tired, or anxious about something completely unrelated to your relationship? Or are you simply being petty? Backing down from an argument and admitting you are wrong – especially if it's not in your nature to do so – takes courage, but will invariably endear you to your lover.

Secondly, are your disagreements a cover-up for something else? Look for the subtext in an argument. Take Tania, for instance, who had a blazing row with her boyfriend because he was talking with his mouth full.

'On the surface it seemed like such a pathetic argument. I was getting ready to go out and I wanted Jon's opinion on the dress I was going to wear. He was flicking through the paper and he just mumbled something through a mouthful of toast. I was furious that he didn't even look at me or give me a decent answer. That sort of laziness is typical of him.'

The issue here is not table manners or etiquette but the fact that Tania felt that Jon was not interested in her dress, not interested in her and not prepared to put himself out in the smallest way. In summary: he Didn't Care. Perhaps if he had been asked (which he wasn't) he would have said that he was just trying to relax before going out or that he didn't feel equipped to comment on Tania's dress or that he didn't feel she would have acted on his opinion anyway. They didn't get to the bottom of the matter though because the argument never progressed beyond John talking with his mouth full.

This type of disagreement is forgettable when it is a one-off, but when these misunderstandings start to characterise a relationship, leaving your partner can start to seem a desirable option. If this is the case, consider whether there are better ways for you to communicate with each other. Spelling out your feelings may seem silly but it might be the best way to get the reaction you want. Imagine the different outcomes if Tania had approached the situation with humour (by snatching away the toast and the newspaper), or with directness ('Look at me, I need your opinion'), or with emotional honesty ('I feel like you don't care how I look'). Maybe they still would have argued, but maybe they would have both taken something on board for the next round of arguments.

The third type of disagreement involves issues of basic principle. Things like whether or not to have children or the fact that your partner travels with his job and cannot spend enough time with you. These can be the hardest disagreements to resolve and it may be necessary to go back to the drawing board and attempt to redesign your relationship. Before you go for the overhaul option, search hard for practical solutions or compromises. For instance, would your partner be prepared to have children in two, five or ten years' time? If his reasons for not having children are financial, would he be prepared to look at ways to save up money? Would both of you be prepared to have children out of wedlock? Before you resign yourself to permanent disagreement, check that you know what his attitudes are inside-out.

If your views on a subject really are irreconcilable, then you need to think carefully about what your priorities are and what sacrifices you are prepared to make. These kind of life-choices are tough and there really are no right or wrong answers. You may have to trust your instincts and simply do what feels right at the time. Counselling can often help you to make decisions when you feel that you have reached deadlock with your partner or are too stuck or bogged down to move on.

IS COUNSELLING THE ANSWER?

There was a time when psychotherapy came with a label marked 'stigma'. Now, in the enlightened Nineties, having your own counsellor is more acceptable. The danger is that counselling gets to be like a quick fit exhaust centre – your relationship's looking a bit wobbly, so go to a counsellor to get it repaired. Unfortunately (or fortunately), counselling isn't a quick-fix option. The counsellor is to the unhappy lover what the hypnotherapist is to the unhappy smoker. Unless *you* have the motivation and the desire to work things out, seeing a therapist won't help. Properly qualified counsellors won't offer you answers or tell you what to do, but they will guide you as you and your partner attempt to find a direction of your own.

Some counsellors say that what their clients experience during a therapy session is similar to the process of falling in – and out of – love. When couples begin counselling, they feel very positive and confident about both the counsellor and the therapy sessions. After a while this initial enthusiasm wanes and the couple may start to question the value of counselling. They may also start to doubt their counsellor. If a couple overcome this doubt and continue counselling they learn that change is a slow process and that results are neither dramatic nor overnight. This full sequence of emotions does indeed parallel the progress of a love affair, from initial excitement to the inevitable cooling down period, followed by a period of acceptance and stability.

Couples can visit a counsellor together or separately. Or they can start off separately and then attend joint sessions or vice versa. A counsellor will encourage you to talk about not only your current relationship and its problems but also relationships that you have had in the past. This can also include your relationships with your parents as a child.

Sometimes people find that what they thought was a new and unique problem is part of a recurring pattern of behaviour. For example, Craig and Lucy went to counselling because, when they started arguing ten months into their relationship, Lucy had responded by seeing one of her colleagues. Although Lucy hadn't slept with her colleague, she admitted things were heading that way and that the relationship was 'definitely more than just platonic'.

When Craig learned of this, his first reaction was to leave Lucy. After another month of arguments and attempted separations they decided to discuss things with a counsellor. When Lucy started talking about her previous relationships, it materialised that most of them had ended because she had been unfaithful. When Lucy was asked why, she said that she thought it was boring to stick with one person for a long time and she liked the diversion of being with someone new. Yet she also said that she was still in love with Craig and couldn't imagine being without him.

When the counsellor delved deeper into Lucy's past she found that Lucy's father had left her mother when Lucy was nine. Questioned about her feelings towards her mother and father, she said that she respected her father but had always found her mother's behaviour too passive.

Lucy thought her behaviour with her colleague showed that she was independent and free-spirited. Over a period of weeks, the counsellor established that Lucy's desire to prove her strength and independence was a way of covering up a very deep-rooted fear that her relationship with Craig would go wrong and that she would be left alone. Rather than waiting to see what would happen with Craig, Lucy had jumped the gun and set up an escape route for herself in the shape of her colleague. That way, she could hop from one relationship to the next without ever putting herself in a 'weak' or vulnerable position. When Lucy began to talk more openly about her fears and anxieties, Craig responded well. On their last visit, they told the counsellor that they were going to do everything they could to make their relationship work.

VARIETIES OF COUNSELLING

One year, the *Observer* newspaper was silly enough to say I had done more through my radio and TV programmes over the past 15 years to aid the British therapy boom than anyone else. When I start to believe reviews and imagine that society changes quickly I simply re-read this letter from an old radio

169

fan: 'Dear Phillip, could you send me a leaflet for Yoga? I think you said it was a vegetable.' No, it is not true that the British have completely warmed to solving their problems through talking treatments alone. Some people still prefer to stick a carrot up their bottom.

Many are indeed confused by the word 'therapy'. If you look at the dictionary it will tell you therapy means 'curative powers' and 'healing', but when you talk to therapists they say they never offer 'cures'. In the words of Leonard Cohen, 'There ain't no cure for life.' I tell psychotherapy clients, 'Therapy is a journey. We will use each other and the regularity of our meetings to help you make changes. In the process, you will probably have feelings about me, including those of dependency. These are stages. The goal remains your greater independence. I will do my best to offer a reliable space for you to say and feel anything you like, possibly for the first time ever. I also offer the guarantee of confidentiality. I cannot exactly predict the outcome. I can only suggest that at the end you will be different.'

People undertake therapy because they feel emotionally stuck. One warning. Psychotherapy is hard on friends, lovers and families because it does produce change. Sometimes, clients remember events which they have had strong reasons to forget, so they must be prepared to face the bad feelings when reclaiming the good. I could add that formal psychotherapy is expensive and favours the articulate.

Now therapy isn't the same thing as counselling although counselling is therapeutic. Counsellors usually work with a much narrower focus than psychotherapists. For instance, marriage counsellors work on marriage; bereavement counsellors work on grief; youth counsellors work on the young and sex counsellors work on daytime television.

One of my counselling clients, weighing in at about 17 stones, had been a junior member of, let us say, the Kray gang. His counselling requirements held an exceptionally narrow focus. 'My wife is frigid and I want her fixed,' he said. Within a couple of months, I had obligingly managed to talk her into routine orgasm, whereat he developed secondary impotence and I had to keep a low profile in North and East London for several months. This illustrates one of the main pitfalls of counselling's narrowcast approach: if you don't get to the root of things you are in danger of substituting one symptom for another as well as attracting an uncomfortable level of consumer disenchantment.

Counselling, then, may resemble psychotherapy, employ a similar non-bossy approach and involve lying on a couch for a period of years; or it may attempt to solve a specific problem face to face in a couple of chairs on a hot, sunny afternoon. Usually, it lies at the cheaper, simpler, talk-can-fix-it end of the spectrum, verging on what you hear on a radio phone-in. The approach is well nigh standard for sexual problems. For instance, when I practise 'sex therapy' I am very insistent we establish a contract containing a clear set of goals from the outset: 'Over eight to ten therapy sessions to use a mixture of behaviour modification techniques and supportive counselling to re-establish your orgasm by next spring or to know the reason why.'

But this 'counselling' is different from 'giving advice' and has to remain voluntary on the part of the client or no result can be achieved. The magistrates in Gloucestershire who recently sentenced a violent husband to 'six months' marriage counselling' didn't know what they were talking about – and nor will the hapless counsellor who has to take him on.

The most complicated therapists (take it any way you like) remain the 'analysts', those shrinks beloved of Woody Allen, usually disciples of Sigmund Freud for whom the evil of all rooting remains sex. Put another way, there is a religion called Freudian psychoanalysis which believes that childhood sexual trauma is responsible for all the neuroses of adult life. The practitioners further incline to the view that knowledge is power. They think if you occupy an ottoman four or five times a week describing your dreams and saying whatever comes into your mouth, your unconscious mind will somehow betray who you really are and this mapping of your true self will

171

obviously lead you to change your ways and habits. I think
there's nothing obvious about this. Freud was an analytical
genius who found it very much more difficult to put any of his
Humpty-Dumpties back together again.

To be fair, analysts can also be post-Freudian or non-
Freudian. The most imaginative practitioners pursue the
unconscious theories of Carl Gustav Jung with an emphasis
on archetypal dreams and picture-symbols. Others plump for
Melanie Klein's extension of Freud's reading of childhood
distress. You may have endured hell as a juvenile, she said,
but was it wonderful for you as a baby? What happened in
your mother's birth canal and did you rate full waitress service
at the breast? If you don't like your grown-up self, could this
have anything to do with cold, casual mothering stopping you
in your tracks as you solicited your daily half-pinta? A skilful
Kleinian will show you 'how it must have been in those earliest
days beyond recall' simply by analysing the pattern of your
present predicaments (though psychologists claim it's
biologically impossible to remember anything before the age
of two!).

Confusion increases because of a US/UK divide. In Woody
Allen's native land, most psychoanalysts are medical doctors.
In the UK they are more likely to be psychology or social
work graduates. Here, medically qualified 'shrinks' work as
plain and ordinary psychiatrists. To make everything crystal
clear, the latter have little to do with 'therapy'. (Almost the
opposite, some people would say – if you see a psychiatrist on
the NHS you may not even get asked how you feel!) Most
generalisations are absurd but a British psychiatrist will
typically use a medical model to offer 'cures' for mental ill-
health. There will be diagnosis of a condition (e.g. schizophrenia) followed by the prescription of a remedy (drugs
through to electric shocks).

The fact that no two countries can agree on a definition of
schizophrenia, and the major cause of drug addiction in the
United Kingdom is the writing of psychotropic scrips by
doctors, only adds to the confusion. The story goes that one

mother of six unruly boys, at the end of her tether with their wayward behaviour, exclaimed: 'You'll all end up in a mental hospital!' And they did – three as patients, three as psychiatrists. Until medicine starts to treat the *whole* of a person, body, mind and soul, as well as enquiring how patients feel inside, it will continue to bear little acquaintance with 'therapy'.

Into this vacuum, naturally enough, come dozens of alternative approaches avoiding this elementary error. Group or Family Therapists may ask patients to attend together to discover how the social thread weaves into the personal problem. They want to assess whether you've been inappropriately labelled by others before you had a chance to choose an identity for yourself. Gestalt therapists, on the other hand, may ask you to forget about analysing *why* you feel stuck but focus 'here and now' on how you *stay* stuck – in thought, word and deed. They want to look at your stuck body language, your stuck speech, your stuck *non-verbal* communication in general and help you to change it. Widespread use of role play and rehearsal assist this effort. A refined version of this, Neuro-Linguistic Programming, actually checks whether individual senses are emotionally impaired. Much of their work is solid, painstaking and realistic, but you could conceivably be asked to say what you would sound like supposing you were a frog. By a succession of 'guided images' you would then be encouraged to learn how to croak afresh to those around you.

Any number of therapies work with body-posture to reach and change the feelings trapped inside. Bioenergetics is particularly helpful for those less verbally skilled who need to express tears or anger. The Alexander Technique can authentically make you physically taller as you learn how to hold yourself free of tension. Primal Therapy encourages regression to childhood, even your own childbirth, as you use a foetal position and an original scream to exorcise early traumas. Even good old friendly hypnotherapy gets to the blocked emotions by asking the body to adopt the path of deep-trance relaxation. And there are at least 50 other ways to break the 'vicious circle' of self-destructive disenchantment which I have no further space to mention.

All I'd say about the 'therapy boom' is don't lose your head. Confronting your personal demons is a serious and potentially dangerous undertaking. It is serious because you have to work hard by feeling worse before you can get any better. It is dangerous because anyone can call themselves a therapist including those in cults, churches or companies pedalling instant salvation. The one thing I have learned from therapy is that if it works it takes time. If it could be done by signing on for a weekend workshop there wouldn't be any problems left.

THE BEGINNING OF THE END (WHEN YOU LEAVE HIM)

It can be a slow process or it can happen overnight. The man with whom you have shared beds, laughs, ideas, interests, happy times and traumatic times has changed in some subtle but quite irrevocable way. The way he brushes his teeth has become irritating; the way he falls asleep in front of the TV bores you; the way he puts his arms around you leaves you cold. When you meet him, you no longer have that thrill of anticipation. If he cannot meet you as planned, you no longer feel that plummet of disappointment. The excitement has gone and when you remember what you used to feel, you wonder if it was ever really Real.

Caroline, a 24-year-old trainee accountant:
'I was just looking at him one morning in bed. He was asleep. I remember looking at him and thinking, 'I don't love you any more.' There wasn't any build-up to it. It was just that simple thought, 'I don't love you.' I knew in a second that all that feeling was gone and I wouldn't be able to get it back. It was devastating because I love being in love. I love that high, butterfly feeling. I suddenly felt very sad and lonely. I lay in bed thinking, 'What am I going to do?'

Falling out of love doesn't always feel like falling off a high

174

cliff. Sometimes it's like walking down a very long slope. Maybe you'll argue a bit more often than you used to and instead of resolving those arguments they will linger in the atmosphere for a few days. Instead of dismissing your differences you'll start to think how fundamental they are. The word 'incompatibility' may creep into your mind. Slowly you begin to plan your escape. You imagine conversations which begin with, 'This is horrible, but . . .' Maybe you'll spend more time apart, have less to say to each other, and instead of craving to be alone together, going out in a crowd will seem more and more acceptable. You think that you still like him, but you wonder whether your relationship is becoming a habit.

Amanda, a 27-year-old process engineer:
'He became less necessary to me. I think at the start I was quite dependent on him. We would spend all our time together and I would confide in him a lot. Then because of various things that happened in my career I began to feel much more independent and confident. We argued because I stopped staying over at his house at weekends, and I didn't call him so much. In the end I felt like I was being stifled by him. I tried to leave him three times before I finally broke free.'

One very good reason to leave a lover is lingering, draining unhappiness. At some point in our lives many of us have fallen completely in love with the wrong man. You can tell a Wrong Man by the constant feeling in your stomach that says, 'I deserve more than this.' You know a Wrong Man by the way he can click his fingers and make you run to him – yet he gives you nothing in return. Suddenly it becomes acceptable to readjust your social life, attitudes, arrangements and moods to suit your partner. When the phrase All Men Are Bastards was coined, this was the sort of man it was intended for.

OK, he may be brilliantly-talented-drop-dead-gorgeous-and-fantastic-in-bed, but he may also be moody, jealous, insensitive, petty or just downright nasty. When we are stuck with the Wrong Man we carry a pair of scales around in our head, constantly weighing up all the bad things he's done against all the nice things he's done. Unfortunately, the scales are biased, giving far too much weight to the nice things and under-estimating the bad things, giving us the illusion that we are in a normal relationship.

As Natasha, 22, said: 'I found myself dismissing all the times he lied and cheated. I believed that the rare occasions when he looked into my eyes and told me that he loved and needed me were the most important ones. Everything else was irrelevant and forgiveable when he looked at me like that. He could be so disarmingly sweet.'

Very often these are the hardest separations even to anticipate, let alone follow through. Objectively, you may know that here is a man who doesn't care enough about you, doesn't listen to you and is making your self-esteem plummet. Yet subjectively, you are still in love, still hoping that things will change, still thinking that if you can just find a way to get through to him, things will change. In the end, the dull ache of dissatisfaction and unhappiness will get through to you. When it does, you'll know what to do.

Katy, a 24-year-old PhD student:
'My relationship with Lawrence became more and more tortured. Every Friday night I travelled four hours by train to see him and when we were together his manner would be evasive or indifferent. He thought that because we lived so far apart it was inevitable that I was being unfaithful to him (as it turned out he was being unfaithful to me). Because of his lack of trust he would phone me at odd hours of the night to check that I was home – sometimes as late as two or three in the morning.

'I knew our relationship had a sell-by date, but I was so infatuated I kept looking for a way to work everything out. Towards the end of our relationship I kept repeating to myself, "You have to leave him." In the end I did and it was incredibly hard. That was a year and a half ago. Now I'm relieved that it's all in the past and I don't have to suffer any more.'

Should you rescue your relationship?

It may seem that your relationship is doomed, but a surprising number of couples manage to salvage something good out of apparent wreckage. Sometimes walking out seems the easiest and most tempting option, but it's worth pausing before you do something irreparable. Relationship counsellors suggest imagining yourself in two years' time: Where will you be living? What job will you be doing? How would your current partner fit into this imagined scenario? In short, can you imagine life without him? If the answer is 'No' or even 'Not sure', analyse your frustration. Forget the huge mindbenders like 'Do I love him?' and concentrate on the specifics:

Are you leaving him for very clear reasons like, 'his constant absence/infidelity/criticism/insults undermine my confidence'; or vague reasons like, 'things aren't as good as they used to be' or 'I need more excitement'? Are you leaving your partner because you disagree about something, however big or small? Small things include the way he never meets you on time. Big things include marriage and having children.

If your partner is doing something damaging to you – damage can be emotional as well as physical – that makes you depressed, frightened, lonely or insecure, then leaving him may be your only route back to sanity. If this is the case, you must put yourself first and take that route. If, on the other hand, you are leaving your relationship for reasons of boredom or conflicting needs then it is possible for you to work things out. Working things out takes time, effort and honesty, and ultimately your relationship may not improve. But if you try, you may succeed and you'll know that you haven't made your decision lightly. Who knows, you could save yourself weeks, months or possibly years of doubt and regret.

MAKING THE BREAK

As the song lyric goes, breaking up is hard to do. There may be 50 ways to leave your lover but most are painful, messy, and occasionally bloody. If you have decided that it really is

177

time to make your exit, there is no prescribed way to extricate yourself, but the following are all methods of damage limitation:

● Do tell him face-to-face.
● Do let him get angry/rant/cry.
● Do give him reasons that make sense.
● Do listen to what he has to say, even if you don't act on it.
● Do say what you're going to do next (move out/lie low for a fortnight/phone him in a week).

● Don't retract what you say when he gets upset or angry.
● Don't pretend you still love him when you don't.
● Don't say it's only a temporary split if it isn't.
● Don't regret your actions a day later – give yourself time to adjust.
● Don't take all of the blame – when relationships break down it's rare that one partner is 100% responsible.

Your choice of language is important. If you are leaving someone who has treated you badly, be very, very rude to him – scream, shout, swear, and pour red wine on his white shirts. If, on the other hand, you have simply had a change of heart, be kind. Tell him that you genuinely cared for him/ liked him/loved him and that you will look back upon your relationship with happiness. Tell him why you are leaving him, and make it clear that this is a decision that you have made and feel sure about. Tell him that your reasons for going are because of the way he and you operate as a couple, not because of how he is as a person.

Yvonne, a 25-year-old pharmacist:
'The conversations we had when we were splitting up were dreadful. If I hadn't been so upset, I would have been embarrassed. Things like, 'I need some space' and 'I still love you, but I can't be with you any more'. I was speaking in clichés. It was like a trite, badly written script. I meant what I was saying

178

but I just sounded fraudulent. He asked me over and over again why I was leaving, and the reasons I was giving sounded empty and shallow. I just knew it was something I had to do. I wish I could have expressed myself better. The whole experience was so painful.'

When men leave women, women seek therapy. This may be shopping therapy, it may be alcohol therapy, but usually it is talking-to-friends therapy. Over a period of days or weeks, women pick over the bones of a relationship and construct a story of what went wrong. By talking, they rationalise, and by rationalising, they slowly come to terms with separation. Unfortunately, men don't warm to this approach because they are not so good at self-disclosure and narrative creativeness. This is why the more you say to your soon-to-be ex the better.

Alistair, a 25-year-old public relations assistant:
'My ability to trust people vanished when Jacqui left me. I realised that for the last three months of our relationship she had been thinking and doing things that she didn't tell me about and which didn't include me. Afterwards, I didn't feel like seeing or talking to anyone. I was on auto-pilot for a long time – going to work, coming home, sleeping, going to work . . . I don't really understand what happened between us. I have no desire to get back into a monogamous relationship at the moment.'

WHEN HE LEAVES YOU

It was a hot sunny day beside the sea when Martin left Eva, 23. It was supposed to be an idyllic weekend spent together after a month of separation. Eva had been doing her finals in Scotland and the seaside break was intended as a romantic reunion. But nothing went right. After a morning in the sun Eva got heatstroke and had to go back to the hotel room to cool off. Martin, meanwhile, got drunk in the bar. When they met for lunch, Martin said that he had been feeling pretty

179

anxious during the last month. Eva quickly interrupted and said, half jokingly, 'About us, you mean? What – do you want to call it a day?' Martin hesitated for a moment and said, 'Yes.'

Love can end when you least expect it to. After two years of studying and spending much time apart, Eva finally had uninterrupted hours to spend with Martin. She had planned their perfect weekend together. She was going to thank him for being so patient while she took her exams and she was going to suggest that they tried living together. Then right at the crucial moment Martin dealt the fatal blow to their relationship.

In the weeks that followed, Eva analysed her break-up with Martin from every possible perspective. Supposing the weekend had got off to a happier start? Supposing she hadn't interrupted him when he said that he had been feeling anxious? Had he dumped her because he was seeing someone else? Was it that they'd spent too little time together in the past two years? Was he jealous that she had a degree and he didn't? Was she too pushy? Was she too passive? Was she too fat? Had she bored him?

Eventually Eva decided that Martin had probably made the decision to leave her several months previously, but delayed telling her because he didn't want her exams to suffer. She wondered how committed he had ever been. In retrospect, she could only remember a few occasions when they had seriously discussed their relationship or the future. Martin always seemed to want things to be light-hearted. Eva realised that much of her relationship with Martin had been conducted in her head. Because she had been separated from him a lot, she had made assumptions about what he thought and felt.

In the end Eva decided that Martin had never regarded their relationship as seriously as she had. She felt foolish for having taken so much for granted and realised that if there had been more of a dialogue between her and Martin she would not have been so surprised when he finished with her.

Eva was devastated at losing Martin but accounting for what went wrong helped her recover. This process of making up a story about a relationship doesn't mean rewriting history and casting yourself as a thwarted romantic heroine (although it can if you want it to). It simply means looking at your relationship in terms of stages: the beginning, the middle and – brace yourself – the end. Think about what happened in each stage and why it happened. What sort of conversations did you have with each other in each stage? What problems did you have? What was going on in your sex life? Each relationship has its own unique evolution – understanding yours will help you come to terms with its end. It will also make you aware of the mistakes you made.

Feeling bereft

Being left by someone you love can feel a lot like bereavement. Especially if your partner was living with you and your day-to-day life included loads of shared activities. Suddenly you have to contend with a big hole where your partner was. Instead of having a morning cuddle and a shower together, you have to face the pre-work routine alone. You no longer watch his favourite TV programmes. You no longer have someone to share meals with. It's interesting that after a few months of being single, these sorts of things can feel very liberating – you're finally free to take complete control of your life and be utterly self-indulgent (see Chapter Two). Along with the good things, you've lost the bad too. Nevertheless, the initial shock of being alone can take a lot of adapting to. It's like a gradual process of reversal. All the 'together things' you used to do have to be revised and turned into 'things I do for myself'. All the habits you've learnt have to be unlearnt.

In Carol Shields' novel *The Republic of Love*, Fay, the protagonist, stands in her kitchen contemplating life on her own:

'Toast, she says to herself, might be the test. She is being whimsical, of course, which is one of the ways she protects herself, but she is partly serious too: can she bear to stand alone in her kitchen on a Sunday morning, or any morning,

181

for that matter, and push down the lever of her ten-year-old
General Electric black-and-chrome toaster and produce a
single slice of breakfast toast? One only.'

Luckily, human beings are amazingly resourceful creatures.
Given time we can adapt to almost anything. People can lose
something as fundamental as one of their five senses and learn
to cope by extending the other four. People who lose their
jobs find other ways to make money and be productive. People
held hostage in solitary confinement can hang on to their sanity
by a thread and emerge years later to tell the tale (read Brian
Keenan's amazing account of captivity in Lebanon), and people
who lose someone they love finally come to terms with loss
and become happy, sociable beings again.

The grief of heartache can be compared to a physical pain.
Sometimes it's there and it's unbearably painful. Other times,
it's just a nagging ache that you can put up with. And sometimes
you can forget about it completely.

If a lost love feels like a bereavement, remember that there
are common psychological stages that accompany bereavement. After the initial shock and disbelief you are likely to
feel anguish, then comes resignation, then comes acceptance.
If it's true that love doesn't last forever, then the flip side of
the coin is also true – grief doesn't last forever either.

Julia, a 22-year-old chef:
'I was so sad. I didn't know how to cope. I thought there must
be some rules about what to do in this sort of situation. Do
you let yourself cry endlessly? Supposing you can't stop? I
decided to put everything that reminded me of Keith – things
like photographs, presents, letters – in a box in my wardrobe.
As soon as I'd done it I felt terrible so I got everything back
out and cried all over again.'

'Never again . . .'
You may believe with unwavering conviction that with the
departure of your partner goes the only chance you will ever

have of love and happiness. Through teary eyes our ex-partners become distorted into romantic idols, sex gods and wise, compassionate gurus. If you know someone who's recently been left by their lover, listen to the way their conversation is peppered with sentences that begin 'I'll never . . .' Notice statements like: 'I'll never meet anyone like that again', 'I'll never be able to trust anyone again', 'I'll never fall in love like that again', and even, 'I'll never be able to sleep with anyone else.'

The 'never again' fear has two aspects. One aspect is the anxiety that we will never be loved again. We believe that we have had our chance of being loved and we've blown it. The other aspect is that sneaking, nervous suspicion that we ourselves will never fall in love in quite the same way again. We will never feel so certain about someone again; so moved or infatuated by them.

Fortunately, these fears are, for the most part, ungrounded. They are the normal kind of anxieties we face when we are forced to stop, reassess everything and set ourselves on a new track.

It should, however, be noted that sometimes there is a tiny, scary bit of truth about the 'never again' fear. For example, if you are feeling so demoralised that you really are convinced you are unloveable, then finding a new partner isn't going to be easy. After all, if you don't like yourself why should you believe someone else will like you? This is why some people need to spend time on their own after a break-up, gradually gathering their self-confidence and rebuilding a positive image of themselves.

It also may be true that we will never fall in love in quite the same way again. Every love affair and relationship is different and sometimes it can be a positive thing that we find new ways of loving. For instance, a relationship that is based on friendship and admiration may not feel so intense or worth dying for as a *9½ Weeks* style romance, but in terms of longevity, and that underrated word, contentment, it's got a lot going for it.

Coping strategies

People react in different ways to being left. Some people feel utterly powerless – their significant other has made a unilateral decision and they are faced with the unpleasant truth that there is very little that they can do or say to change that decision. Others feel angry and betrayed, as though all the time they have spent with their partner has been wasted and they have been treated unfairly or cruelly. Others feel lost – they based their life around their partner and they feel that overnight everything has become hopeless or meaningless. Of course, people can also feel relieved and have a sense of optimism and excitement about the unpredictability of the future. A combination of all these feelings is normal.

Steph, 31-year-old nurse:
'He was very upfront and honest. He cooked me a meal and when we had finished eating he told me that he had made a mistake and that he wasn't being fair to himself or me. He said that he couldn't carry on having a relationship with me. I was very much in love with him and I felt like a big book was being closed. I had a sense of being barred from the past – all the precious times we had spent together seemed remote and unrepeatable. For some absurd reason, I focused on a time on a Greek island when we got lost together and made love in an olive grove. It was such a happy day and it turned into the most unbearable memory. I kept wishing to be back in the past when everything was OK. Wanting that and knowing it was impossible was very painful.'

After the initial shock of being left it's vital to develop some coping strategies. Rule number one is to put yourself first and be completely selfish. Try some or all of the following.

● Talk. Talk to your best friends. Talk to your parents. Talk to people who care about you and will listen. Don't feel guilty about burdening people – remember that you will do the same for them in the future. Sometimes you might want to talk to relive past occasions with your lover or you might want to take an overview of your whole relationship and speculate about what went wrong. You may be disgustingly sentimental, but draw comfort from the fact that sentimentality is far less nauseating for other people when it's felt in retrospect.

● Ask people to acknowledge that your relationship has ended. Mel, 26, was upset that her friends tried to cheer her up by giving her false hopes about her ex. 'They kept telling me that he still liked me and it was just a matter of time before he came back to me. This was totally untrue – Jake and I talked very honestly and I knew for sure that our relationship was over. There were two people who said the right thing. One of my work colleagues came over one day and said that she wanted to say how sorry she was that I had split up with Jake. And my father wrote me a short letter saying he had heard from my mother about Jake and me and that he hoped I wasn't broken-hearted. I think I really needed the separation to be recognised.'

● Keep a diary. Write down all your feelings, especially the most intimate sadnesses that you can't bear to tell your friends. Use your diary as a dumping ground. But observe one rule: make sure the last line of your diary entry is always positive or, if not positive, accepting. Never end on a down note.

● Emphasise the positive. Remind yourself of all the good things in your life. Reward yourself for being strong and self-sufficient. Pay yourself compliments and believe in the compliments that other people pay you.

● Make a plan. When we're feeling down it's always easy to let things drift and reduce life to the bare essentials. To give you a feeling of control, plan a day out, a holiday or a new design for your flat.

● Write a letter to your ex. The urge to perform post mortems is irresistible after the break-up of a relationship. Rather than confronting your ex in person or on the telephone, write him a long letter about all the anger, frustration and sadness you feel. When you've finished the letter, put it in an envelope and hide it at the bottom of a drawer. Get it out a month or two later and see if you still feel so angry. If you don't, congratulate yourself on making progress. If you do, think about posting it.

● Buy yourself a present. Make it something that you consider a luxury. It could be a brand-new bed with a big fluffy duvet and some soft toys; an aromatherapy massage; a guitar; an expensive lipstick; a giant sketch pad and an easel; an aquarium; a new hairstyle – anything that feels self-indulgent.

The first weekend that Caroline, 30, was on her own after her long-term boyfriend left her, she went to a bookshop. 'I should have had a shopping trolley: I bought modern romantic fiction, I bought poetry, I bought classics. I even bought self-help psychology books. I thought that if I didn't feel like going out I could just sit at home and read. I love books and I don't normally allow myself time to read. I think for about a fortnight I lived in novel-land.'

● Change your routine. If there are times or places that are acute reminders of your ex, avoid them. Take a different route, eat in a different restaurant, listen to a different radio station, get in touch with old friends. Sometimes it's necessary to wallow, but wallowing is different from being masochistic. Don't make yourself suffer when you don't have to.

Mark, 25, said the turning point came when he got in touch with some old college friends whom he'd known before his relationship with Anne began. 'I found that I was staying at home being introspective. Forcing myself to go out and socialise was a huge effort but it helped to fill the hole left by losing Anne.'

● Treat yourself like your own best friend. If your friend was miserable, you'd try to be kind and caring and you'd make sure she was looking after herself. You certainly wouldn't pick on this time to be critical, harsh or judgemental. Treat yourself in the same way.

HOW TO LET GO OF A GRUDGE – IN GENERAL

Couple relationships are not the only ones to cause long-standing suffering. *All* relationships can turn sour and give us a sense of grudge and grievance that holds us back.

Susan, for example, works in the accounts department of a large law practice. Normally she is a very helpful person but she will never process cheques for snooty solicitor Andrew because he once made a sarcastic joke about her weight. 'I take real pleasure,' drawled Susan, 'in delaying his business. I want him to feel as embarrassed as me. If you can't get mad, get even, that's my motto.'

Retaliation seems to come to us naturally and we've all done it at some point: 'I shall never speak to you again!' – 'And I shan't talk to you either!' It's a kid's way of coping with frustration. You don't know what to do so you start a war. A dispute which ought to be handled by negotiation gets frozen into a grudge and you preserve every detail of the insult forever. In the process you end up by hurting yourself as much as others.

Susan confessed this is exactly what happened when she over-heard Andrew making fun of her appearance. She felt mad as hell but powerless to speak to him. She'd already been having trouble with depression (the reason she'd come to see me). Handling frustration and making important decisions were the main triggers. Instead of taking effective action she'd binge on pick'n'mix at home, and she could never make up her mind whether to marry long-standing boyfriend Alex because he was often overly critical. 'Critics,' she said, 'I don't need!'

I asked whether her parents had been hard to get along with: 'You bet – my father took a degree in negative empathy. I haven't spoken to him for ten years after he slapped me when I got back one hour late from a date at the age of 19'. Even as a child Susan would go into a sulk when she couldn't get her

187

own way and a great deal of patience from Mum was needed to bring her round.

Of the two common types of grudge this is the sort that needs to be avoided because it fails to bring you any lasting benefits. It's the 'bad grudge', the 'shooting yourself in the foot' grudge or the grudge that 'cuts off your nose to spite your face'. It's the grudge where you hold all the pain and anger inside yourself and it festers. You are the one who becomes the victim. Meanwhile, you do silly things which you think are going to punish your enemy but all too often rebound on your own head.

For instance, Susan is failing to get her message across to Andrew. What she'd like to say is, 'Stop making unpleasant personal remarks about me – I hate it!', but all she's achieved is a poor level of work performance. Perhaps she'll be sacked when her supervisor next looks at the records? Far from troubling Andrew this would probably make his life easier!

With her father, she wanted him to understand that slapping a grown-up daughter is a completely unacceptable personal violation. But all she has actually achieved is confusion. Her dad has probably filed the episode away under 'children are crazy'.

It's not only that bad grudges fail to convey the right message to the other person. They also cost someone like Susan time and trouble that could be better spent having fun. By bearing a grudge she has not only boycotted her dad, she has also stopped herself from visiting her much-loved mum and this really does mean 'cutting off her nose to spite her face'.

If Susan is an example of holding a bad grudge what does it mean to hold a 'good' one?

If an offensive person in your life seems unable to change their unpleasant behaviour you need to reach a point of decision where you tell them enough is enough: 'Since you can't respect me and my values I no longer wish to have contact with you – here I draw the line.' But you do this to their face.

Take the case of Doreen, who finally discovered her daughter had been sexually abused by her husband 17 years earlier. All her family and friends were urging her to forgive and forget his 'mistake'. They said it no longer counted because husband and wife had lived together in reasonable happiness for nearly 20 years.

When Doreen came to see me she said through gritted teeth that she did *not* feel able to forgive her husband the teeniest bit. By keeping the abuse secret for so long he'd made her feel guilty, foolish and enraged. Love? She now detested him. She didn't want to spend another night under the same roof. Doreen was not 'bearing a bad grudge'. She was hiding none of her feelings. She was telling her husband exactly what his behaviour meant – that it was unforgiveable. Perhaps God could help him but she certainly couldn't.

Easy perhaps to spot the difference between good and bad grudges when crimes of abuse or rape are involved. But what about someone like Maria, a 23-year-old hotel worker, whose mother-in-law, Virginia, would never speak to her? When Virginia called her son on the phone the line would go dead if Maria answered. It was obvious the older woman held a bad grudge because Maria had dared to steal her precious son. The question was, should Maria continue to put up with the rudeness to keep the peace?

It's always helpful to try and see what's going on behind the scenes in these situations. How does the difficult person benefit from holding their grudge against you?

Very quickly Maria was able to tell us that Virginia was a lonely, possessive woman who had a lot of trouble thinking anyone else deserved a good time. She was bitter about growing older and resentful of the freedoms young people like Maria enjoyed which she had not. In other words, her bad grudge was just the tip of the iceberg and actually allowed Virginia to punish her daughter-in-law for all the major disappointments in her own life. Maria had done nothing wrong – Virginia simply couldn't face change.

As I listened, Maria's face brightened and she gradually shifted her posture. It became evident she was seeing things very differently and it was a happier young wife who said,

'It's really *her* problem, isn't it? I'm going to tell her she either starts speaking to me or she's no longer welcome in my home. I'm happy to build bridges. But if she's going to treat me like dirt I'm not going to be her doormat. She'll be the loser by her own choice.'

Understanding all this gave Maria new options in a situation where she'd always been the casualty. The key to the puzzle is realising that those who hold bad grudges do so from a position of weakness not strength. Virginia, for instance, didn't want to admit she had any personal problems or any responsibility for the conflict. Pretending it was all Maria's fault solved everything!

Joan, a 25-year-old divorced photographer, felt the same about the break-up of her marriage to Robert, a computer dealer: all the blame was his. When she discovered her husband having a casual affair, she cut up his business suits, gave his vintage wine to the homeless and bad-mouthed him on a local radio phone-in programme. This may appear tempting but it's never a healthy strategy, says Laura Schlessinger (author of *10 Stupid Things Women do to Mess up Their Lives*), because all you prove is that you can behave as badly as the one who hurt you. None of the real emotional issues gets addressed: you let yourself feel angry when you really need to be sad. You don't request support from family and friends.

Schlessinger insists that turning a bad grudge into a feud never helps. Taking an 'eye for an eye and a tooth for a tooth' seems attractive but the raw pain of your loss will *still* be there, waiting to be dealt with, however many eyes and teeth you damage. It's only macho men with thin skins who need to believe themselves perfect. Women know that life is messy, relationships foul up and we all make mistakes.

Clinging to a bad grudge, says Susan Heitler (author of *From Conflict to Resolution*) is ultimately about hiding the truth from *yourself*. If you listen to the other side and negotiate a compromise you will have to hear about the flaws in your own character. You will also have to *change*! A grudge, she says, is using anger to conceal your real desire. Grudges are basically about boosting your personal security and not being able to deal with failing. 'I think of a (bad) grudge as a mixture of garbage and sludge.' You really don't need one in your life.

Easy to say, but if you happen to feel like Virginia or Joan how do you learn to stop bearing grudges?

Well, it would do no harm to try to like yourself more. There can be nothing so terribly wrong with you that you need to cover up all your feelings. It's not your fault that some people don't respond. In fact it would be a ridiculous world if everybody in it thought you were wonderful because we all have such different personalities.

The next step concerns conflict. If you try to 'win' in a personal relationship then the other person must lose and that means you both lose because the relationship will lose. As I often say to clients, partnership isn't a matter of 'who's right or wrong'. Being a 'contractually correct' spouse earns few brownie points. The only thing that will help your relationship survive is whether you two guys manage to make each other feel wanted.

Third, try to make more allowances for chance in life – not everyone is out to get you. If someone doesn't instantly return your call it doesn't necessarily mean they want to avoid you. People are *also* busy so try again later.

Inevitably, we also sometimes cause offence to others so it's useful to practise the S word. Learning to say sorry is an art in itself but also one of the great human faculties (no other animal says sorry). Starting is often the problem but as soon as you break the ice, I swear it gets easier.

Even if you don't need to apologise, it is never a bad idea to tell someone with whom you are falling out: 'You've hurt my feelings – have I (unintentionally) hurt yours?'

Growing older and wiser is all about the quality of dialogue you can have with yourself. It's a tough thought to face, but none of us is perfect. We all have an 'ordinary' side. Even presidents and princesses, under some circumstances, can be as dull as a drunk in a bar. Let yourself feel more fallible. When you're out in the car and you make a left turn without signalling and the other driver gives you the finger, why bother to retaliate?

Killing them won't improve your driving or theirs. Saying sorry with your facial expression would be good for *you*.

Lastly, overhaul your emotional reflexes. Maybe, like Susan, you once needed to avoid seeing your parents. But is it still true? Say to yourself 'I needed to get away from them then. Now I feel stronger and maybe I could restore contact. It will be difficult at first but I've also a lot to gain. There's no harm in trying.' Ask who's really paying the price – you or them? Perhaps it was nobody's actual fault? If youth, fear and insecurity made you cut the link, perhaps age, fear and insecurity lay behind their motives? We're all a long time dead – ask yourself if you seriously want to leave the planet angry.

Great all-time grudges
1. Dean Martin and Jerry Lewis – the comedy duo feuded from 1956 until Lewis gave Martin a surprise birthday cake on his 72nd birthday.

2. Meg Ryan and mother Susan Jordan were estranged for four years after Ryan decided to marry fellow actor Dennis Quaid whom Jordan had deemed 'unsuitable'. Jordan previously abandoned her husband and family when Ryan was only 15.

3. Patti Davis and parents Ronald and Nancy Reagan – separated by Patti's fiercely critical autobiography and provocative nude photo sets in *Playboy*. Still estranged.

4. Problem page writers Abigail Van Buren ('Dear Abby') and sister Ann Landers hardly talked for years due to competitiveness in the world of agony columns. 'It's all gone and forgotten now,' says Landers.

Some grudges are less easily dismissed – for example, those based on deliberate unfaithfulness, as we shall discover in the next chapter.

Chapter Eight

Infidelity – His and Hers

In that dark movie *Blue Velvet*, Kyle MacLachlan falls in love with high school sweetheart Laura Dern. Frame by frame you can measure them getting involved. She longs to kiss; he longs to undress. There's the physics and chemistry of an inevitable match. But not for one moment does this passion prevent Kyle MacLachlan leaping into bed with the voluptuous Isabella Rossellini. When Laura Dern finally realises she's been betrayed, the expression on her face sums up a gulf between the sexes: 'How could you possibly sleep with *her* while loving *me*? How could any man? That's something I could *never, ever* do!'

On all surveys of sexual behaviour this century, men consistently emerge as the greatest betrayers. Annette Lawson's investigation of adultery six years ago found that 60% of married men had at least one extra-marital affair by the age of 40 compared to 39% of married women. The massive Wellcome Trust survey 'Sexual Behaviour in Britain' (1994) concluded that men cheat approximately two and a half times as often as women even though the figures probably under-reported the actual amount of infidelity. Indeed, the figures should be taken with further salt: some researchers are convinced that women consistently tell lies about their own faithless activity and always have done.

Now anyone can understand the compulsion to roam if things at home are bloody awful. When people need to separate, having an affair is a time-honoured method of achieving the break. But why, when love is bliss, when you've got Liz Hurley in the bedroom waiting to give you multiple orgasms, would you cruise Sunset Boulevard in search of an AIDS test?

A woman would say: 'If he loves me he'd think about what would hurt me and wouldn't do this. I've never denied him sex. Surely this must mean he doesn't love me?' A man would say, as Trevor Eve did in 'The Politician's Wife', 'If you can't tell the difference between making love and fucking then I'm sorry. *You're* the one I love.'

Granted that every man will argue that he should have his cake and eat it, and every right-thinking rat doctor will say men are programmed to scatter their genes in every available woman, there are five basic male complexes which foster infidelity.

1. The divided self

At the heart of masculinity is a kind of schizophrenia. Men tend to be split into Jekyll v. Hyde, heart v. head, love v. sex. The two sides rarely enjoy a nodding acquaintance. Little boys learn to distrust subjective feelings. The myth of masculinity is that they must be objective like father and impersonal, unlike mother. Sex is not just about falling in love, it's a means of keeping score and measuring male progress. At puberty, it becomes impossible to dissociate sex from a lust for power over the woman in a contest which is essentially against other men in a game of 'genital theft'. 'When a man marries his mistress,' said Sir James Goldsmith famously, 'the position of mistress falls vacant.'

Case history 1

'I first fell in love when I was 16 and lived with my boyfriend Rick till I was 21. We went to the same university on the same course and he really did love me. However, I'd also met this wonderful man when I was 15 who said, 'You're too young. I'll come back for you when you're 21.' And funnily enough, he did turn up at my 21st birthday party. He was wonderful, swept me off my feet and I stayed the night with him. When he returned to college, my boyfriend was waiting for me and screaming. 'Have you slept with him? Have you slept with him?' I felt bad enough without lying so I said, 'Yes, I did.'

Whereupon, my boyfriend reeled off a list of 10 other women on campus he'd had sex with in the past six months, people I'd known in the college bar who must have been laughing at me behind my back. What a toe-rag! I realise I was no saint but I don't know how I could have been so stupid. I think he was saying, 'I want you but I'm too young to be tied down and I also want to play the field. So if you could hang on while I have another 30 women, we'll be fine!' However, he's married and I gather he hasn't changed one bit!' (Alex Conn, 28, food scientist.)

2. The intimacy barrier

Not only do they live life in compartments separating head from heart, men find a conflict between the drive for sex and the drive for intimacy. Women who may happily integrate the two find this a difficult, even a crazy concept. However, it is the source of that justification which men adopt when caught with their trousers down – 'What you don't know can't hurt you', or 'Out of sight is out of mind.' Men buy sex by the yard, make love to anonymous bodies or half-cropped photographs of the same. Women, by contrast, relate better to bodies with names.

Case history 2

'I've always had affairs but hardly noticed. That's difficult to explain. But looking back over 10 years of marriage, there's this peculiar pattern. I seem to have gone to bed with most of my wife's friends. There were no seductions. All were as much to blame as me. I comforted one woman when her dog was run over and she put her hand down my trousers. I bumped into another when driving in the car and she asked if I wanted sex. Another rang and flirted down the phone and afterwards said come round in person. Yes I've "cheated" but so did all these women. All were able to lie and still go on being friends with my wife. I didn't really lie. I simply emphasised the truth differently. But I love my wife, and that's true.' (Bryan, 33-year-old film editor who sought counselling for addiction to adultery.)

3. The sex barrier

Just as men have trouble sharing a woman's view on intimacy, so women often misunderstand a bloke's view of sex. It's summed up in that terrible phrase 'I never refused him', as if all that counted was access to a vagina. In the same way, most journalists missed the point about Hugh Grant's encounter with Divine Brown. His opening remark when he picked her up was: 'Aren't you gorgeous?' What he meant was that her suggestive pumpkin lips, inflated hips, sleazy skirt and slutty conversation offered a perfect screen on which he could project his sexual Mr Hyde. It's possible to think that Liz Hurley's wholesome personality and flawless physique render her useless for these purposes. What men seek when they stray is rarely the love of a good woman. What men seem to prefer is some risky, fetishistic, sado-masochistic, abusive, androgynous, fantasy-filled private underworld. The penis, like the Starship Enterprise, is an imperial vessel and it wants to boldly go everywhere.

Case history 3

'I've only been the other woman once. He still loved his wife as the mother of his kids but six years ago she started rationing sex and he turned to me. I think women have no idea what effect they have on their husbands/boyfriends when they won't make love. They need to get real about the sex thing, especially when the man has always been very active. Sexual needs also change with age and it's very hard to turn to your wife and say, 'I want to do whips and suspenders, please.' At the start of an affair, since sex is upfront, you can negotiate the entire menu. In my experience, if husbands try to change the menu at home, wives want to know if they've begun an affair already.' (Diana, 31, solicitor).

4. Incest taboos

High on the list of controlling male 'splits' is that between the images of 'Mother' and 'Whore'. The Trevor Eve character hints at this when he effectively says he wouldn't dream of 'fucking' his wife. She might say that's the problem. Whatever they did on the front seat of his MGB when courting, he's now got it into his head she must be shielded from real sex. It's not just about enjoying erotic variations. As husband/ partner, he can no longer let himself go with the mother of his children, the woman he has come to revere or fear and towards whom his feelings may include protectiveness as well as denigration. It's as if the new mother becomes sacred cow. In some families, wives are actually called 'Mum'. Many men cannot screw the woman who not only bakes their favourite pudding but knows all their faults and covers the mortgage. It's just too much power to give away.

Case history 4
'For me love is all-consuming. It begins in the brain and spreads to my other extremities. For men, sex begins in the other parts and only occasionally reaches the brain. In my marriage when things became rocky I gave it 110%. I tried to love and look after my husband even more. I questioned myself to see where I was at fault. I've since wised up. When things get rocky for a man, I realise he turns to another woman. One of my husband's friends told me the divorce was all my fault. He said: "You spoiled everything by finding out about his mistress." It's just too silly. Another said: "When I was 16, my father took me to a brothel." The message *I've* learned is that sex happens outside the family.' (Marion, 41, fitness instructor.)

5. Love phobia
For some men the split may go deeper still. Dislike and fear of women leads to a fury complex. For some men, love is The Enemy. Mum and girls in general have somehow let down the little boy so the Big Man, prey to his inner child, decides to be unfaithful to all the women he subsequently attracts. Many men see love as a trap. If you ask them to say the L- word, they think you are the secret service of an enemy power attempting to break their resistance or asking them to rat on

their buddies. The more these men love, the more they fear loss of self/ego/identity. Cheating on a partner is like taking out an insurance policy against emotional vulnerability. If they marry, beware when babies are born – these are the men most likely to start a new affair in competition.

Case history 5

'I need a secret life. I learned to survive in my family by concealing my feelings and always having an escape route. I suppose I just got good at lying to get away from their prying. Also, a man is a double winner if he can have lovers on the side. Then he's really in control. I remember the smile on my face one afternoon when I went from the arms of Rose to Thalia to Pat then drove around in the car with Alice with my hand halfway up her skirt thinking if they only knew how they'd all been deceived. And another day when I deliberately went to bed with Jen at precisely the same moment Alice was supposed to arrive for our date and seeing the look of disbelief in her eyes when I told her she couldn't come in because I'd already got company. I felt like a king.' (Stuart, 31, newspaper executive.)

But – it is not true that men are always rats. Dr Glenn Wilson, Reader in Human Personality at London's Institute of Psychiatry, says: 'Men may separate love and sex as part of novelty-seeking. But it is not normal for men to seek sex with others when first in love – there is usually a sustained honeymoon period. What we've come to realise is that long-term relationships will almost inevitably include the occasional excursion.' David Bowie has said that after a lifetime of promiscuity, 'Monogamy is really exciting.' And remember that Phil from 'East Enders' turned down sex on holiday 'because I love my wife'. There's always hope in the soaps.

If the complexes listed above represent men's motives, how can you tell if your partner's cheating?

HOW TO TELL IF YOUR PARTNER'S HAVING AN AFFAIR

The process begins with elimination. In order for an affair to happen, an erring party must devote time, sexuality, organisation, money and subterfuge to the event. There will be a specific number of visible changes in both outward and inner behaviour but one can still fail to total it up. Lipstick on the collar is rare; it may even be a badge of innocence in a kiss from Mum. The interested party must deduct from more subtle clues.

By all means start with physical clues. Lovers generally avoid lovebites but passionate humans are careless of digging in their nails, from neck to buttock. Reckless coupling can also injure. One man said he'd sat on a drawing pin to account for the inflammation caused by falling out of bed on to his mistress's broken vibrator.

Is there a new pride in appearance? Is he dieting? What of the new hairstyle? And that sudden attention to late-night hygiene? Why should he shower when returning after hours? Unless he has incriminating evidence to launder, what does it mean that he's finally discovered how to operate a washing machine after six years of living together?

Sex holds a certain perfume. So why is he applying extra cologne at home as the clock strikes one? And what of bed? Has sex recently ceased or increased? Can he still come? Are orgasms faked? Is that routine order of caresses muddled? Does he suddenly know how to inflame your senses with a flick of his fingers for the first time in living memory? Does he suddenly realise how to use tongue and teeth to please?

Is there guilty nocturnal attention? 'Yes, of course I'll fetch you a drink/extra pillow/mogadon/blindfold, my darling-darling.' New varieties of sex may be extremely welcome but they are totally suspicious.

So are new patterns of absence. Even abbreviated, truncated, interrupted intercourse takes time. Laugh if he says he's about to play poker: Freud is listening even if you've gone deaf. It's too pat to offer such an easy excuse for games in the small hours. Unusual sociability? Unprecedented devotion to work? Four punctures in a month? Oh come on! One man took up the flute and tooted his way through London for five years before his wife requested a recital. Curious – he still couldn't manage a solitary musical sequence.

Money is another giveaway. Pity the woman who discovered she was maritally adrift when she visited her florist. She wanted to send flowers to Aunt Joan but was told the account, though still in joint names, had recently been moved to her husband's place of work and the outstanding amount was up by a mere 427% in one month. Pity the woman who found her family in mortgage arrears, the loot having gone to a far more expensive

good lord, I almost forgot, I've got to take the dog to the vet

we haven't got a dog

lady. One tabloid newspaper recently contrasted the annual 'cost' of a mistress with that of a wife and got the former wrong (total £2,000) by some £5,000 a year since hotel bills alone can top £120 per thrill. Independent experts in fact suggest checking all joint household expenditure for hitherto unexplained excesses.

Telephones tell tales. The re-dial number never lies. Don't forget the car phone, especially if someone feels compelled to visit the garage at midnight. As a matter of fact, lovers must communicate, if only to arrange or cancel their next rendezvous. So pay attention when they make for the phone and observe those expressions of sick panic when inconvenient calls come in. Think of the man reduced to announcing he was being blackmailed by a gang of international arms dealers simply because his girlfriend thoughtlessly dialled him at home.

Panic is an inward sign. In the restless cheat, it tends to blend into generalised psychological arousal or distil into hysteria. The villain is excited; nervous; alert; speedy and shaky. Desperate to control events that in their nature elude such grasp, he is constantly adrenalised. Life cannot continue on its automatic path; the pilot must manually negotiate every pocket of turbulence lest the big secret escape: that both plane and contents are way, way off course. More so since the secret wants to come out. Who wouldn't wish to proclaim the ecstasies of new passion? Hence the second inner sign of estrangement is a tedious, nagging irritability, as if all this neurotic stress were the 'partner's' fault for obstructing the new route to bliss.

A third indication is blank emotional withdrawal. Perhaps a normally boastful, attention-seeking ego suddenly doesn't need you any more, has nothing to say about its daily triumphs, tricks and coups? I have to think that in the nature of things egos don't voluntarily forego attention.

Fourth and almost worst is compensatory over-attention. From slugs into overnight paragons; from lousy father into doting Dad; from difficult critic into PR-speak. When the flowers arrive, please sit down and say you've got to talk. Don't fly off the handle. Just check the florist's bill.

How people justify infidelity

There's an old blunt saying that you don't have affairs on your own doorstep. Affairs are tolerable, it seems, provided they are conducted out of sight and out of mind, perhaps in Birmingham if you live in Brighton. There is clearly some truth in this. It is often miserable to have to work for the boss you used to sleep with whether you got tired of him or he of you. However, there is also a lot of nonsense talked too. Cleopatra was not the first person to sleep her way to the top. And when it comes to infidelity, the most likely candidate for simple reasons of availability and excitement is often your next-door neighbour or spouse's best friend. Together with work colleagues, these categories yield adultery's archetypes.

1. Gerald

Gerald is a GP, married with four children. 'But I do have an on-going affair with air hostess Elaine, the 24-year-old wife of a neighbour. It's a gentle sort of thing. We just escape once or twice a month and spend one day and night together. It's like that. Very quiet and we just need each other. It might sound odd but we've been doing it for three years. It is a real part to my life. I do love and admire my wife and of course my children. I have *absolutely* no intention of leaving them. And it's very important that Jean should never know of this. I couldn't bear to hurt her. She is my real main life, after all. It's only because I trust Laney that I can do this.'

2. Jude and Jo

Contrast this genteel approach with the blasé wisdom of 'affairs are just part of life's rich pageant'. Jude and Jo are predictably American although they live in London and do have British counterparts. They have decided to enjoy the odd affair, surfacing approximately twice a year on a strictly permissive premise. 'We're the kind of people who were always going to have affairs. We knew this about ourselves long before we ever got together. But we also have a wonderful house, three gorgeous kids and we don't want things split up by deception and mistrust. So we made this rule. Affairs OK – but only with people we both knew, liked and respected. It doesn't mean we compare notes in advance but rely on the other's judgement. Then it's up to the one involved to proceed as discreetly and considerately as possible. It's not so strange, really. There isn't any fear of betrayal and life does feel safer.' It can also sound shocking, of course, until you consider the further possibilities.

3. Henry
Henry and Christine have two children. He is an academic lecturing at local conferences. At one centre of learning, work completed, he bedded a colleague. The outcome was no college comedy by novelist David Lodge. 'It was pretty wonderful for a time. Every day I was in London – or within striking distance – we would get together. But I began to feel less and less comfortable with it. I really couldn't stand the dishonesty – that's what everyone says, isn't it? I ended it. I went there to tell her and we talked. She was very upset but I explained that Chrissie and I were thinking of having another baby and I couldn't carry on. The real shock came when I got back home. Chrissie had already got her telephone call (from my mistress). I tried denying it all but there was no escape. She had times, dates, places, coincidences, the lot. Chrissie *was* pregnant. She was devastated. I wonder now what I ever saw in my lover. The vindictiveness of that phone call shattered me. Our marriage has survived, but only just, only by a miracle.'

4. Kate
Kate, 27, a bank worker, was rendered distraught by her husband's betrayal. She waited till his fling had ended, then evened the score: 'I was left with this sensation of impotence and no self-esteem. So I rather clinically decided to make it one-all. I felt like someone in search of a victim, albeit a willing one. I was determined to find a lover, not to flaunt in my

husband's face, just to swing the abstract scales of justice. I ended up feeling sorry for my new bloke, because he got rather fond of me, but that didn't matter as much as my new feeling of significance. It worked in restoring most of my confidence.'

5. Michael
But one problem with affairs is their natural unpredictability. Michael, married to Wendy, then met Linda and bounded into bed with the sex object of his dreams. He envisaged a romp through the *Kama Sutra*. Instead he shed 13 pounds in four weeks, finding himself head over heels not just in sex but in love: 'I would sneak out of Linda's room at midnight and back to Wendy feeling sated but then start playing tapes in my head of what we'd been doing. I couldn't sleep or eat. After a few hours away from Linda, I was desperate to see her face, hear her voice. I told her I'd fallen in love and she couldn't believe it. There was this constant churning longing in my gut. After three months, Linda was ready to accept my feelings as real. But I was trapped. What to do? Lose my love, or lose my two kids? And I remember I *did* have a choice about making that first phone call.'

6. Rosalind
Ros also regrets impetuosity. 'I was pregnant with our second child and felt so damned good inside I couldn't say no when this beautiful young actor spun me a line about sex and fecundity. I went into his hotel without a murmur and wore him out. We continued until I was past seven months then made the stupidest mistake over a letter and got caught by my husband. I've heard of men going haywire during pregnancy because they feel overlooked or during mid-life crisis or whatever but didn't know women were also at risk. My husband still makes deadly sinister jokes about not being the father of his own offspring.'

7. Robert
When all's said and done, most affairs are based on the

tendency to separate the marital from the sexual impulse. Frenchmen are supposed to marry for children or charcuterie, reserving concupiscence for mistresses. Both sexes seek variant loveplay in their illicit liaisons. This is certainly one motive behind Robert's involvement with Petra (her working name), whom he's been seeing and paying for over 11 years. It perhaps also helps explain why men seem to have so many more affairs than women – some of the women because they are in business have 'multiple' partners. 'Petra reads my mind. She knows when it needs soothing, when it wants to play dirty, when I want to dominate and when I want her to include a friend. I can suggest any behaviour or scenario to her and I know she will arrange it. My wife is a wonderful mother, organiser and warm lover. But I could never expect her to satisfy my mild sado masochism, my troilism, nor my urge to turn sex into risqué psychodrama. At least, it's never crossed my mind to risk it.'

8. Jilly
If marriage itself has dimmed the sexual impulse, then extra-marital attractions obviously increase. Most sex research says bedroom boredom is the main culprit, especially when female partners are straying, but for Jilly married to Benji there was this further incentive: 'I never felt as if I'd been young. I got married straight from my father's home into my husband's. As a teenager, I was serious and did homework not boyfriends. Benji was my first lover. When he seemed to lose interest in sex, or – ouch! – had to work up an interest, I yearned to know whether this was because he was undersexed or I was not attractive. I had no scale of comparison. That's where Rickie came in. I couldn't believe what I was doing, almost anywhere and anytime. And there were two others. It didn't make me happy but I did feel very desirable. And it gave me the courage to haul Benji off for counselling.'

But what if we focus more closely on the whys and motives behind female infidelity? Isn't there an obvious question looming:

SHOULD YOU SLEEP WITH MARRIED MEN?

Of course not, but then nor should they sleep with you. We do many things that we shouldn't. We do some things because they are the lesser of two evils, like having an abortion. The question is not really, should I sleep with married men? The question is, should I be sleeping with *this* man right now? Is he enhancing my life or detracting from it?

Your answer will include your own judgements about the sanctity of marriage and may be governed by your feelings for his spouse. Some people say he wouldn't be on the market if the marriage truly mattered. Others say the marriage would have a far greater chance of mattering if you both kept your clothes on. There's truth on both sides – but some marriages are already dead in the water and having an affair is often the only way back to dry land and a possible new beginning. Facts are facts: having an affair is one of the principal ways in which we arrange the transition from one relationship to another and I'm bound to say not all relationships should or could last for life.

The problem of cheating, as Princess Diana has explained, is also about our dislike of overcrowding: 'There were three people in my marriage.' She naturally hated the competition. Nor is it an accident that generally we bond in *pairs* – short of living alone, it's the *smallest* number of people with whom we can share our daily experience. Since all children grow up seeking parental attention, we have an in-built tendency to like as much attention as we can get. Possessiveness and jealousy are the natural consequences. So when you look at your sleeping arrangements there's more than a moral question. You need to ask, 'Am I the exceptional sort of person who really has no sexual jealousy or do I need to minimise the stress and provocation to my sense of identity by remaining largely monogamous?'

There's another way to consider the issue. At what stages or passages of life are we most likely to be unfaithful or promiscuous? The answer is:

1. When first discovering sex in the adolescent years.
2. When major relationships collapse and we are looking to shore up our damaged self-esteem and confidence.
3. During any identity crisis following a primary change in our circumstances, e.g. having children, losing a job, getting older.

Or listen to my colleague Adam Phillips: 'As small children, we can't help but be faithful to *our parents*. We organise our lives around them. And yet growing up can involve challenging them, betraying them, letting them down. If our survival, at the beginning, involves something like monogamy, our development soon involves something like infidelity. We may need a background of safety, but we only discover anything new by taking risks. In other words, our stories about childhood prepare us for our stories about adulthood. There is only one mother and father in the world – one Mr or Miss Right – but there are a lot of men and women. It is possible that when we think about monogamy we usually think about it as though we were still children, not adults. As though monogamy were just the opposite of promiscuity, *rather than one way, among others, that we may choose to live*' (my italics).

Now we will probably find that cheating on other people is undoubtedly bad for them but not a great deal better for us. Time and energy spent on duplicity feels shabby; knowing we're causing pain and distress to others leaves us with a guilty conscience. But you cannot feel these emotions in advance. In a universal sense, as Phillips suggests, we only really learn from our own experiences. So while I am hopeful some people will learn from their infidelity and eventually refrain, I am also certain that others will go on being unfaithful and breaking hearts. The art is not to get speared and punished on the lance of someone else's learning curve in the meanwhile.

For example, Reece was a young man who'd been a fat teenager. You could tell he was immensely satisfied with himself now that the weight had vanished and women found him very

207

attractive. But if you probed and questioned really hard, you would discover a wide-eyed schoolboy on his first trip to the funfair. He flirted with everyone. He wanted to go to bed with everyone. But he always made a joke of it.

That was actually one of the giveaways to his personality. He wouldn't be serious. You could never pin him down about his real beliefs or wishes. Did he like you? Did he love you? Who could say? He wasn't ever going to make a verbal commitment. Words were his screens and he acted like a romantic spy. If God was watching, he knew Reece was actually bedding five women at the same time.

There was Jenny the dancer (who came round in her overcoat and nothing else); Mandy the student (who got the elbow when Reece double-booked himself at three one afternoon); Anna the journalist (who also bumped into Mandy at the VD clinic when things really went haywire); Elaine the anthropologist (who should have known better) and Alice the model (who was a sucker for his particular cute blond look). Five grown-up women all being dangled on a string. The moral is: if you don't want to go to bed with a cheat, find out from his friends what he's like underneath.

On the other hand, you may feel blasé and gung-ho. What does it matter to you who else he's seeing as long as he bothers to see to you properly? After all, there are women who go through phases of only wanting one thing from a man, are there not? But if instead you feel jealous and distressed, with or without good reason, how can you best handle it?

DEALING WITH JEALOUSY

One Friday evening quite by chance, Daniel (28) and Eleanor (26), who've been going out for three years, met some of Daniel's office colleagues in a bar. Included in the group was a single, good-looking brunette called Marilyn.

The conversation only lasts ten minutes before Eleanor begins to feel uncomfortable. She knows she's always had a tendency to get hot under the collar where Daniel and other women are concerned. It's not that he does anything provocative. Eleanor simply notices the strong bond of attachment that exists between her bloke and this attractive young woman. They seem to pair off so naturally and obviously have an excellent understanding.

Eleanor doesn't imagine for a single second that Daniel is having an affair, but she feels almost as distressed as if he were. Fantasies take over and in a blink of an eye she's already imagining her relationship might crumble.

We've nearly all got a vulnerable spot where the tiniest pressure can cause a major eruption with absolutely zero warning. In her sudden panic, Eleanor simply hates seeing Dan so focused on somebody else. To her intense surprise, she finds she doesn't want him to talk to Marilyn at all.

'But it's crazy,' she thinks. 'I'm going crazy. He needs to relate to people at work. There's nothing going on between them. So why do I have this awful pang? Is there something wrong with me?'

The answer of course is there's nothing wrong with Eleanor or anyone else who feels the same. In a situation like this, when your lover has a strong rapport with someone else, you're perfectly entitled to feel jealous. For nearly all of us, it's the most natural feeling in the world.

If you look inside the green-eyed monster you can see why. Jealousy is based on experiences we've all shared, from moments of getting overlooked or feeling rejected. We all know what it's like to be 'left out'. We all remember people who didn't bother to keep their promises to us. The result is that in competitive situations many of us can quickly lose our confidence. Life is full of contests but for every winner there have to be several losers, and losing hurts. In these situations, it's easy to become paranoid. We are tempted to blame other people for our losses. We imagine they are enjoying good fortune but only at our expense. A stream of jealousy rises from the surface of our daily reverses and rejections.

Psychologists say jealousy begins at birth. We can learn to feel jealous before we even know the word. Studies suggest that by the age of two, the lives of young children can be dominated by 'sibling rivalry' – jealous feelings between or about brothers and sisters. These remain intense until the age of nine but may persist into later life. It's tough discovering as a toddler that there are other people in the world besides ourselves and natural to dislike the experience, but the process is perfectly normal. Dr Glenn Wilson of London University again: 'Jealousy is clearly a survival behaviour. Siblings compete for mother's attention to make sure they get their share of the milk supply and aren't abandoned.'

And if jealousy is so widespread and natural, why does a person like Eleanor feel embarrassed by it? Perhaps she's a victim of fashion? Jealousy was widely derided by sexual liberals in the Seventies as a backward and unacceptable emotion. Yet no emotion can be without purpose. By all means separate 'normal' from 'pathological' jealousy. But if you come home unexpectedly to find your loved one in the arms of another, you do not tiptoe out of the bedroom, apologise for interrupting and offer to make them both a cup of coffee. You scream and shout and demand to know what the hell they think they're playing at.

Not only is jealousy part of nature but you can even use it to your own advantage as I always try to point out to my clients. Jealousy focuses your close personal priorities by showing who you really care about. If you were never jealous, it's hard to believe you were ever in love.

Jealousy in other people can also give you an insight into their needs and how to meet them. Take Joe (25), who's married to Alison (27) and reacts really badly when baby Paul is born. Joe was a proud father who handed round a big bunch of cigars on the great day itself. But after nine months of his wife's pregnancy and three months of breast-feeding Joe feels less wanted. Little Paul seems to know by radar as soon as Joe is about to persuade Alison to fool around or have sex and there've been several nights when Joe's moped off to the pub. He feels more loved for his payslip than his personality.

Observing these jealous flashes, Alison gradually understands that Joe is silently signalling for attention. She thinks, 'Perhaps the baby is taking over too much. What can I do? Paul needs the best of care at this vital stage in his life and Big Joe can be a pain in the bum. But what's the point of having children if Joe and I end up like strangers? We need more hands to help. Maybe I'll get my mum to babysit for us on Fridays and we could see where we go from there.'

Two Fridays later, Joe begins behaving like a more responsive father.

You can always examine possessive reactions from others to similar profit. But perhaps the most important way of using jealousy is to gain insight into your own needs and values. The products and lifestyle you crave and covet most will say more about you than many a psychological profile.

For instance, are you still a frustrated teenager? Maybe you have a dream of driving down a boulevard in LA in an open-topped Mercedes and envy all the movie-stars you see on TV who can enjoy your dream? OK – use that envy! Going to Beverly Hills may be out but what stops you saving up and taking yourself off to a second-hand car dealer and getting an MGB that will provide some of the necessary buzz?

Or maybe you feel desperately jealous of a girlfriend who's bought her house and you'll never afford that for at least five years? OK – react positively and do what you can! Within your budget decide if you can redecorate the kitchen or fit some new French windows. By taking action you'll feel in better control. It's even possible to construct something that's prettier than her property and therefore put you in an altogether better frame of mind.

And that's the beauty of jealousy in all its natural glory. Not only does it protect your romantic interests, it says you're full of passion for the other good things of life. It indicates what you want for the future. Even if you can't hit the jackpot it points you in the directions you need to go. Not bad for an emotion usually dismissed as 'primitive'.

The sensible approach is not to think of yourself as disabled by these green-eyed emotions but to discover what we call the 'usable bits' of your jealous feelings and convert them into positive action and energy. Eleanor, for example, needs to confide to Daniel that she has this jealous tendency and he should stick by her side at parties with strangers – at least until she has got comfortable with them. By looking at what we're jealous of and accepting the implications, we get to know ourselves that much better and can very definitely live life more happily.

Like any emotion, jealousy tips us into reaction before we can think. We replay old tapes in our mind full of our worst nightmares. And these messages get stuck unless we can take a step back, pause for breath, and turn these feelings to our advantage. Ask yourself, 'How can I get what I want?' not 'How can I spoil other people's pleasure?'

How jealous are you?
So which category do you fall into? Are you using jealousy effectively – or is it using you? Read the following monologues and choose for yourself:

DON'T SAY: 'What a beautiful figure. She must be a terrible person. I bet nobody likes her. It's either the breast-feeding or her middle name is Liposuction. She must have spent *thousands* on plastic surgery. Dolly Parton eat your heart out. But it's not fair on people like me. I can't compete. With women like that walking around nobody will ever look at me. I'm going to have another custard cream.'

SAY THIS: 'I'd like to look like that. Of course she's put a great deal of time, trouble and money into her appearance. I know I couldn't undergo any surgery. But there's no reason why I shouldn't make more of my looks. My legs, for instance, always get into shape quickly. Should I finally go to the gym? Will that help? I don't know but I think I'll give it a try for three months. I've got nothing to lose – except a few extra pounds!'

DON'T SAY: 'My sister's always had the attention, I hate her.

212

She's been ruining my life ever since I was three. Why does she have to get the boyfriend who's the stockbroker while I'm stuck with Maurice, the great chandelier salesman? There's no justice when I'm always struggling to make ends meet. It's the same old story – to them that have shall be given. If I had a voodoo doll, I'd make it look like her and stick pins in it.'

SAY THIS: 'It's difficult for me having a sister who's so successful when I've had so much bad luck. But I know she can be a good friend. I have to take a leaf out of her book and get some self-confidence. She's excellent at solving financial problems. Perhaps she could help me with some business contacts if I ask? I really think it's time Maurice and I sorted out our financial relationship. I'm going to get nowhere unless we pull together. I'll make an appointment to see that financial adviser. Nothing ventured, nothing gained.'

DON'T SAY: 'Is there some secret law that says men always get the promotions? There's no way that guy is better than me. He must have bribed the interviewer – probably sleeping with him by now. Mother always told me men played dirty and now I believe it. I've worked in that sexist place for two years waiting my turn. A stranger with rat fur on his chin walks in off the street and they give him the position. I'd like to go to his funeral – soon. He wouldn't be missed. I give up.'

SAY THIS: 'I was very disappointed not to get the job I'd set my heart on. It will take me a couple of weeks to recover. But I'm damned if I'm going to be beaten. I'm really well qualified for the position but perhaps I can use a little revision on computer skills and systems. Maybe that was the difference between us as candidates? I've heard this guy is a systems whiz. Maybe if I was that good I'd have got the promotion? It hurts but I have to admit he's well qualified. But I hate this feeling of coming second. If all it takes is some extra homework, I'm game. I never want to be this miserable again!'

Another view of jealousy

Claude Steiner is a Californian clinical psychologist with a special interest in multiple relationships. He says that jealousy is a much misunderstood emotion. He breaks the monster down into two separate beasts. The first has to do with control, the second with love. *Control jealousy* is where a partner is primarily regarded as property. The jealousy therefore is a dislike of losing control of the property. *Deficit jealousy* is to do with a sense of uneven or unfair balance in relationship giving.

For instance, Gillian and Paul have been married for six years. If Gillian cares for Paul, cooks for him, cuddles him when he's low and holds him close at night when he's full of tension, she is understandably going to be irked when he is always too tired to talk to her in the evening, ignores her needs, spends every Saturday at the match and is a lazy lover. For all the nurturing she is putting into the relationship, she gets very little back. When Paul then proceeds to give 'nurturing' to his sister's flatmate under the guise of working late, it's not surprising that Gillian becomes violently jealous. He has tipped the already uneven balance right over.

Every therapist who has ever worked with a jealous couple agrees that the jealousy must be acknowledged and brought out into the open. If, however, the jealousy is of the 'control' type, Steiner hints that the problem is insoluble. You either decide to put up with the situation or you separate. 'Controllers' are sometimes dangerous. When they accuse you of sleeping with every man you meet they may turn violent. An escape plan is a wise move.

Deficit jealousy – like Paul and Gillian's – is easier to work with. By getting the couple to examine the whole relationship and not just the incident of jealousy, they are able to employ a kind of lateral thinking about the partnership. Paul can see that by altering his behaviour towards Gillian she will become happier in the marriage. Gillian can see that if she became happier, the extra-marital incident would lose its heat.

But Gillian needs to get over more than simply this one incident. She needs to come to terms with the fact that her life has altered. Paul has made it clear that he may go to bed with other women, if only occasionally. How can Gillian not only accept this but start to feel OK about it? The answer lies in Gillian finding alternative interests and building up her own self-esteem. It doesn't necessarily mean she should rush off and have affairs in order to compete, although that might well become part of the independent lifestyle she needs to adopt.

Of course, there's a risk that by developing herself and her interests Gillian may eventually become so independent or so involved with someone else that the partnership ends. But letting things slide and allowing the jealousy to smoulder on is no guarantee that the relationship will endure. Indeed, the couple's original fear, voiced to their counsellor, was that if they couldn't do something to cope with the jealousy, it would mean the end of them as a couple anyway.

And there is the real possibility that the partnership will survive because Gillian begins to feel a whole person and not just a reflection of Paul. One of the reasons people find jealousy so hard to handle is fear: fear of a powerful emotion and of what it uncovers. In a situation like Gillian's one of the obvious anxieties is that the relationship will be exposed as a poor one. Yet since changes in behaviour can overcome such problems, the partnership has the option not only of surviving but also, astonishingly, of improving.

Jealousy usually vanishes when its underlying paradox is exposed: *some anxious people need to feel their relationship is under threat before they can be certain it's worth defending!*

215

Chapter Nine

Who Needs Friends?

'Friends are the families of our own invention,' writes Irma
Kurtz, 'Cosmo's' resident agony aunt. 'However much we love
our lovers, we women simply cannot live without our friends.'
Researchers at the University of the South Bank have called
them 'families of choice'. At a time when matrimony is in
retreat and the extended family fast becoming extinct,
friendship is the social lifeline we create for ourselves. We
nearly all depend on this network to cope with the stress of
work, play and love – that trio of potential excesses.

'Some of my friends are like an extended family and some
are playmates to go shopping with or get drunk. I have several
friends who are incredibly special, a source of inspiration, my
confidants, my sounding boards, my critics, my emergency
services. I'd be lost without them. I feel blessed because of
them.' (Chantal, Kensington)

As employment grows ever more competitive, female net-
working becomes the obvious way to find many jobs. Faced
with a male conspiracy to retain the top positions, women have
been compelled to explore their own secret reserves of
affiliation. These days, it's not just what you know but who
you know and how well. Families have always promoted their
junior members; now families of friends do the same thing.
Getting to the head of the queue means relying on friends to
tip you off with the best information and ideally helping cut
corners towards that all-important employment interview. And
naturally they hold your hand when necessary through the
anxieties of applying.

Secondly, thirdly and fourthly, friendship is there to pull
you out of the bushes when you collapse in a boozy coma;

217

stop you giving your heart to every passing psychopath and lend you a few quid to get your car unclamped.

So we often need friends, as Chantal has just made clear. But do we *all* need friends? And are we equally adept at making and keeping friends? Is there a script we need to learn? Does friendship follow certain rules? And can men be 'just friends' without the penis rearing its head? This chapter aims to answer these questions while helping the shy improve their social contact-making.

FRIENDSHIP PROS AND CONS

For those who don't know, friendship has clear advantages. According to social psychologists, close friends help us develop emotional stability and even maintain physical health; they can stave off loneliness, depression and sometimes prevent suicide. Friends provide anchor points for our opinions, beliefs and reactions. Through their responses to us, friends let us build up a picture of our good and bad 'sides'. A friend validates many of our perceptions and confirms that our thought world is sound. Close friends, in other words, offer free personality testing right from adolescence into later life. They reduce the fear of the unknown, a role they've probably been playing since the days when humankind first discovered there was physical and emotional safety in numbers. Good friends value our opinions and boost our self-esteem.

The great psychologist Alfred Adler once claimed that every suicide is a reproach or a revenge – an attempt to remind friends how much the recently departed would be missed. Friends worthy of the name allow us to take some responsibility for them too since a true 'friendship transaction' must be reciprocal.

In short, all these positive elements of friendship serve to support our personalities. Different friends offer different deals. Some are good for idle, some for religious debate, some are agony aunts. Others are there to take us to the cinema.

Against this, I suppose you could say friends have been

known to let you down. They may steal boyfriends, or gossip behind your back. They can get obsessed about something till you want to throttle them. But all the same, *most* friends do none of these things too often! Friendship has more benefits than drawbacks.

A greater pity, therefore, that some people clearly lack friendship skills. This is rarely their fault. They grow up in families or substitute families which teach them positively not to mix.

Shyness

The trouble is some families are themselves anti-social and replete with shyness. Mum 'hates' causing a fuss in the shops in case she draws too much attention to herself. Dad can't stand asking for directions when he gets lost in case he needs to make small talk which he's hopeless at. The kids simply tend to copy their parents.

THE STAGES OF FRIENDSHIP

Childhood lays down the foundations not only of our good relationships but also of our bad ones.
1.   During infancy, you make friends and 'play' with those on your doorstep. Proximity decides.
2.   At six years of age, the child begins to realise that cooperation has value but she remains self-interested.
3.   At seven, friendship becomes collaborative. Play is social but friendship is regarded as possessive and exclusive. A 'best' friend cannot have other friends and remain a best friend!
4.   At 12, the girl comes to realise that one person cannot fulfil all her needs. Whereas boys tend to identify with a posturing gang of mates, girls form close, confessional friendships.
5.   From 12–13, friendships begin to switch from the same to the opposite sex. During adolescence, aware-ness changes in several ways. A girl notes the

219

complexities of relationship from 'pals' to 'best friend for life'. She creates a personal directory of personality types and develops her own theories of what makes people tick. She probably spends time in groups or cliques 'hanging out'. These form a safe base from which to try out tentative relationships with the opposite sex. (Parents who discourage gangs are probably delaying their child's adult development.) Friendship takes centre stage superseding home life as a source of informed guidance. A girl sees that other people also have personal needs and finds out how to manage the competing claims of these with her own.

6.   In her early 20s, a woman is still establishing her identity and often seeks mutual friends or mentors with characteristics she envies or tries to copy. Friends tend to define rather than support her self-image.

7.   Late 20s – she begins to settle into longer-term relationships which become the primary focus. These can be used as an excuse to drop unwanted friends – friends she's outgrown at this point.

8.   A woman in her early 30s will tend to have different friends to do different activities – sport, entertainment, work – rather than one multi-purpose 'best friend'.

9.   By the mid-30s, all is again up in the air as long-term relationships hit rocky patches and friends may be dumped overboard after divorce or when making new alliances.

Within the family, this poverty of communication matters less. Dad grunts at Mum. She knows he wants her to pass the ketchup. Mum smiles a bit when she goes off to work and the children understand she's saying goodbye. But when the children of such a family have to fend for themselves in the big wide world, these low level communication and social skills prove their absolute undoing. There's not much point grunting at a potential employer when she asks you to highlight your three greatest strengths and weaknesses. It's even more risky to go to a party and try nodding your way into an intimate, sexual experience.

So you could say shy people generally come from shy families who help them perfect their shyness. Some families even label a child 'the shy one' to prove how socially adept the rest of them are. However, social learning can nearly always be unlearned, revised or elaborated. If you want to facilitate friendship with a newly encountered stranger, these are the guidelines:

■ Practise eye contact without staring; hold your body in an open, accepting posture.

■ Think and take a breath before speaking. Without preliminary air, there are no words. If you exhale before speaking your voice will sound strangulated and ill-at-ease.

■ Get your facial muscles moving – shy people look hostile not anxious, because they immobilise their features. Say 'Me-You-Me-You-Me-You' to yourself very quickly as a cheek-warming exercise before entering a room of strangers.

■ Tell other people when you feel shy so you have nothing to hide and can relax – most people will sympathise. Those that don't aren't worth knowing.

■ Listen to other people actively, nod when they make a point. Make them talk about themselves by asking open questions which demand a response that is not just 'yes' or 'no'. If you concentrate on them you'll forget about you. They'll enjoy the attention.

■ Practise your social skills on shopkeepers, door-people, waiters and telephonists where it doesn't matter if you fluff.

■ Remember that self-disclosure is a key factor in establishing friendships; so is humour and the ability to roam 'to-and-fro' in conversation rather than indulge in long, boring monologues.

■ Negative information about yourself should be disclosed early. Positive information later. Otherwise you are more likely to be disliked.

221

The friend-free

Contrary to popular belief, not everybody wants friends. Different people have different drives for friendship. Some self-assured people are strong enough to do without the incidental reassurances provided by constant or daily social contact. Writers and artists tend to be solitary. So do farmers and fisher-folk. For others, friendship needs are governed by a kind of critical mass phenomenon. Once we've acquired a certain number of friends, we don't need any more! There is equally a critical threshold before we feel motivated to do anything about feelings of loneliness and isolation.

Finding a friend

As I always found myself saying to callers on the radio, nobody is going to beat a path to your house, break down the front door and demand to be your best friend. For that to happen, you need to circulate. Moreover, you need to circulate widely. Think about it. Out of any given group of 100 people, you could probably only form a close friendship with about three. So when a couple of people fail to respond to your first attempts at friendship, don't conclude 'nobody wants me'.

On the other hand, if you ask yourself, 'What do I want to do with my time?' rather than 'Does anybody like me?' you will inevitably take a rather important step *into* circulation. Practically all major leisure activities involve other people – from skiing, hang-gliding, sailing to politics, gardening, dancing. Group dynamics work their own magic. For instance, people's feelings change due to simple proximity. When 'enemies' meet for peace conferences, like the Israelis and the Egyptians did, they usually end up liking each other a lot more than when there was no contact. However, friends made at work or play may not readily turn into best friends serving under all circumstances.

Deepening a friendship

Having met a stranger, how do we develop a relationship? Attraction is the first point and here you should *not* rely on

222

instinct alone. What you'll probably find is that the people you attract are either very good or very bad for you. Size them up carefully!

At the outset, your gut feeling will pick up something familiar or recognisable about them. When you get talking, you'll find they've either had similar problems to you in the past so can be really helpful and sympathetic. Or they've had similar problems to you in the past and actually want you to pay for their share as well as your own!

In experiments where strangers had to pair off in a crowded room, those who were the last to be selected were all found to be nature's loners, either the children of divorce or they had suffered a family calamity. Some were adjusted, some were decidedly not. So don't rush into any new relationship – with friend or lover. Take a good, recently packed parachute in case you need to bale out.

THE RULES OF FRIENDSHIP

1. Friendship develops like any other relationship. If you sense it's stopped growing, you start to lose interest. Don't take your friends for granted – if you think you are doing so, give them a call.
2. As friendship increases so too do outward displays of affection, plus time spent together talking.
3. People have personal limits on how intimate they wish a friendship to become. Learn to respect the physical and mental boundaries.
4. As friendships grow deeper, paradoxically, the relationships *can* become more casual again. The overall timespan of the association will decide.
5. In the maintenance of a friendship, fairness is the buzzword. Quarrels between friends are caused when it's felt the balance is unevenly set. Equity says you ought to get roughly as much out of the relationship as you put in. People respond to inequity by feeling unhappy, guilty or angry. Even over-equity can be negative: the person who

223

gives too much can be pressurising, just like at school –
always tagging along and wanting to join in your games!

6.   But conflict in relationships, if managed correctly, can also
develop them. The more openness there is about distress
and the consequences of a particular behaviour, the more
the bond of attachment can deepen and improve. Ripe
friendships, like good marriages, must have their ups and
downs.

Growing out of friends

Friendships also alter with your own circumstances. Lottery
winners, alas, nearly always lose their old acquaintances. Those
who improve their educational circumstances can also end up
knowing more and feeling cleverer than the 'stupider' mates
they left behind. Research suggests the drive for friendship in
any case declines after the age of 30 except where there's
serious disruption to life such as divorce, career change or
death of spouse.

Friends or lovers?

Research also shows that violent physical exercise and dancing can create the necessary state of arousal for sex – so be
careful if you dance with your friends! The quality of a
relationship is largely decided by the activities taking place
within it not, as used to be thought, the feelings dictating the
activities.

Nor are friendship and love so very different from each
other. They're like stopping points on a continuum: one may
easily lead to the other. It's marvellous to be good friends with
your sexual partner. However, when there's uncertainty about
whether to step over the borderline of friendship to sex, this
may well be because you sense, unconsciously, that the friends
may not suit you sexually. It is undoubtedly more difficult to
stay on good terms with a friend-turned-lover than to become
friends with a lover-turned-friend . . .

THE TALE OF MIKE AND MAGGIE

Can heterosexuals have platonic relationships with the opposite sex? Yes, but there may be complications, some of them unforeseen, as Mike explains: 'We met at university. I was in love with Diana, Maggie's best friend. I think Maggie fancied me sexually – partly out of rivalry with Di – but it caused no problems as Maggie and I discovered we could relate in lots of other respects anyway. When Diana finished with me, it was Maggie who helped – but platonically. She gave the supportive hugs and told me I wasn't the fiend Diana described.

'I left college and got a job. Maggie stayed on as a hard-up graduate. The relationship then became one where we were almost best friends but I used to help her out financially. We'd write loads of letters, have the odd dinner, go on holiday occasionally and I'd always be slipping her the odd fiver or paying for a big shop in the supermarket. I remember one time she lived on three potatoes for a week. It was not quite brother and sister – more like a serious mutual admiration society.

'Then after one boozy dinner in Camden Town, I took Maggie home and suddenly looked at her sexually for the first time in years, and she looked at me. She was wearing this long, black, satin dress – I think it was an evening gown of her grandmother's belted at the waist. But I noticed her lips, breasts and buttocks in that order. She was enormously intuitive and said at once, 'Michael, how strange, it never occurred to me before – but what a *good* idea.'

'Perhaps it wasn't so strange that two people so compatible and friendly by day should also suit each other after dark. We already knew from conversation that we shared certain sexual attitudes – we both liked to do the same, slightly kinky things. So we did them. And the sky didn't collapse. It didn't feel like incest. We didn't recoil in horror. In fact, it didn't rock our friendship in the slightest, and presented no more stress than *not* having had sex in the previous six years. And we carried

225

on for quite a while – being friends who also went to bed with each other. There was never the undying romantic passion of love's dream but we were longer in the tooth than that and extremely sexually compatible.

'However, to cut a long story short, I eventually married someone else and Maggie also found a boyfriend who proposed. And that marked the end of our long friendship. Because the fact that Maggie and I had *been* lovers, that fact alone, was enough to ensure that her husband could never accept a continuation of our friendship. He killed it stone dead. To this day, years later, we never speak to each other and I often wonder whether I lost a scintillating friendship only because we couldn't keep our hands off each other that night in Camden Town?'

WOMEN AND FRIENDSHIP

The social network is vital for both sexes, but women generally have the potential for more intimate, more open and more interdependent relationships with friends than do men. The flip side of this is that women are more vulnerable; they can be more easily hurt by friends. And few things are as hurtful as suddenly becoming second fiddle to your friend's new lover.

Kelly, 22, student: 'I have a friend called Liz who is terrific fun and can be very supportive and loyal. But she is absolutely *terrible* when it comes to men. When she is not in a relationship she insists that I come out with her constantly, that we tell each other everything and that we are 'closer than sisters'. As soon as the next side of beef lumbers over the horizon, it's goodbye Liz. She doesn't bother to return calls, she can't possibly meet for a natter, she's got no time to discuss anything except her latest *boeuf,* and he *always* has to tag along with her like some bovine body-servant.'

Everyone knows a Liz, and shakes their heads indulgently when they think of how awful she is, but cast ye not the first stone! Haven't you, at least once, dumped your friends for some guy with a broad smile and a comfy double bed? Haven't you sworn undying friendship to your best mates, vowed that you'd always be there for them, and then forgotten their birthday/vital job interview/name as the blood rushed to your head? No? Well, the chances are that your friends notice a definite change in your personality when *you* fall in love.

But this is hardly a major crime. As we saw in Chapter One, simple time constraints, let alone the overwhelming demands of romance, mean that a new relationship will inevitably change your behaviour patterns. Your priorities are quite rightly rearranged, and all but the most demanding friends should understand that you need to take time for your relationship. Problems arise when you let things get out of hand. Kelly describes her own feelings on falling in love as 'very weird. In one part of my mind I know that I'm acting as though I'm on drugs, distracted, forgetful, and only really focused on one thing – my lover! But I'm not being hypocritical. Unlike Liz I try very hard not to forget about my friends.'

Just as love is not some automatic process that you can switch on, sit back and enjoy, neither is friendship. Making friends takes effort, and so does maintaining them. People who are bad at 'keeping up' their relationships with friends tend to rely on a circle of people with whom they routinely come into contact. As long as the routine continues everything is fine, but if they fall in love and drop out of the loop they may find it's a different story. Even if you are normally a loyal companion you cannot rest on your laurels – your friends will be severely put out if they find you've always got 'better things to do.'

Managing to integrate your love life and your social life is a bit like juggling. Keeping all your balls in the air is rarely a natural talent; you have to work hard to juggle successfully. What can you do to keep everything aloft?

● Don't isolate your friends from your lover. Your friends will feel left out, your lover may wonder what's wrong with him, and you will severely limit your options.

Sam, 28, designer: 'When I fell in love with Bill I was very worried that he wouldn't get on with my mates – he was so different to them. I would always find an excuse not to bring him along to parties or evenings out, and I quite enjoyed keeping my friends in suspense, having an air of mystery hang about my love life. Bill didn't seem too bothered, although he was sometimes curious, but my friends got angry, and one even accused me of being ashamed of them. Eventually I introduced them all and realised that my fears had been groundless. Admittedly they don't have much in common, but they get on fine, and it's like a weight's been lifted off my shoulders. I see now that it's better to let people come to their own conclusions.'

● Equally, don't try and force them to like each other. This will simply turn your friends off your lover, and create some awkward tensions. You and your lover may be attracted to one another for different reasons than those that bind you to your friends, and if they have little in common you will be attempting to force a round peg into a square hole.

John, 25, systems' analyst: 'Jacqui's friends were very nice, but they weren't *my* friends, and I couldn't really talk to them. But she couldn't simply accept that and come to some sort of amicable compromise. I didn't see why we always had to do things en masse, but she had to have it both ways. She said that she wasn't happy unless I was with her, but whatever we did she was always agitating to get her friends involved too. Whenever we were out she'd phone them up, and if I ever tried to cry off for a night she'd turn drama into a crisis. I think her friends were as fed up with constantly having me around as I was with them.'

● Make some time to spend with your friends, without your lover around. Make sure they know you haven't abandoned them, and that they haven't been supplanted. *Don't* spend the whole time talking about Him. Be interested in *their* lives, and on no account be patronising about their love lives. Few creatures are as universally disliked as one half of a nauseating couple telling someone else how 'unlucky' they are and that they 'don't know what they're missing out on'.

● When you are out with your partner and your friends together don't spend the whole time gazing into his eyes and whispering sweet nothings. Your friends will quickly regret having asked you out. Remember, you are out with *them*, so don't exclude them.

● If, at the end of the day, your friends are still critical and demanding, it may be time to reassess the friendship. You may feel that you have made a real effort to keep your relationship going, but that you are now being asked to jump through hoops. The uncomfortable truth is that as people mature they may simply outgrow their friendships. Few things are as likely to change you as falling in love and developing a deep and committed relationship. If your friend is unwilling to accept this, or your friendship is not strong enough to adapt and take a new form, then it probably is time to move on.

Jill, 32, secretary: 'Judy and I were best friends at college, and moved in together for six years afterwards. She really was closer to me than my own sister. We often talked about what would happen if one of us fell in love and wanted to settle down with a man, but I guess Judy never really faced the possibility seriously. When I did meet Tom (now my husband) she became very difficult, and often accused me of having betrayed her, or having changed too much. But we lived together for another 18 months before Tom and I got engaged. Well of course I wanted to move in with him, but Judy saw this as the final betrayal. She was incredibly angry with me and our friendship ended quite bitterly. I wrote to her asking her to be my maid of honour but she never replied to my letter. Perhaps she felt I was just rubbing salt into her wounds.'

Friendship has a lot in common with love. In many ways Sternberg's Platonic Love describes it well – intimacy and commitment without passion (see Chapter One). Both of them need maintenance, communication and compromise to last. With a little hard work you can avoid being forced to choose one over the other.

Chapter Ten

The Single Life – Part Two: The Difficulties

Joke for the millennium – Q: What's the burning issue for women in the new century? A: Is it okay to fake orgasm during masturbation?

Something strange has happened. While the media binges on sex, lots of people aren't getting any. Our leaders wallow in sleaze but many of their citizens remain aloof. Thought for the decade: the politicians and the British Royal Family could be the last ones doing it. We may have fewer taboos but we also have fewer encounters. We can literally have each other but all too often we say no. As you approach 30, this is the typical scenario.

Boy meets girl. After three weeks, they find the time to go out to dinner. They discuss job stress. They eat the food of love – exotic mushrooms, wild strawberries – but it makes no impression on them. They think the candlelight is some sort of remedy for tired eyes. She's frazzled and didn't bother to 'fix' her appearance. He's dyspeptic from the shouting match he had with his account manager. They do like each other. They think, in the abstract, about their respective attractions. They could get a wonderful romance together if God gave them six months off on a desert island. But after coffee (decaffeinated) they take their separate transport home. He doesn't dream of making a pass – nobody does in the middle of the week. She wouldn't say yes if he did. She'll be asleep before her head hits the pillow. The alarm is set for 6.30 and she's got to stay focused.

Fifteen years ago, boy met girl. They agreed to date later that day. They knocked off work at 4.30, dashed home, primped and preened. He collected her by car to cut off her escape at the end of the evening. The romantic meal would be carefully chosen to fill her stomach with spice and her veins with a measure of pure alcohol. Both would be playing a game, with her running just fast enough to let him catch her if she wanted him to. The meal was foreplay and the only major decision was timing – would they do it on the first date, the second or third? Whatever was decided, the evening was just an episode in that long-running saga of Let's Make Love. And both were keen.

So just what changed in the Nineties? Recent surveys suggest that, without taking any kind of vow, more and more individuals find themselves without a love life, especially after those heady late teens/early 20s. In the USA, 23% of single men and 32% of single women remained celibate in 1994. In Britain, the Wellcome Foundation survey, published that same year, reported that 'half the single people and more than three quarters of the widowed had enjoyed no sex at all in the preceding month', and seemed to confirm that affairs were less common than had previously been supposed.

Today, when women end an important relationship, their average period of unplanned celibacy is from one to three years. But this trend is *not* deliberate. Sensuous men and women haven't forsworn their hormones, decided sex is silly or plotted to become trainee hermits or nuns. There is actually something wholeheartedly positive about turning your back on the routine games-playing of falling into bed with the next charming idiot who asks. We now live in a much more grown-up world than we did before.

In the Nineties, many dates have not even been predicated on the idea of having sex. It is now possible to be friends with other men and women, to touch them affectionately, to ruffle somebody's hair, to massage their neck, even to share a couch or bed without having to go further or define your sexual orientation. By contrast, Seventies' people felt honour-bound to try sex simply because parents had told them they shouldn't.

However, giving up playing games only partly accounts for the change. The bulk of the trend comes from a revolution in

232

the way we live and work. Accidental celibacy is a consequence of computers and tough government making all of us more competitive. Personal lives have shrunk; Nineties' offices don't close at five p.m. – people are expected to stay until the work is done.

In today's cocktail hours, we practise word-processing not adultery . . .

Case one

> *Megan, 32, Oncologist:*
> 'The options for women have been refined. We are first and foremost building our careers and it's extremely tough. We aren't looking for a breadwinner. Second, because of our careers, we don't have the time to go out and find someone. Third, we are no longer accepting inferior goods. Men have to fit a tighter prescription. We've sort of fine-tuned the shopping element in looking for a man. I know exactly what sort of a guy I'm looking for and if I can't get him I don't want a substitute in the wrong style or shape that doesn't fit my requirements – I'll look elsewhere. Women are being a lot more choosy about whether someone comes up to their expectations – everyone's just standing and holding back a bit. It's one of the side effects of our success in life.'

Successful individuals like Megan find themselves keeping sex at bay. Her essential conditions for a decent love life are to be able to allot time and tenderness to an affair. She prefers to put her emotional life on hold because there are no opportunities. But there are compensations.

> *Megan again:*
> 'I have intense conversations with men friends which, in the past, I might have had with a lover. Taking sex off the agenda allows you a certain freedom – to call a

guy at midnight, no strings attached, to seek advice or just unwind. God knows, with this job you need to.'

The workforce is now 50% female. In the USA, women are expected to own half of all small businesses by the year 2000. In the UK, 10% of the most important managers are women and in some industries the figure is between 20 and 30%. The new social science of 'values research' has highlighted a 'genderquake' amongst women currently aged 18–34 who appear to value autonomy, work and education *more* than having a family or parenting. Duty is a higher calling than love. For them building a career is a number one priority; pleasing a man merely optional. And as we know, women often feel they need to work twice as hard as any male to gain recognition. The recession has reinforced this sense of discipline at a time when companies are keeping fewer staff and demanding longer hours.

Case two

> *Laura, 26, PA to company director:*
> 'I get glimpses of men with whom I think it would be just wonderful to be involved. I look and think: 'You're adorable', but I know I haven't got time for dinners, conversation, foreplay, chat, sex, post-coital sweet nothings, sleep and getting up for work the next day – which for me starts with phone calls before seven. I like sex and romance on a high level but the idea of a quickie is ludicrous. I miss sex but am not sure if I don't get the next best thing sometimes by talking with close friends – male or female. The system has told me I'm responsible for myself and must pay my bills to survive – so that's what I'm doing.'

Open sexism is a further depriving factor for some. There is a sad reluctance on the part of executive single women to fall in love because malicious gossip may suggest a) 'She only gets anything done by using her sex appeal', or b) 'She's having an affair and must be unstable.' A comparative dearth of suitable male partners for women over the age of 30 also contributes (the men are married, too recently divorced, withered on the vine or looking for something a tad younger). But after work-related pressures, the biggest factor in the trend towards greater celibacy is . . . the trouble with men.

I'll put this as delicately as I can. One woman told me: 'I've captured the last civilised man on the planet. God knows what I'd do if I lost him. In my view, the rest are cheap fakes.' A certain jaundice there, perhaps, but another has also said: 'Until the male of the species evolves a bit more, I'd rather spend my time with girlfriends. Today, confident young women are not thrilled because some person with a penis makes a cheap suggestion.'

Case three

Jenny, 27, social worker:
Women need to keep a roof over their heads. However, that no longer entails attracting a man first. I prefer my freedom. I don't have to be wonderful sexually to get anything. I've had enough bad lovers to know what a good one feels like. Eventually, I want a whole package – love, sex, commitment, intelligent conversation *and* Haagen-Dazs. But I won't necessarily need to marry for it. I'm also avoiding unsuccessful men. I never thought it would matter but I find that men lose their confidence – and hence attractiveness – if I'm earning while they're broke.'

In other words, the consequence of a lot of experience *may* be an improved sense of discrimination. You get to know what doesn't work for you, be it the one-night stand, the unhygienic male, the professional philanderer, the chauvinist, the heavy drinker or the bloke with more overdrafts than Nick Leeson. Such men may become technically competent lovers but

235

independent women require emotional payback too.

However, as they say in the movies, a good man is hard to find. And there's little evidence to show he's also looking for a good woman. According to Dr Beverley Alimo-Metcalfe of the British Institute of Management, 'the divorce rate for high-earning women compared to men is about *four times* greater.' This is 'largely because many men feel threatened by well-travelled women who are successful and earning as much as, or more than, they are.' So many men still insist on calling the shots.

Case four

> *Gail, 31, assistant editor on a woman's magazine:*
> 'Not having sex eventually plays on your mind. At the features desk not many of us are having sex at the moment but we're thinking about it all the time because of the magazine. You start to wonder, is celibacy really bad for you? Maybe our situation is really awful? I do feel a bit frustrated but on the other side it's not worth getting involved with the wrong people just for sexual gratification. I channel my energies into my work, that's what makes me feel really great. I really love coming into work on a Monday morning. I sometimes thank God I'm back at work after the traumas of the weekend. It really helps having a loyal bunch of working girlfriends who are always there to talk to.'

IS NOT HAVING SEX HARMFUL TO YOUR HEALTH?

Physically, no. If you're talking individual survival, people need water not sex. Many women go through 'Sleeping Beauty Syndrome', where their libido is put on hold ready to be awakened in the future, while men simply have wet dreams or absorb redundant sperm into the bloodstream. Other celibates, who remain acutely frustrated, should probably avoid handling heavy machinery in case of accident! And there is no evidence to suggest that celibate sportsmen are better performers than those who make love the night before the match – or even at half-time. So a Government health reassurance: temporary celibacy is not medically harmful. The only serious health dangers are in *having* sex, if you participate in unsafe sexual practices.

The man's case

Gerald, 30, personal trainer, London:
'Half my female clients are accidentally celibate. They're going flat out for work, getting in early and doing the full hours. I'm the same. I used to chat anyone up – the more the better. But that energy is now going into work. Everyone needs to get fit to keep up with the pace. It's all or nothing – you can't be a little bit pregnant and you can't be a little bit promiscuous. Hardly anyone can have both a successful career and personal life it seems to me. Men are affected like the women – company directors are either divorced or too exhausted for sex with their wives after travelling abroad or whatever. One multi-millionaire client on his second or third divorce said to me 'Gerry, if you need a friend get a dog.' Now the trend is for people to be just friends, even share a bed but not have sex. These days, sex is for the unemployed.'

Case five

Christina, 28, widowed two years, working as a supply teacher:
'There are certain things you neglect when you're not having sex. You don't look after yourself quite so strenuously. I mean, sometimes you might not quite bother shaving under your arms, you might leave it another week; you might not bother getting your legs

waxed quite so often. I've also put on weight though that was down to stress. I'm drinking too much. I suppose a bit of me is afraid of being unfaithful to his memory. What I miss most is lying in bed late on Sunday morning and having a cuddle with the Sunday papers all over the place and maybe leading to sex or not but at least having that option. One cruel irony about being on my own is that I have loads more money. You start paying for things you don't really need, or even taking your friends to restaurants when they can't afford it and always picking up the bill. I know one thing for sure. If I had died and not my husband he wouldn't have stayed celibate. It's a personal pattern with me. This is my third sabbatical from men – I did the same between relationships in my early 20s, waiting for Mr Right.'

THE GOOD NEWS IS . . .

Accidental celibacy usually comes from higher expectations and raised standards. Women are voting with their feet against men who can't satisfy them. There is more understanding of the power of emotional 'process'.

Case six

Melanie, banker, 39, celibate three years:
'For the last three years sex just hasn't happened. Fundamentally, I think I find work much more exciting. It's more fun to close deals than be chased around the bedroom. I didn't choose to put the shutters up; I didn't say that's the end of sex. I simply discovered I prefer my privacy and the company of my cat. Since I broke up with my boyfriend, I've given up housework. My cooker has never been used. I get other people to clean for me. Now I make it plain to men I'm not available and I put my libido into my work. I don't miss

sex because I don't miss the kind of men who used to supply it, especially my ex who wanted a trophy wife. Any new relationship would *have* to be with a man who adores a rich, powerful, independent woman. He'd need to know there's nothing material he can offer me – apart from himself.'

Case seven

Angelika, 30, accountant:
'I have absolutely no doubt whatsoever that if I wanted to go out and have sex tonight I could. It wouldn't be the slightest problem. I think we are quite lucky being "Thatcher children" that we've been given the confidence to choose for ourselves. For two years my choice has been to stay out of a man's bed. It wasn't planned but I've never wanted sex for sex's sake. Some people would rather have sex than play tennis – I'd rather play tennis. I'm very monogamous. I've got an enormous number of close male friends and this is the first night in 12 I've stayed home. Last summer I went walking in the Andes with two great chums. They probably both fancy me but I never flirt. I caught my last boyfriend two-timing me after a tip-off from my cleaner. I told him to get out of my life. No, I wasn't icily polite. I said, "Fuck off and die, I want you out of my house." '

The end of a relationship demands a time of mourning, not jumping into bed with a new man because you can't face sorrow. Sometimes you need to avoid having an affair in order to concentrate on education, spiritual growth or a critical phase of your career. We all know meaningless sex is meaningless.

We also know that accidental celibacy is rarely lifelong. After all, no economic turndown lasts forever. Successful women attract successful men. Angelika again: 'If this evening I met somebody who was completely and utterly great fun and just was terrific and all the rest of it, I wouldn't say what a shame I can't because I don't. I would be very happy to take him to my bed.'

But singles still have families

In the mid-1970s, the *Futurist* Magazine predicted marriage and the nuclear family would be extinct by 1992. Despite this spectacular miscalculation it is still chic to say the family is in crisis. Figures for divorce and lone parents, proclaiming war between the sexes and down the generations, bolster this opinion. It's certainly true that if you marry today, you have a 40% chance of divorcing before you die. Divorces over the last 20 years in the UK have doubled, from 74,000 to more than 150,000 every year. Three million people in this country will experience a broken marriage during the 1990s. But marriage is *not* the family and if you read between the battle lines it's possible to notice that families are flourishing.

For a start, nobody can really be born outside one, real or adopted. Humans are biologically and therefore psychologically dependent on family care. In times past, various French aristocrats left babies in the wild to be raised by wolves or owls, to see if they would blend with nature and talk like Adam. To their chagrin, they found that children without close human relatives and relationships, if they survived at all, simply grew up to be gibbering idiots. Or, looking at a more contemporary example, perhaps you get dumped at birth on a Birmingham church doorstep by a teenage schoolgirl in despair. Yet this proves that the miracle of adoption can plant a West Midlands accent into anyone.

Most adopted foundlings, with the help of counsellors and researchers, go to tenacious lengths to try to find out where they come from and to which family they belong. We have this principle enshrined in law. All adoptees have the right to know which family tree connects them to the social forest. We instinctively recognise this natural bond. For the same reasons, most experiments to raise babies communally away from their

240

natural parents have failed. The parents seek out the children and the children their parents. For 50 years, some German and Polish mothers have been searching for families kidnapped from them by the Nazis, just as today Cambodian refugees look for missing brothers and sisters after the terror of their killing fields, and American fathers still hope to find those sons unaccounted for since Vietnam.

Why this persistence? I believe because the family is indelible. Freud may have been wrong about the significance of sex as the only cause of neurosis but he was right to put his finger on the importance of early childhood family experience as the determinant of future behaviour. What happens is that family genes meet family habits and blend a family style. When you get married, most of the problems arise because your family's way of doing things tends to clash with his. You may grill tom*ay*toes; but he fries tom*aa*toes. The old joke – 'When two people become one, the important question is which one' – emphasises the subtler union: at a wedding ceremony, it is two families which are trying to merge, not mere individuals, because we tend to carry our families around in our heads. Or, as W. S. Gilbert put it: 'I can trace my ancestry back to a protoplasmal primordial atomic globule. Consequently, my

family pride is something inconceivable. I can't help it. I was born sneering.'

In further proof, let's add that the single and celibate also have family-derived difficulties. The main issue in my field of counselling is often how to wrestle with those negative 'voices' in your brain constantly reiterating: 'She's no Einstein, she couldn't total a chequebook!' The voices mainly belong to Mother or Father or Grandparent, demonstrating that in this respect all unhappy families may resemble each other in their destructive capacity.

Yes, but what about the demise of the nuclear family? Don't more people live alone (single-person households have doubled from one in eight in 1961 to one in four today)? Isn't the proportion of childless women, today one in ten, on present trends going to hit 17% by the year 2000? Don't 37% of marriages end in divorce (in 1990, 55% of all divorces involved children under 16, the majority under 10)? Doesn't this mean that every week, 2,900 children are told their parents are no longer going to stay together? In the face of such collapse, how can you possibly suggest the family is flourishing?

The answer is that only family customs are changing. As the divorce rate rises, so does the cohabitation rate. The proportion of single women cohabiting aged 18–49 has risen from 8% in 1981 to 20% in 1988. These alternative types of family are replacing our brief historical flirtation with the nuclear variety. We may not be able to keep grandparents under our roofs due to age and health needs but the new 'blended' family, whether based on marriage or not, means that most of us know some step-children and many acknowledge wide-ranging parental responsibilities. Indeed, a pair of thirty-something cohabitees may form a household containing his, hers plus their children, in a 'family' including exes, new spouses plus their kids too!

In fact, our family future seems to be following the path forged by Scandinavian countries, where there is a shift from patriarchal society to a more egalitarian one. The standard relationship between breadwinner and homemaker is giving way to a greater sharing of household tasks while both adults work part-time. Oh yes, the two 'partners' also maintain their separate *single* households. And have a new word for it. The Danes call it 'living-apart-together'.

Chapter Eleven

Changing Times

Being able to cope with change is perhaps the most useful gift for the times we live in. Women are newly in charge of their sexuality and fertility. But knowing when to say 'Yes' to sex and love is as important as the ability to say 'No'. Your independence will only survive if you keep making the right choices. In this chapter, we'll look at the rules governing when and how you should change your mind.

A BRIEF HISTORY OF CHANGE

Change is it! The universe starts with a big bang and just keeps on truckin'. Whatever the whisper from your plastic surgeon, ageing is inevitable. You live in seasons and cycles – solar, lunar, hormonal. Growing up, leaving home, losing grandparents are all predictable landmarks along the way.

Change is natural in all healthy relationships. You wouldn't want to dress at 20 as you did at 12. And you don't want to put the same thoughts in your mind at 20 as belonged there at 12. Ditto your heart and your love life. If you don't 'work' on your relationships, they'll die. You constantly need to find new solutions for your age and stage. Some of the biggest crises occur when one partner outgrows the other.

For example, Janet aged 23 and Steven aged 27 meet in America on holiday. They start an affair that rocks the world. For weeks on end, they are high on each other, on life and on the endless possibilities for their future. They party till dawn like Roman Emperors. They instantly know they will marry.

Scene cuts to England ten years and two children later. Partying is now the last thing on Janet's agenda. She's bothered about the health of her family, the link between asthma and air pollution and has joined the local primary school as a Parent Governor. Steven, by contrast, is still playing all night, still getting drunk twice a week and spending more in a month than he earns. When they visit a marriage counsellor, he complains, 'You're not the woman I married – you've changed!!!' and she complains, 'And you haven't changed! That's the problem!'

Change is also the hallmark of the twentieth century. My father was born into a village without electricity. He began writing with chalk on a slate, only graduating to a Waterman's fountain pen, and went on to work in the same company for 44 years. My children, techno-cybernauts by comparison, exchange information about mood-altering substances on the Global Internet and will never work for one company for 44 years. Within a single lifetime we've left the Middle Ages and reached sci-fi meltdown.

So the environmental message is clear: you either manage change or it will manage you. You need to be proactive: change is done to you unless you do it to yourself. As the hippy therapists used to say: 'If you always do what you've always done you'll always get what you've always got.' They didn't mean you could sit back and expect the Good Lord to provide. They meant you'd get stuck and left behind in this land of total challenge unless you constantly equipped yourself with new skills and adapted to shifting circumstances.

Why is it so hard to change? It isn't, it just feels that way to some people. You can easily tell change-haters from change-lovers. The former say, 'Isn't this great, we don't have to make any new decisions and can avoid any unpleasant surprises!' The latter say, 'For God's sake, let's do something new today, there's nothing to look forward to!'

Change-haters like to eat the same food, go to the same shops (by the same routes), take the same holidays, cling to the same jobs and sport the same hairstyles for years on end. Their relationships tend to be littered with rejections as partners move on. Change-lovers, by contrast, are restless for new sights

and sounds and attract more companions than they know what
to do with. They willingly swallow raw sea urchin Japanese-
style and go back-packing in Nepal. Their motto runs: 'This is
life, not a rehearsal for it.'

Yes, but why are people born one way or the other? They
aren't: it depends on what happens to them in childhood. Kids
are nearly always conservative and hate change. This is
reasonable since they're trying to learn everything for the very
first time. Good parents introduce change by tiny degrees, so
the child can adjust and gain in self-confidence. If small
children are deluged with unwanted upheaval (divorce, deaths,
abuse, rejection, instability) they resist. Instead of learning to
trust themselves ('I'm okay whatever happens around me') they
try to control the world so it won't hurt them again ('Everything's got to be in its proper place'). As grown-ups, they
become over-rigid, even superstitious, and rarely develop risk-
taking skills.

But don't adults need stability and continuity just like
children? No, grown-ups need challenge and flexibility or they
cease to be able to take effective decisions. The great
psychologist Erik Erikson said, 'If you can't create and innovate
you will stagnate.' On the other hand, there's no point in variety
for its own sake.

Take the case of Muriel, who was invited on to an assertion
training course. She was introduced to the YES/NO exercise.
The facilitator said: 'Your homework is to say "Yes!" to three
things you normally say no to, or "No" to three things you
normally say yes to. Please report back next week.' Fired with
enthusiasm, Muriel quit her rented flat, dumped her boyfriend
and resigned from her job as warehouse supervisor. Did it make
her happy? No, it made her homeless, lonely and unemployed.
The moral is: unplanned change solves nothing.

So how can you survive a huge life change *safely*? It's been
compared to a journey in four stages. The difficulty is that any
gain involves a loss, so we always react to change by feeling
shocked. The natural mood is *denial*. People say 'She mustn't
be dead!' after some fatal accident. Or it can be as light-hearted

247

as 'I'll never climb that!' when ordered up a rope in the school gym. You make a mental attempt to seek refuge rather than take a sudden change on board and this is perfectly normal.

Next comes *resistance*. You justify your denial. For instance, a father will continue searching for his missing daughter long after the authorities want him to give it up. Or you beg your parents for a note to let you off games because you might possibly sprain your ankle. You gradually realise that the problem cannot be avoided and subtly protest about the adjustments it'll be necessary for you to make. This weighing up of costs includes the depressed and bitter phase of mourning. But equally, even happy changes bring some sort of stress as we look into the small print behind our leap into the 'unknown'.

The third phase of surviving change is *exploration*. You 'reframe' the problem. You now begin to see and accept that somebody's death could make some sort of sense. Or visualise yourself producing a major athletic feat successfully. At a certain point in any transition, people stop feeling bad about what they are losing and work out in detail how life is going to carry on.

The fourth phase of the change journey is conscious *commitment* – the moment you think, 'I *will* do it!' Now you can grasp all the joys and excitements of your new opportunities. Unwelcome changes can at last be endured openly. You are able to celebrate the life of a person you've lost without bursting into tears, or shin up most of the rest of that rope without embarrassment or panic – or negotiate a refusal. You've come from protest to grumbling, from grumbling to considering your options and from there to a new and deeper level of self-determination.

Yes, you say, I see all that but I still worry about changing my life! Then here's a 10-point check-list to get you through.

1. Try to accept your feelings at each stage of the process. Your task is not to be a robot but react to the blows of fortune if they fall. Don't do a Muriel and attempt to finish

all four stages overnight. Tell yourself it's reasonable to be *un*reasonable in stages one and two. If you want to get your head under the duvet in *denial* – fine. You're the expert on your needs. If you catch your boyfriend snogging another don't start by weighing things up to see if he's justified, ventilate your fury. If your boss decides you're surplus to requirements, tell everyone you think the decision is *insane.* Remember, you need to buy emotional time when faced with unacceptable change. You can always come up with a different explanation afterwards.

2. Question your inner fears. Most procrastinators have one trait in common: they operate on a mindset from child-hood. For instance, they hesitate to end unsatisfactory rela-tionships because 'I never get what I want.' What they really mean is, 'I never got what I wanted *when I was a child*.' Time has moved on but they ignore the adult powers they now possess. 'Mummy' and 'Daddy' are no longer around to squash their wishes but a sort of 'inner parent' still does the same job. You need to engage this 'voice' in discussion. Demand to see on what evidence you are judged to be an unworthy human being – you'll find there isn't any!

3. Always rehearse your major decisions. Think through the consequences. If you want to move house, go and walk round the new area first. Try out the shops, buses, cafes, libraries, cinemas and sample the local services before get-ting committed. If you want to end a relationship, visualise and write down all the likely repercussions under 'gains' and 'losses' and be honest when you do. Write an outline script and read it on to cassette to see if it will do the job you expect.

4. If you *are* quite stuck, it's probably better to make small, unrelated life-changes that don't really count to build up your confidence. I've said shy people need to make idle

chat with shop-keepers and doormen before chatting up new partners. Stuck people need to change their hairstyle, wallpaper, spectacles or other minor accessories rather than plunge into changes of house, lover or job. Better to start by painting the kitchen red than by painting the town.

5. If you're going into therapy, remember that analysis is only half the story. Lots of people can explain to you why your life may be troubled. The important point, as Marx once said, is to change it. Discuss at the outset with any counsellor or psychotherapist the goals you want to reach. Ask them how they measure 'progress'. There's no point in letting someone take you to pieces if they don't have the first clue about how to put you back together again, or how to sustain you in the meantime. If you don't like the therapist, find another one.

6. Don't try to change others – you can't, or at least not directly. As Freud's pupil Alfred Adler said: 'The only person you can change is yourself; the only thing you can change is how you respond to what others do.' This is an invaluable message when dealing with difficult lovers or family. You can't make them praise you or take an interest in your life. You can only calculate your reaction if they don't. It's possible to give notice – 'Ignore me again and I'll walk out', but that's as far as it goes. On the other hand if you don't 'always do what you've always done' there's a good chance others *will* change their behaviour in return.

7. Don't dawdle over changes. For instance, confront unreliable friends *before* their behaviour amounts to abuse. Try to work out where you stand on the slippery slope of their rejection. After too much lapse of time or too many insults, you may lack the confidence or energy to resist a bully so keep a high opinion of yourself by responding early. Remember that every major life-change entails some crisis of self-esteem so you need to protect your interests.

8. Don't use change itself as a means of blurring or evading your problems. If you're stressed up to the eyeballs a change is not as good as a rest. It may simply involve additional work. You need proper breaks. Those who try to run away from their troubles are never better off – the troubles follow too.

9. Remind yourself that nobody enjoys an overdose of change – not even the change-lover. If everything is up in the air and we can't begin to take life one day at a time we simply end up dazed and confused, staring into headlights like bewildered rabbits.

10. Finally, try to look at events through different people's spectacles and from multiple viewpoints. Imagine how the people on Mars might regard your problems, or what God (or perhaps Zeus) would have to say. Then focus energy where you can make a difference. Act on issues you can control. Transition is bliss when you sit in the driving seat and don't have to stop for unnecessary passengers.

Chapter Twelve

Taking Care of Yourself

SAFER SEX

SAFER SEX

Just two or three decades ago, sex without protection could have resulted in pregnancy or what doctors called a 'trivial, treatable VD'. Nowadays, because of HIV and AIDS, unprotected sex can kill you. The treatment won't cure. Using a condom has become an obligatory part of modern sexual etiquette.

There are three ways to guard against the sexual transmission of HIV. Firstly, abstain from sex; or secondly, ensure that you and your partner are not infected, and only ever sleep with each other again, or thirdly, practise safer sex. Viewed in this way, the third option is the most – and probably the only – practical solution. After all, lifelong abstinence is simply not viable; a lifetime of mutual monogamy is hard to achieve and, as cynical as it may sound, it can be difficult always to be 100% confident about your partner's sexual activities.

What's risky and what's not

Human immunodeficiency virus, or HIV, is carried in semen, blood (including menstrual blood) and vaginal fluids. The virus enters the body through cuts or sores in the skin. Unprotected penetrative sex, either anal or vaginal, with an infected partner, allows the mingling of these body fluids and is the highest risk activity in terms of HIV transmission.

The 1996 *Aids Reference Manual* describes penetrative sex using a male or a female condom as a 'much less risky activity'. In other words, assuming that the condom doesn't tear or split and is used properly the risk of HIV transmission is minimal compared to the risk of having unprotected sex. Using a condom properly means rolling the condom down the entire length of the penis to lessen the chance of it coming off during sex, putting it on before any sexual contact takes place (not just before ejaculation), and holding the condom in place when your partner withdraws.

Withdrawal should take place as soon as possible after your partner ejaculates so that there is no chance of the penis becoming flaccid and semen leaking out. It is also important to check that the brand of condoms you are using has been checked for quality and safety. Look out for the kitemark on the box. It should read: 'CERTIFIED TO BRITISH STANDARD BS 3704'. Check the expiry date too.

The fact that oil-based lubricants such as petroleum jelly can damage the rubber of the condom is pretty well publicised, but other everyday substances such as suntan oil, massage oil and bath oil (and even lipstick cream and ice cream) can also weaken condoms. One study in 1988 showed that baby oil destroyed up to 95% of a condom's strength after just 15 minutes. If you are using a lubricant with a condom, choose a water-based one such as KY Jelly.

Oral sex is also much less risky than unprotected sex, especially if you are receiving rather than giving oral sex; yet it is still possible for transmission of HIV to happen this way. It is advisable to avoid oral sex if you have cuts, infections or ulcers in your mouth or throat or if your partner has abrasions or sores on his penis.

Forms of sex that are safe include self-masturbation, using sex toys on yourself, and massaging and stroking your partner's body. Kissing is fairly safe and masturbating your partner is fine so long as semen doesn't come into contact with any skin cuts or abrasions, or even a rash such as eczema.

Who's at risk?

It can be misleading to think that some people are more at risk of HIV than others since everyone has an equal chance of becoming infected if they are exposed to the virus. This aside, the following groups of people are more at risk because of their behaviour or the circumstances in which they find themselves:

● homosexual or bisexual men who have unprotected anal sex with a large number of partners;
● anyone who received blood transfusions or blood products before 1985 when blood started being screened for HIV;
● people who have received blood or blood products in countries where screening is not routine;
● intravenous drug users who share needles or syringes;
● people who have had unprotected sex with a large number of partners (especially prostitutes) in high risk countries such as Thailand.

When you sleep with a new partner, assessing him (or her) for 'risk' not only feels very calculating, it can also verge on the impossible. If a man has slept with three partners in the last ten years is he safer than a man who has slept with 30? Supposing one of the partners of the first man had a bisexual lover or she was very promiscuous? Supposing she had a boyfriend who had a lover who injected drugs or who received a 'dirty' injection while travelling in Africa? The logistics can become mind-boggling. The answer is a simple cliché: it's better to be safe than sorry.

Safer sex in practice
If condoms are so readily available, easy to use and give us peace of mind after the event, why does it sometimes seem so difficult to reach for one at the crucial moment? The answer is because we are excellent at thinking of excuses. Take the following examples:

● 'They're a passion killer'
This is up to you. If, when you are about to make love, you have to get up, get dressed and walk to the nearest branch of

255

Boots, then condoms will kill your lust. If, on the other hand, you whip one out from beneath your pillow and apply it to your partner's penis while sitting astride him, it's unlikely to cause more than a small blip in your passion. The trick is to use condoms erotically – massage his penis as you unroll the condom or interrupt oral sex to put one on.

Or if you want to be as enthusiastic as Emma, 23, you can surprise your lover by putting a condom on him using your mouth. 'You just hold the teat of the condom in your mouth between your lips, you put the rim on the head of his penis and then you just use your lips to push the rim down the shaft.'

● 'My boyfriend hates them'
Some men dislike condoms because they claim they diminish sensation during sex. The truth is, today's condoms are made of such thin rubber they shouldn't cause *anybody* a major loss of sensation. Often the anticipation of wearing a condom is worse than the actual physical experience. Again the answer is to be seductive rather than clinical – treat condoms like a sex toy, not a washing-up glove. Also, if wearing a condom makes him take longer to ejaculate, point out the fringe benefits.

● 'I'm allergic to them'
This is not an excuse, it's a valid objection. But many people who think they are allergic to condoms are actually allergic to the spermicide used on condoms. This can be remedied: experiment with different brands until you find one that uses a spermicide that suits you. Or if you *are* allergic to latex, try using a female condom made of polyurethane.

● 'Sex can never be completely safe'
It's true that penetrative sex can never be 100% safe. Hence 'safer' sex, not 'safe' sex. Condoms can have holes in them, they can split or they can come off during sex. But if your partner wears one you will both be drastically cutting down the risk of catching an STD (sexually transmitted disease),

including HIV. Look at it this way – if you are choosing to enter a potentially dangerous situation you want to take as many precautions to safeguard yourself as possible.

CONTRACEPTION

Women now have greater control over their fertility than ever before. The range of contraceptives currently marketed means that women can choose birth control methods that are suited to their particular needs. Some methods of contraception are one-off methods – you use them and throw them away – others exist which offer years of almost 100% contraceptive cover.

You can review your choice of contraception as your life situation changes. What suited you three years ago when you were in a casual relationship may not suit you when you enter a serious relationship and start to think about your long-term fertility. These are the alternatives:

The combined pill
The pill has come a long way since the 1960s when doses of hormone were very high and side effects were common. Today's pills contain very low doses of hormone, they regulate the menstrual cycle so that heavy bleeding and cramps are rare and, used properly, less than 1% of users in a year will become pregnant.

How does it work?
All commonly prescribed pills, with the exception of the progestogen only pill or 'POP', contain a combination (hence 'combined' pill) of the two female hormones, oestrogen and progesterone. The pill prevents conception in three ways: it stops ovulation, it changes the mucus around the cervix so that it is more hostile to sperm, and it alters the lining of the uterus so that if conception were to take place, the fertilised egg would have difficulty implanting.

How do you use it?

Pills come in 21-day packs. You take one pill a day for 21 days and then stop (or you take a placebo pill) for seven days. During the pill-free days your uterus responds to the lowered levels of hormones by shedding its lining. This bleeding should be lighter than a normal period.

Pill users need to be aware of the things that interfere with its efficacy. If you vomit or have diarrhoea during the 21 days when you are taking the pill, you will not have full contraceptive cover and you will need to use a condom in addition to taking the pill (see the pack for more details). The same applies if you are taking antibiotics.

What are the pros and cons?

The pill is one of the most effective and convenient contraceptives available. It offers sexual freedom, and if you decide that you want to try to conceive or switch to a different type of contraceptive, you can stop taking it straight away. The drawbacks of the pill are that it offers no protection from cervical cancer or STDs, including HIV (this is the case with all hormonal contraceptives) and it may cause side effects such as weight changes and mood swings, especially in the first three months of use. It's also vital that you remember to take it every day – if you've got a terrible memory, it probably isn't for you.

Sally, 23, legal clerk

'I found it took my body a long time to settle down to the pill. The first brand I tried was one of the popular combined pills and it was a disaster. I had low level bleeding almost continuously for four months before I stopped taking it out of frustration. Then my doctor tried me on a triphasic pill. I still had slight bleeding before the seven pill-free days, but it wasn't nearly as bad. Now my body has adjusted totally to the pill and I think it's an excellent contraceptive.'

Progestogen-only pill (POP)

The POP or mini-pill is similar to the combined pill, but it does not contain the hormone oestrogen. It prevents pregnancy by changing the cervical mucus and making implantation of a fertilised egg difficult (it suppresses ovulation in some women, but not all). The POP is suitable for women who cannot take oestrogen for medical reasons.

Most women are offered the combined pill rather than the POP since the former is better at preventing pregnancy. It is also more important that the POP is taken at the same time every day for it to be effective.

Implants

The most common type of implant is called Norplant and it was launched in the UK in October 1993. Implants offer long-term contraceptive cover and they are as effective, if not more so, than the combined pill.

How does it work?

Implants are inserted by a doctor under the skin on the inside of the upper arm where they release a low dose of progestogen to the body. The slow delivery of hormone prevents conception by suppressing ovulation, changing the cervical mucus so that it is hostile to sperm and making it difficult for a fertilised egg to become implanted in the uterus.

How do you use it?

The main advantage of implants is that once they have been inserted they can be forgotten about. The insertion procedure, which takes place in your doctor's surgery, lasts about 20 minutes. The implants come in the form of six soft silicone rods – once they are in place they can remain there for up to five years.

What are the pros and cons?

The main advantage of implants is they are such an effective, reversible method of contraception – for the first few years they offer virtually 100% protection. However, they are not quite the wonder-contraceptive they first appear to be. The main drawback with implants is that they can cause side effects, which in some women can be quite severe. About 60% of women experience irregular bleeding in the first year after insertion. Others experience mood swings, weight gain, nausea and acne. Unlike the pill, which you can simply stop taking, implants need to be removed by a doctor.

Injections
Injections are another highly effective method of hormonal contraception, offering almost 100% cover, but doctors tend to recommend them for short-term use only (some women have injections while they are waiting for their partners' vasectomies to take effect). The names of the two most common injectable hormones are Depo-Provera and Noristerat.

How does it work?
Injections prevent conception in the same way as implants.

How do you use it?
A doctor carries out the injections every eight or every 12 weeks.

What are the pros and cons?
The main advantage is the reliability of injections. Disadvantages include the fact that fertility may take some time to return and women may experience side effects similar to those associated with implants.

The Diaphragm or cap
Diaphragms and caps are devices made of rubber that are inserted high up into the vagina before sex. Diaphragms are dome-shaped with a metal rim and fit round the entire cervix. Caps are smaller and cover the entrance to the cervix.

How does it work?
Diaphragms and caps are barrier methods of contraception that prevent pregnancy by making sure that sperm never enters the uterus and fallopian tubes. They are used with spermicide, which provides extra protection by immobilising sperm.

How do you use it?
A doctor or nurse will show you how to insert a cap or diaphragm the first time you use it. You then insert the device – with spermicide – anything up to three hours before you know you are going to have sex. The diaphragm or cap should be left inside the vagina for at least six hours after sex.

What are the pros and cons?
Caps and diaphragms do not interfere with the body's natural hormone balance (which some women consider an advantage). You will also be protected against several sexually transmitted diseases including gonorrhoea, chlamydia, and the wart or human papilloma virus, which is thought to be linked to cervical cancer. The disadvantages are that caps and diaphragms are tricky to insert if you are not used to them and they have a much higher failure rate than hormonal contraceptives. Also, you need to be able to anticipate whether you will have sex if you are going to be away from home.

Male and female condoms
Condoms are the most popular barrier contraceptives. The male condom fits snugly over the erect penis, while the female condom lines the inside of the vagina.

How does it work?
Both the male and female condom prevent semen from coming into contact with the woman's body. This means that sperm never have a chance to travel to the fallopian tubes – the place where conception takes place.

261

How do you use it?

Once mastered, applying a condom to the penis or inserting a female condom into the vagina is pretty straightforward. Male condoms should only be put on while the penis is erect – use the finger and thumb of one hand to pinch the end of the condom and use the other hand to roll the condom down the length of the penis. Hold the condom in place during withdrawal and then wrap the condom in tissue and dispose of it in a bin (see also Safer Sex).

The female condom should be inserted into the vagina before you have any sexual contact with your partner. Insert the ring at the closed end of the condom high into the vagina so that the ring sits just behind your pubic bone. The ring at the open end of the condom should lie flat against the vulva. Withdraw the condom after your partner has ejaculated and dispose of it in the same way as a male condom.

What are the pros and cons?

Condoms are the most easily available contraceptive. You don't need to have them fitted or prescribed by a doctor, you can walk into any supermarket or chemist and buy them, and instructions on their use are inside every packet. As well as offering effective protection from pregnancy they can also prevent sexually transmitted diseases, including HIV. They have no effect on hormone levels, don't impair fertility and are free from side effects. The disadvantages of condoms are that they can occasionally tear or slip off during sex; they necessitate some amount of planning ahead for sex; and some couples complain that condoms interrupt lovemaking.

The sponge

The sponge is another barrier method of contraception. Like male and female condoms they are used once and then thrown away after sex.

How does it work?
The sponge is made of polyurethane foam which has a built-in spermicide to immobilise sperm. It also blocks the entrance to the cervix so that sperm cannot pass through to the uterus.

How do you use it?
You put water on to the sponge to activate the spermicide and you then insert it high up into the vagina. There is a loop attached to the sponge to help you remove it after sex.

What are the pros and cons?
The sponge is not really a contraceptive in its own right. It has a pretty high failure rate compared to other methods and it is best recommended for times when fertility is low. The advantages of the sponge are that it is widely available in chemists and it's comfortable to use.

The IUD
IUD is short for intra-uterine device. IUDs are small T-shaped devices made of plastic with a thin coating of copper. They are very effective at preventing conception (although they offer slightly less protection than hormonal methods) and, once they have been inserted into the uterus, they can stay there for several years.

How does it work?
An IUD prevents pregnancy in two ways: by preventing the sperm meeting the egg and by changing the lining of the uterus so that, if conception were to take place, the fertilised egg would not be able to implant in the uterus.

How do you use it?
An IUD is inserted into the uterus by a doctor. The fitting may be uncomfortable and cause pains like menstrual cramps for a few hours afterwards. After insertion an IUD can be forgotten about.

263

What are the pros and cons?

An IUD starts to work as soon as it is fitted and it offers long-term contraceptive protection. One of the main disadvantages of the IUD is the slightly increased risk of getting pelvic inflammatory disease. This is a condition that is associated with infertility, so most IUD users tend to be older women who have already completed their families. IUDs can sometimes cause periods to become heavy and painful and between three and 15 women in every 100 will spontaneously expel their IUD – usually during their first or second menstrual period following insertion.

The IUS

The IUS, or intra-uterine system, is the latest type of IUD. It is inserted into the uterus in the same way as a traditional IUD, but once it is in place it slowly releases progestogen into the body. This makes it as effective as the hormonal methods of contraception.

Natural methods

What with pill scares in recent years and worries about the possible short- and long-term side effects associated with other methods of contraception, some women opt for a natural approach to birth control. This means having intimate knowledge of your menstrual cycle and a partner who is both patient and sympathetic.

How does it work?

The principle is simple: identify the days in your menstrual cycle when you are likely to be fertile and then abstain from sex or use a barrier method of contraception.

How do you use it?

The key to natural birth control is pinpointing ovulation. There are several ways to do this. First of all you should keep a detailed diary of your menstrual cycle; ovulation usually happens 12 to 16 days before your period. For example, if your cycle is a regular 28 days, you will probably ovulate on the 14th day. Secondly, you can monitor your cervical mucus. Fertile mucus is wet, slippery, clear and stretchy, whereas non-fertile mucus is slight, sticky and cloudy. Thirdly, there are changes in the cervix around the time of ovulation – it becomes softer and it opens slightly. If you decide to try natural methods it's advisable to seek expert help.

What are the pros and cons?
The advantages of natural birth control are lack of cost, universal availability and absence of side effects. Women say that they enjoy learning about their bodies and taking control of their fertility. The main problem is that natural methods can be unreliable, especially if you have an irregular menstrual cycle, if you are not very experienced at detecting changes in your body or even if you don't have very good will power.

The good news is that drug companies are working on technology to make ovulation detection much easier. Unipath manufacture a personal contraceptive system that measures hormone levels in urine. An electronic monitoring system informs you of the days on which you would be most likely to conceive.

Sterilisation
Sterilisation is the most drastic method of contraception there is. Although in some cases operations may be reversible, this is rare, and sterilisation really should be thought of as permanent. Most women who choose this option are in the 40-plus age group and have completed their families. The operation itself is quite straightforward: using microsurgery, which leaves minimal scarring, a surgeon will cauterise or use clips or rings to block your fallopian tubes.

Occasionally, fallopian tubes have been known to heal themselves and sterilised women have become pregnant, but again this is rare. Women who request sterilisation will receive counselling before they have an operation.

Emergencies

What happens when contraceptives fail? Or when you don't use a contraceptive when you should have done? Fortunately, there are two alternatives to a couple of weeks of anxiety and dread. Firstly, you can take the morning-after pill. Secondly, you can have an IUD fitted.

The morning-after pill should really be called the '72-hours after pill' since you have three days in which to act after having 'unprotected' sex. A doctor will prescribe four pills; two to be taken on the first occasion and two to be taken 12 hours later. This will prevent the implantation of a fertilised egg if conception has taken place. An IUD can be fitted up to five days after a contraceptive failure. Again, it works by preventing the implantation of a fertilised egg.

New directions

The perfect contraceptive is one which is 100% safe, 100% effective, has no side effects, doesn't interfere with lovemaking, is easy to use, is widely available and sings to you. This sounds like a tall order, but the research for new methods of contraception continues, and the old methods are constantly being refined. Here are just some of the things that may be available soon:

● Vaginal rings – a flexible plastic ring that you insert into the vagina for 21 days out of 28. Once in position the ring releases a low dose of progestogen.
● The polyurethane condom – already available in the US, the 'plastic' condom is thinner than traditional condoms and has the added bonus that it can be used with oil-based lubricants.
● The melatonin pill – a pill that contains the hormone melatonin instead of oestrogen and progestogen. Melatonin is thought to be a natural contraceptive which works by inhibiting ovulation (provided health risks are ruled out).
● Contraceptive patches – these would release a low dose of hormone through the skin in the same way as hormone replacement patches.

● Contraceptive vaccines – scientists are very excited about these. In the twenty-first century it looks as though vaccines will be available to make you immune to your partner's sperm. Alternatively, vaccines for men will make the male body produce antibodies to sperm. Vaccines may also be able to disrupt the implantation of a fertilised egg in the uterus or prevent a sperm cell from penetrating the outer layer of an egg.

● Microspheres and microcapsules – one of the problems with current contraceptive implants such as Norplant is that the silicon rods stay under your skin until they are surgically removed. Microspheres and microcapsules, on the other hand, are made of biodegradable materials that can be placed under the skin by injection or implantation. They release a slow dose of hormone and then dissolve away naturally after a period of one to 18 months, depending on the type being used.

● The male pill – the male pill has been promised by doctors for a very long time. Now it looks as though the final product may be a combination of a pill and an injection. The injection will deliver testosterone to stop sperm production and the pill will contain a synthetic version of the female hormone progesterone. A Brazilian drug company says it expects to be first in the market with a product made from gossipol, an extract of cotton which works by deactivating the enzyme responsible for sperm production, and this will not require an additional injection. However, 'the field is full of talk'.

● Nasal sprays – designed to be sprayed into the nostrils several times a day. They would work by preventing ovulation.

● The abortion pill – this is currently available in the UK as a non-surgical way of ending a pregnancy. Doctors are now looking into the possibility of using it as a once-a-month contraceptive.

SEXUAL BODY MAINTENANCE

Looking after yourself sexually doesn't mean conforming to out-of-date ides about female attractiveness. You don't have to be tall and thin or blonde and busty. A sexy body is about taking care of yourself. This means taking the right sort of exercise for you – whether it is aqua-aerobics, yoga, a run round the park or a pre-work swim – taking care of your skin and hair, eating healthy foods and feeling relaxed about your body and your sexuality.

Sexual body maintenance also means understanding your body so that if something goes wrong, you can respond practically. Knowing the way your body works sexually and learning about the complex rise and fall of hormones that dictate not just the menstrual cycle, but levels of sexual desire, can give you a great sense of control.

The breasts

The breasts inspire the same sort of anxiety in women that the penis does in men. Are they too small? Do they point in the right direction – or directions? Are they a source of admiration or a source of ridicule? What sort of underwear shows them off to their best advantage?

The breasts are a sexual display and women spend thousands of pounds on enhancing their shape and size. They can be enlarged or reduced with surgery; they can be firmed with lotions, tonics and sprays; and they can be accentuated or hidden with expensive or uncomfortable bras. The truth is that breasts naturally lose their elasticity with age, and after having children, gravity can take its toll. If you don't want to resort to surgery or expensive potions that may not work, the following are tried and tested methods of breast maintenance:

● Have your breasts measured by a professional bra-fitter. Seven out of 10 women wear the wrong size bra, meaning that their breasts are crushed or don't receive adequate support.
● Eat a balanced, nutritious diet. Crash dieting can cause drooping and stretch marks.
● Basic hydrotherapy treatment can tone breast tissue, even if the effects are only temporary. Shower the breasts daily with cold water (the colder the better). This stimulates blood flow

to the breasts and makes the skin tighten. This principle has been used in the design of a breast treatment called Aquamaid – a bra with cups containing gel that is put in the freezer and then worn for five to 10 minutes a day.

● Go swimming. Swimming is the best all-round exercise for breasts, partly because no gravity is involved, but also because the arm movements tone the muscles that lie beneath the breasts.

NB: Size only matters if your lover has a breast fetish. Any woman who is 'over-endowed' will naturally capture attention, some of it unwanted. Inside a relationship, however, such attention tends to fade. Even long-term partners of actress Pamela Anderson don't spend all day saying: 'Oh, I'm so-oh glad you've got big breasts!' Probably as many men prefer partners with less obtrusive bosoms. For the record, when rubbed against a hairy chest, large naked breasts are extremely uncomfortable for any man on top or beneath!

Many women suffer from cyclical mastalgia, which is breast pain before a period. This pain can make the breasts exquisitely sensitive to touch – even turning over in bed at night can be agonising. Although there are few medical treatments for breast pain, complementary medicine can often help. A therapy called applied kinesiology which involves massage may alleviate symptoms. Evening primrose oil is also an established remedy.

The sex organs

A general practitioner once commented that she treated more cases of vaginal infections such as thrush in the period after Christmas than at any other time of the year. She claimed that the reason for this was that women used lots of highly perfumed soaps and bath potions that they were given as Christmas presents. Cosmetic products such as perfumed tissues and sanitary towels, genital sprays, and scented soaps and bath products are not just unnecessary, they can also destroy the delicate pH balance of the vagina and make you vulnerable to infection.

The moral of the story is that when it comes to genital hygiene, less is more. The female reproductive tract has an amazing ability to look after itself and washing with plenty of water and a small amount of plain unfragranced soap is all the day-to-day care that you need. In the long term, however, there are several things you can do if you want to keep your sex organs in good shape:

● *The sex workout*

You can tone up the muscles around the vagina by practising Kegel exercises or pelvic floor exercises (see 'Great Kegel Sex', Chapter Six). These are the muscles that you can contract to 'hug' your partner's penis during sex. Well-toned pubococcygeal muscles don't just improve your sex life, they also improve the 'fitness' of the organs surrounding the vagina, making future problems such as prolapse and stress incontinence less likely.

To practise Kegel exercises, imagine that you are trying to stop urinating in mid-flow. Tense the muscles as hard as you can and count to ten. Now slowly relax the muscles in stages (imagine a lift descending in a five-storey building). Contract the muscles again, this time in stages, and repeat the count to ten. Do this sequence several times. As your muscle control improves, try counting to 20 instead of ten and take more time to relax your muscles.

A British urologist, John Firth, has designed a weight device that can be used to help women practise Kegel exercises. A hollow plastic cone containing variable metal weights is inserted into the vagina and the pubococcygeal muscles can be contracted around the cone. The device, which has a cord attached for removal, looks similar to a tampon.

● *Know your body*

Unerotic though it is, sex can sometimes give rise to unpleasant symptoms, particularly if you have sex very frequently or you have sex before your vagina is sufficiently lubricated. Symptoms can range from simply feeling sore to suffering a full-blown attack of cystitis. Some women have more resilient urogenital tracts than others. Sam, 29, is one of the unlucky ones:

'From the age of 17 to the age of 21 I was stuck in a horrible cycle of sex-related symptoms. After a period of having lots of sex I would get a horrible stinging sensation when I went to the toilet. After a couple of days it would get worse and I would go to my doctor, who gave me antibiotics. Then by the end of the antibiotics course I would be suffering from thrush. Even when I finally thought that I had recovered, I hadn't, because, somehow, my partner reinfected me with thrush. Over the years, I've learnt various strategies to avoid these sorts of symptoms.'

If you know that you are vulnerable to sex-related symptoms, take precautions: make sure that you are sufficiently lubricated before you make love; empty your bladder after sex; practise good sexual hygiene (for example, never have anal sex followed straight away by vaginal sex); and if you are a cystitis sufferer, wash with warm water after sex and avoid sexual positions that you know will irritate your urethra.

● *Smear tests*

Cervical cancer is one of the few diseases that can be detected before you actually have it. There is a time period known as the precancerous stage during which cervical cells undergo abnormal changes – the smear test is designed to detect these changes.

The procedure involved in a smear test is straightforward. A device called a speculum is inserted and opened inside your vagina, and using a tiny brush or a spatula, the doctor takes a sample of cells from your cervical opening. (The speculum cannot be lubricated because lubricating gel can contaminate the smear, but it can be warmed with warm water.) The sample of cells is put on to a glass slide and sent off to a laboratory to be examined microscopically.

If you have an abnormal smear test, this does not mean you have cancer and it doesn't mean that you necessarily have precancerous changes. It simply means that you will be asked back for a repeat smear test in a few months' time. If abnormalities persist or are severe, your doctor will send you for further investigations.

Women should have a smear test every two or three years. If you have had genital warts in the past, you should have a smear test annually. This is because some types of wart virus put women in a higher risk group for cervical cancer.

SEXUAL HEALTH

If you've ever looked at the sex section in a medical textbook the range of infections can seem overwhelming. There are names like trichomoniasis, bacterial vaginosis, vaginitis, candidiasis, monoliasis . . . and that's just to name a few. Most genito-urinary infections can be divided into three types: fungal infections, such as thrush; bacterial infections, such as cystitis; and viral infections, such as herpes. The first two types can usually be treated with anti-fungal medications or antibiotics. Treating viruses is slightly more difficult, but there are anti-viral drugs on the market that can help.

If you have any unusual or worrying symptoms, you will need to seek medical help straight away. Many women feel nervous or uncomfortable about consulting a doctor about sex-related illnesses, but doctors are accustomed to treating these sorts of problems. If you don't want to go to your general practitioner, you can go to a clinic that specialises in genito-urinary (GU) medicine or sexual health.

The following symptoms may be signs that you have a sexually transmitted illness. Alternatively, some of them may be symptoms of a gynaecological problem that is not directly related to sex. Whichever, both should be checked by a doctor.

● Small, painless protrusions or raised areas anywhere on the genitals (possible cause: genital warts).
● Any unusual vaginal discharge, particularly one that is foul-smelling, frothy or discoloured (possible causes include: bacterial vaginosis, thrush, gonorrhoea, chlamydia, trichomoniasis and vaginitis).
● Pain or tenderness in the lower abdomen (possible causes include: pelvic inflammatory disease, cystitis and gonorrhoea).
● Pain on urinating (possible causes include: cystitis, genital herpes, thrush and trichomoniasis).
● Painful sores anywhere on the genital area (possible cause: herpes).
● Painful intercourse (possible causes include: many vaginal infections, cystitis and vestibulitis).

Silent infections
It is important to realise that many sexually transmitted infections can be symptomless and as a result your body doesn't give you any warning signs. This is why it is essential to have a check-up at a genito-urinary clinic if you have had sexual contact with a partner who has symptoms of an infection – even if *you* don't.

Some women who have had unprotected casual sex opt to have a check-up, simply to eliminate the possibility of infection. For example, a bacterial infection called chlamydia is the most common sexually transmitted disease in the western world, yet only one third of women who are infected notice that anything is wrong. Untreated chlamydia can have profound effects on the reproductive system, gradually creeping through the cervix, uterus and fallopian tubes to cause pelvic inflammatory diseases or PID. Untreated PID can go on to cause infertility.

Raising your sexual energy levels
Sex at its best is an erotically charged and exhilarating experience. At its worst it can be a chore or a duty – something that you fit in between falling into bed at the end of the day and

falling asleep. At the beginning of a relationship, exciting sex is easy, but when a relationship is well established it can become routine and slip down your list of priorities. Good sex is like a good relationship – you need to make time for it.

Discover your sexual energy cycle (see also 'Menstrual Rhythms', Chapter Five).
Our sexual energy levels are dictated by how well we are feeling. They are also dictated by hormones. Some women find that their sexual energy peaks in the middle of their menstrual cycles (usually around the 14th day), which is when they ovulate. In purely biological terms this makes good sense: the time when you are most fertile is also the time when you are most lustful. Other women find their desire is at its height just before they menstruate. Still others have the best sex when they are menstruating.

The trick is to discover your own unique sexual energy cycle. Keep a diary for two or three months, noting the times when your libido hits its high points. When do you have most sexual thoughts, dreams and fantasies? When do you initiate sex most? When are you most likely to masturbate? Is there a time when you find it easier to reach orgasm? Alternatively, are there times when you have absolutely no interest in sex?

If you can discern a pattern in your levels of desire, act upon it. If you feel at your sexiest around mid-cycle, make lots of time for sex then. Go away for the weekend with your lover. Make sex especially erotic. Exploit the highs that your body gives you.

Are you sex-stressed?
What do you think about when you make love? Some people would argue that if you are thinking *anything* you are not giving yourself up to the pure physical, sensual experience of sex. But given that it's almost impossible to switch off totally, it is worth considering whether your thoughts fall into the category of sexy or stressful.

Sexy thoughts can focus on your lover: how gorgeous he is;

274

how much he turns you on; how much you love the way he touches you; how connected and close you feel to him. Or they can focus on you: how sexy and aroused you feel; the delicious sensations you are experiencing; what you want to do next. Sexy thoughts can also be ones that drift off into the realm of fantasy. These sorts of thoughts can make the difference between OK sex and great sex. They can also boost your libido level.

Stressful thoughts are the psychological equivalent of a cold bucket of water. If you are worrying that you look unattractive or ridiculous; that you are taking too long to reach orgasm; that you don't feel aroused enough; or even if you are preoccupied with a problem at work, then you are denying yourself the possible intensity of sex.

One way to boost your sexual energy is to challenge stressful thoughts. Ask yourself why you have them in the first place. How valid are they? Can you get rid of them by sharing them with your partner? Can you cure yourself of stressful thoughts by changing the way you make love? Sometimes simple changes are enough: try making love at a different time of day; give your partner explicit instructions about what you want him to do; make foreplay twice as long so that you are really ready to have sex. Above all, when you make love, resolve to clear a worry-free space in your head beforehand.

Stay sexually active

Some people report that their levels of desire diminish when they have a lot of sex, but it's actually more likely that infrequent sex will deplete your sexual energy. In fact, couples who get out of the habit of having sex may find that when they do get around to making love, they simply don't feel as aroused as they used to. This may be especially true of women.

The simple answer to this is to stay sexually active. If you are single, sexual activity can include masturbation and sensual self-massage. Just because you choose not to be part of a couple, you do not have to be asexual. Allow yourself the luxury of sexual fantasies and erotic thoughts – treat masturbation with

275

the same indulgence that you would sex.

If you and your partner have not made love for a while, get back into the habit of sex slowly. Spend time touching each other. Cultivate your desire gradually and relearn what feels good. If you don't feel like having penetrative sex, don't. Instead, experiment by giving your partner a massage. Kiss and cuddle each other. Have a bath together. Ask him where and how he likes to be touched. Find his erogenous zones and get him to do the same for you. Reread Chapter Six on 'Great Sex' and choose your favourite bits . . .

So BACK TO LOVE

One of the most important properties of love is that it varies from society to society. Tell a Papuan Indian that you have 'fallen in love' and she won't have a clue what you mean. The movie star Shirley MacLaine once said: 'I lived for eight years in the Far East. God knows what Japanese men are thinking about during sex. I never found out. They certainly weren't thinking about "falling in love".' She'd probably say something similar if she went to the Near East, sampling Iran, Iraq or Saudi Arabia.

This leads to a simple but profound conclusion. Relationships based on romantic love can only flourish in countries where men and women enjoy equality.

This book was written in part to celebrate your ability to choose both love and lover. *Cosmopolitan* hardly circulates in those countries where men are naturally deemed more important than women and their sexual needs are catered for by a mix of chauvinism and polygamy. The moral is equally simple. Love is not a right we can take for granted but a hard-won privilege. It isn't understood by visitors from countries ruled by Ayatollahs. All societies have sex. Only some link it to love. Many reduce it to 'duty'. The way we associate love and sex demands some care and consideration.

I hinted in Chapter One that falling in love doesn't necessarily mean you should have sex. Conversely, having sex need not imply that you have somehow miraculously fallen in love. I will add this. Sex is only good (and sometimes great) if you care about the person on the other end.

The actor John Travolta seems to have got it right. He says he only goes to bed with 'friends'. By this he means that you need to establish some level of emotional connection with another human being before you can really expect to enjoy them physically. True Love isn't necessary for Great Sex. But having an amicable feeling about your partner *is*.

Chapter Thirteen

Cosmo Quizzes

1. HOW IMPORTANT ARE RELATIONSHIPS IN YOUR LIFE?

Pick one answer to each question and add up your scores at the end:

1. Where do you see yourself in ten years?
    a) dropping off the kids at school after kissing your husband goodbye;
    b) missing a date because you stayed after hours to put the finishing touches to a vital project at work;
    c) getting the boat to Thailand for the next leg of your round-the-world odyssey?

2. After an intense but troubled relationship your partner leaves you. Do you feel:
    a) that you would do practically anything to get him back;
    b) relieved but lonely;
    c) exhilarated that you are young, free and single?

3. How do you feel when you're not in a relationship?
    a) contented;
    b) desperate to get a man;
    c) usually you're not bothered, but occasionally you get a twinge of loneliness?

4. You see a pair of young lovers canoodling in the park. You are single. Do you:
    a) not really notice them;
    b) feel a pang of envy;

c) wonder if you'll ever be that happy?

5. Yet another one of your friends is getting hitched to the bridal cart. Are you:
a) happy for her;
b) mystified as to why she would want to tie herself down;
c) desperately jealous?

6. When you're out with a female friend are you:
a) keeping an eye out for the talent;
b) deliberately sharking for Mr Right;
c) going out solely to talk to your mate?

7. Your partner says he really needs to have a serious talk with you that evening, but the boss says that you have to stay late and help her with a make-or-break presentation. Do you:
a) tell the boss you've got more important things to sort out;
b) arrive home late and say you're too tired to talk;
c) tell you partner that you're really sorry, and promise that you'll make time tomorrow?

8. Your lover threatens to leave unless you agree not to spend Sundays with your folks. Do you:
a) make up some excuse to explain to your parents why you can't make it any more;
b) tell him he's a jerk and dump him;
c) tell him that you can't do that, but you'll try and make more time for him in the rest of the week?

9. Your partner gets a job in another city. Do you:
a) stay put but try and spend every weekend with him;
b) regretfully go your separate ways;
c) move there with him?

10. You discover that your partner is having an affair. Do you:
a) kick him out;

b) give him an ultimatum – it's her or you;
c) decide that a piece of him is better than nothing?

11. Your partner wants to get married, but insists that you give up your job. Would you:
a) make it clear that your career is more important to you than marriage;
b) agree and pack in your job;
c) tell him you'll think about it and then talk him round?

12. Your friends want you to come away for a big weekend in a country house, but your partner doesn't want to go. Do you:
a) have a crisis of indecision and conflicting loyalties;
b) tell him you'll think of him when you're in the ballroom;
c) tell your friends you've already got something planned?

13. Have your past relationships ended bcause:
a) he wouldn't commit;
b) you wouldn't commit;
c) some other reason?

14. If your relationship was in trouble would you:
a) be prepared to spend a significant amount of time and money going to a counsellor;
b) do your best to talk it over and sort it out:
c) feel fatalistic and give up?

15. If your partner hated cigarettes and you smoked 40 a day, would you:
a) give up;
b) cut down and try not to smoke near him;
c) carry on regardless?

16. When you were a kid playing with your Ken and Barbie toys, did you:
a) pretend they were opposing spies on secret missions;

b) have them helping each other in a hospital;
c) play house with them?

17. You've tried your hardest but your friends really don't get on with your partner, and vice versa. Do you:
a) change your friends;
b) change your partner;
c) just try and keep them apart?

18. Your partner's family are very religious, and they want you to convert and get married in a huge ceremony. Otherwise they threaten to try and turn him against you. Do you:
a) ignore them, and count on your partner's love;
b) tell your partner that you find his family and religion too disturbing to cope with;
c) convert and go through with the wedding?

19. Your partner is a classic rogue and treats you pretty badly. All your friends say he's no good for you. Do you:
a) dump him;
b) give him one more chance;
c) tell your friends they're wrong, he loves you really, they just don't know him like you do, etc.?

20. Your granny warns you that you're going to end up being an old maid. Are you:
a) petrified – suppose she's right?;
b) amused – the old dear's always harping on about marriage and kids, but she doesn't mean any harm;
c) confident – you're in no hurry, and you know there are plenty of good men out there?

How did you score?
1.	a) 3;	b) 2;	c) 1
2.	a) 3;	b) 2;	c) 1
3.	a) 1;	b) 3;	c) 2

4. a) 1;	b) 2;	c) 3
5. a) 2;	b) 1;	c) 3
6. a) 2;	b) 3;	c) 1
7. a) 3;	b) 1;	c) 2
8. a) 3;	b) 1;	c) 2
9. a) 2;	b) 1;	c) 3
10. a) 1;	b) 2;	c) 3
11. a) 1;	b) 3;	c) 2
12. a) 2;	b) 1;	c) 3
13. a) 3;	b) 1;	c) 2
14. a) 3;	b) 2;	c) 1
15. a) 3;	b) 2;	c) 1
16. a) 1;	b) 2;	c) 3
17. a) 3;	b) 1;	c) 2
18. a) 2;	b) 1;	c) 3
19. a) 1;	b) 2;	c) 3
20. a) 3;	b) 1;	c) 2

If you scored between 20 and 32:
It's safe to say that you don't spend your time daydreaming about Mr Right. In fact you might find that if he came along, you'd have no room to fit him in. Relationships and commitment are not your thing, at least not yet. You have other priorities. Perhaps you are very focused on your career, and not willing to jeopardise your prospects. Perhaps your friends provide all the support and intimacy you need, and you don't want to risk curtailing your social life. Either way, the words 'steady relationship' ring alarm bells for you, conjuring up images of tetchy partners, loss of freedom and the end of youth. This negative and partial view of what it's like to have someone love you could be revised in the light of a more experimental approach to experience. Why not say 'yes' next time someone asks and cohabit for a week or so to see if it's fun? Being independent doesn't have to mean being lonely.

If you scored between 33 and 47:

You are trying to keep a balance in your life between your need for love, support and understanding, and your desire to be free and independent. There are so many demands on your time, from so many conflicting sources, that it can be a real headache deciding your priorities. Do not despair – everyone is in the same boat – and look at the discussion of the difficulties of finding a place in your life for love in Chapter One. The main thing is that you have the will to try, without letting the urge to find a mate dominate your existence.

If you scored between 48 and 60:

Being in a loving relationship is important for lots of reasons – it may even be a biological necessity for humans. But you can overdo it. When the over-riding concern of your life is to secure a man it may be at the cost of your friends. There are few things more boring than a dedicated man-hunter, and you don't want to end up like the women in *When Harry Met Sally*, carrying boxes of index cards of the available men they know. More to the point, when you do lay hands on some manflesh, panic may blind you to a number of other factors, from his overbearing parents to how little you two have in common. At the end of the day if you become complete prey to the mating instinct you'll get the opposite of what you wanted: potential suitors will be scared!

2. THE CONFLICT QUESTIONNAIRE

Conflict is growing both at home and in the workplace. How well do you handle the emotions arising? Please tick *one* preference per section.

A. If someone is cross with me I typically:
1) grow flustered and lose control of my words;
2) escalate the conflict by shouting;
3) retreat and try to avoid a scene;
4) say sorry even though it's not my fault;

5) count to ten and ask for an explanation;
6) try to joke my way out of trouble;
7) send the other person to Coventry.

B. If I'm angry with someone else I typically:
1) shut up;
2) grow icily polite;
3) say firmly how much I dislike their behaviour;
4) look and feel wounded;
5) dump my feelings on a colleague, subordinate or family member;
6) suppress my irritation till forced to erupt;
7) write them off as beneath contempt.

C. If someone is angry with me my mood is usually one of:
1) guilt;
2) fear;
3) panic;
4) hurt;
5) self-control;
6) defiance;
7) anger.

D. If I'm angry with someone else I usually feel:
1) alarmed in case they hate me;
2) afraid in case I hurt their feelings;
3) comfortable because I'm making my point;
4) too emotional to think straight;
5) anxious in case I hit them;
6) exhilarated because I can shout;
7) enraged with everyone.

E. Finally – guess how many murders occur in the US workplace each year?
1) 50;
2) 400;
3) 700;

4) 1,100?

Scoring
Give yourself marks as follows:

Section A	Section B	Section C	Section D:
1) = 0	1) = 4	1) = 0	1) = 1
2) = 0	2) = 5	2) = 1	2) = 4
3) = 2	3) = 10	3) = 1	3) = 10
4) = 1	4) = 1	4) = 1	4) = 1
5) = 10	5) = 0	5) = 10	5) = 3
6) = 3	6) = 2	6) = 3	6) = 2
7) = 0	7) = 3	7) = 2	7) = 0

40 points – you truly excel at managing conflict;
20–35 – you handle anger with skill;
10–19 – specific responses need more practice;
Under 10 – till now, confronting anger has not been your strength.

The correct answer to E is 3)!

3. HOW HIGH IS YOUR LIBIDO?

Pick one answer to each question and add up your scores at the end:

1. How many times would you like to have sex in a week:
a) twice or less;
b) between two and five times;
c) five times at the very least?

2. When you make love with your partner do you usually:
a) have sex once;
b) have sex twice;
c) have an extended sex session that can last for hours?

3. To unwind after a stressful day would you rather:

286

a) have a luxurious bath and a sensual massage;
b) watch television and listen to music;
c) have sex on the living room floor?

4. If you haven't had sex for a month, are you:
a) climbing the walls;
b) pretty frustrated;
c) indifferent?

5. It's a sunny Sunday morning and you wake up with your partner beside you. Do you:
a) leap out of bed and suggest going for a walk;
b) leap on your partner and demand sex;
c) stay in bed dozing, talking, and perhaps getting around to sex when you're both fully awake?

6. You meet a gorgeous man at a party and you end up in bed together. Do you:
a) find the prospect of sex irresistible;
b) enjoy kissing and touching but save sex for when you get to know each other better;
c) wonder what you've got yourself into and suddenly feel inhibited?

7. You are talking on the phone to your new boyfriend who lives on the other side of town. It is midnight and he says he's feeling horny. Do you:
a) jump in a cab and go round;
b) tell him you can't wait to see him the next day;
c) tell him it's late and you both need some sleep?

8. You're not seeing anyone and you meet up with an old flame. After a few drinks do you:
a) suggest going to bed to relive old times;
b) become sentimental and tell him that you still fancy him;
c) enjoy his company but know that episode of your life is over?

9. Does foreplay take:
a) about a minute – you get turned on very quickly;
b) take between 10 and 30 minutes depending on your mood;
c) ages – you need loads of touching and kissing to make you feel aroused?

10. Do you ever worry that:
a) other people talk and think about sex more than you do;
b) your desire for sex gets you in trouble;
c) everyone goes on about sex a bit too much?

11. If you had to summarise your sexual relationships which statement would be most accurate:
a) my desire for sex matches that of my partner(s);
b) my lack of desire for sex has led to arguments;
c) my partner(s) has been pleased/overwhelmed/intimidated by my powerful sex drive?

12. How often do you masturbate or fantasise about sex:
a) every day;
b) probably about weekly, at least monthly;
c) it's been more than a month?

13. You see a stunning male model featured in a magazine. Do you:
a) think how wonderful it would be to seduce him;
b) get a kick out of looking at his body;
c) appreciate his good looks but don't dwell on the pictures?

14. A colleague you've always liked tells you that he finds you sexy. Do you:
a) feel thrilled and see him as a sexual opportunity;
b) simply enjoy the flattery;
c) think that his comment is inappropriate?

15. A good example of feeling lustful is:
a) wanting sex so much that you would do it in a public place;

b)   managing it twice in one night;
c)   tearing off your clothes as soon as you get home?

16. If your partner wanted sex all the time, would you:
a)   quickly get tired of his constant demands;
b)   try and keep up with him;
c)   breathe a sigh of relief that you've found a man who can keep up with you?

17. Do you think you'll still be interested in sex at:
a)   55;
b)   65;
c)   75?

18. In order to feel like having sex, do you need:
a)   no prompting at all;
b)   to be in the right mood;
c)   to be wined and dined and then given a hot bath and a sensual massage?

19. Your lover has been offered a job 200 miles away. Are you:
a)   worried at the thought of not being able to spend much time with him;
b)   worried that your phone bill will be huge;
c)   distraught that you'll only make love on weekends?

20. Your best friend says that she is cheating on her long-term boyfriend because she doesn't get enough sex. Do you:
a)   understand completely;
b)   think she should accept a small sacrifice for the sake of the relationship;
c)   think she's mad – what's sex got to do with love and commitment?

How did you score?

1. a) 1;	b) 2;	c) 3
2. a) 1;	b) 2;	c) 3
3. a) 2;	b) 1;	c) 3
4. a) 3;	b) 2;	c) 1
5. a) 1;	b) 3;	c) 2
6. a) 3;	b) 2;	c) 1
7. a) 3;	b) 2;	c) 1
8. a) 3;	b) 2;	c) 1
9. a) 3;	b) 2;	c) 1
10. a) 2;	b) 3;	c) 1
11. a) 2;	b) 1;	c) 3
12. a) 3;	b) 2;	c) 1
13. a) 3;	b) 2;	c) 1
14. a) 3;	b) 2;	c) 1
15. a) 3;	b) 1;	c) 2
16. a) 1;	b) 2;	c) 3
17. a) 1;	b) 2;	c) 3
18. a) 3;	b) 2;	c) 1
19. a) 2;	b) 1;	c) 3
20. a) 3;	b) 2;	c) 1

If you scored between 20 and 32:

When it comes to sex you can take it or leave it. This is not to say that you have an inadequate love life – simply that you also appreciate other aspects of relationships. Commitment and intimacy are maybe more important to you than what happens between the sheets. Your libido levels may simply be a matter of choice, or the result of upbringing. Maybe you were taught that sex is more for male than female pleasure? Naturally, things can change – it only takes a new attitude or a new relationship. Women reach their sexual peak after thirty, and many report a flowering of sexuality towards the menopause, so don't close your mind. Perhaps learning more about sex and your own sexual response would mean you could enjoy it more, moving it further up the agenda?

If you scored between 33 and 47:
Bedroom frolics may not occupy your every waking moment but you still know where to put good sex – at the top of your wish list. If the mood is right there's nothing you'd rather do, and if your partner makes the correct moves he can reduce you to putty. But there's more to you than lasciviousness. On a sunny day, your place is outside, and sometimes you'd rather talk than take off your clothes.

If you scored between 48 and 60:
You fall into an exclusive minority of people with high sex drive. If you were a dynamo you could light a street. You've probably got a rich fantasy life too, and work hard to make some of it come true. The only problem is finding the man who can keep up with you. The male of the species always claims to have only one thing on his mind, but with you he'll have to decide whether to put up or shut up. Many women probably feel as strongly as you about sex, but few can admit it. In today's new moral climate, where there's a lot more talk than action, it can be hard to get the satisfaction you crave – and deserve! Stick with it, because you'll put a great big smile on some lucky partner's face. While a high libido is perfectly healthy, and lots of fun, the danger is that you may neglect the other side of partnering. Remember, sex is often best when the rest of your relationship works too, and conversely, when it doesn't, your sex life may be the first thing to suffer. And you'd *hate* that!

4. HOW INHIBITED ARE YOU?

Pick one answer to each question and add up your scores at the end:

1. You walk into a room at a party where a porno film is being played. Do you:
a) threaten to phone the vice squad;
b) whip off all your clothes and suggest re-enacting key scenes;

291

c)   mingle discreetly with the audience?

2.   You want to shock your partner. Do you:
a)   get undressed with the lights on;
b)   answer the door naked;
c)   go for his prostate?

3.   Your boyfriend suggests anal sex. Do you:
a)   politely but firmly decline;
b)   tell him he's disgusting;
c)   produce a tube of KY Jelly with a twinkle in your eye?

4.   Your friends are discussing how messy sex is. Do you:
a)   regale them with tales of your flowback;
b)   laugh along with the others;
c)   excuse yourself from the conversation?

5.   If you heard your parents having sex, would you think:
a)   it's disgusting at their age;
b)   good on them;
c)   it's a bit embarrassing?

6.   A new lover proves to be very vocal when he comes. Are you:
a)   pleased that you've found a man who's not ashamed to let the world know how good it feels to be with you;
b)   petrified in case the neighbours hear;
c)   amused and keen to join in?

7.   You're at a dinner party with a mixed group of friends and someone suggests playing strip poker. Are you:
a)   too embarrassed to stay;
b)   tempted to lose as many hands as possible;
c)   reluctant at first but get into the spirit after a while?

8.   Your friend tells you about a party she went to that turned into an orgy (where safe sex was practised throughout of course). Are you:

a) intensely jealous;
b) disapproving of her loose morals;
c) curious but not exactly keen on the idea?

9. You're on the beach in Greece where everyone else is nude. Do you:
a) feel silly with your clothes on, and strip off without a second thought;
b) move to another beach;
c) go topless?

10. You and a friend go to an Ann Summers shop She urges you to buy a vibrator. Do you:
a) blush and tell her not to be ridiculous;
b) buy the most expensive one on offer;
c) buy some sexy lingerie instead?

11. You decide your sex life needs spicing up. Do you:
a) try a new position in bed;
b) cover yourself in whipped cream and get your partner to lick it off;
c) buy a clitoral stimulator?

12. Your partner accuses you of being strait-laced. Do you:
a) tell him that you are the normal one;
b) feel hurt but refuse to rise to the bait;
c) graphically prove him wrong?

13. Your boyfriend challenges you to see who can write the most erotic letter. Is yours:
a) way too steamy for a sex magazine;
b) guaranteed to have him howling at your door;
c) replete with coy euphemisms?

14. Your partner visits you at work and suggests that he provide some on-the-spot executive relief. Do you:
a) retire to a handy bathroom;

b) tell him it's for the bedroom, not the boardroom;
c) use the nearest cupboard, stationery room or photocopier alcove?

15. When you phone your partner do you:
a) end up having phone sex;
b) suggest some things you'd like to do to him;
c) ban the 'F' word?

16. You've gone to see a counsellor about feeling down, and she asks you to tell her about your love life. Do you:
a) clam up;
b) spill the beans, leaving no detail untold;
c) feel slightly self-conscious but reply to her questions?

17. You and your partner have gone to see a doctor about an STD. She asks you about the last time you had intercourse. Do you:
a) let your partner answer;
b) claim that you can't remember;
c) give a quick résumé of this week's sex?

18. You and your mum are watching a nature programme, but she's not paying attention. Suddenly two lions start graphically shagging. Do you:
a) change channels as quickly as possible and hope she didn't notice;
b) call her attention to the spectacle on screen;
c) watch without comment – it's only natural?

19. Your partner offers to swap fantasies with you. Do you:
a) agree on the condition that he goes first;
b) tell him one that'll give him goosebumps;
c) tell him that your fantasies are for private consumption only?

20. Your partner wants to do a 'Cosmo' sex quiz with you. Do you:

a) answer all the questions openly and truthfully;
b) refuse on the grounds that they are simply trivial nonsense;
c) want to look at his answers but keep yours to yourself?

How did you score?

	a)	b)	c)
1.	a) 1;	b) 3;	c) 2
2.	a) 1;	b) 2;	c) 3
3.	a) 2;	b) 1;	c) 3
4.	a) 3;	b) 1;	c) 2
5.	a) 1;	b) 3;	c) 2
6.	a) 3;	b) 1;	c) 2
7.	a) 1;	b) 3;	c) 2
8.	a) 3;	b) 1;	c) 2
9.	a) 3;	b) 1;	c) 2
10.	a) 1;	b) 3;	c) 2
11.	a) 1;	b) 2;	c) 3
12.	a) 1;	b) 2;	c) 3
13.	a) 3;	b) 2;	c) 1
14.	a) 2;	b) 1;	c) 3
15.	a) 3;	b) 2;	c) 1
16.	a) 1;	b) 3;	c) 2
17.	a) 2;	b) 1;	c) 3
18.	a) 1;	b) 3;	c) 2
19.	a) 2;	b) 3;	c) 1
20.	a) 3;	b) 1;	c) 2

If you scored between 20 and 32:
I expect you're thoroughly cheesed off with being told that you need to loosen up. Like it or not, you are decidedly lacking in the freedom of self-expression department. Perhaps your inhibitions only apply in the arena of sex? Few areas are regarded as so personal. There are very real fears of earning rejection or scorn, and it is with good reason that most of us are careful about how much we reveal. But you can swing too far the other way, and cut yourself off from a lot of exciting territory. Being more open and less inhibited could do wonders for your self-confidence. Check out some assertion classes as a way to make a new start.

If you scored between 33 and 47:
You have very definite limits to how open you are – and with
whom. You might be bold and daring with a trusted lover. But
you can still be self-conscious , and very private about some
intimate issues. Most of the time this is probably sensible –
friendships and relationships involve a constant, delicate
negotiation between our desire to open up and trust, and our
fear of being hurt. It is healthy to have a touch of cynicism
and maybe to keep a little in reserve (especially if you're
British!). Few of us would feel comfortable about shedding our
clothes and diving headlong into an orgy. We would be embarrassed about our bodies, embarrassed about our performance
and just plain embarrassed about being embarrassing. But
supposing your British reserve also denies you the chance of
true love and passion? How will you know unless you take
the plunge and risk looking stupid just for once?

If you scored between 48 and 60:
You are a real free spirit. When you're in a party mood you
throw caution to the wind and let nothing get in the way of a
good time. And with your friends and lovers you're honest,
open and upfront. In lots of ways you are a very lucky person:
either you're naturally free of the burden of guilt, shame and
self-consciousness that afflict the average Joanna, or you've
somehow overcome all those inner demons. Your sort of
openness can be a gift. You can give information about yourself,
making it easier for friends and partners to trust you and to
become intimate with you. You can deal well with difficult
emotions because you won't be afraid to express what you
feel. And you are more prepared to experiment and enjoy
aspects of sexuality that many people fail to sample. The one
danger is that being uninhibited can sometimes also mean
being inappropriate. Even if *you* have no difficulty with taboo
subjects, it may be wise to tread softly where others are
involved, and even to respect their hang-ups. A loud, boorish
extrovert telling them to 'lighten up' will simply confirm their
worst fears and prejudices.

5. HOW BISEXUAL ARE YOU?

Pick one answer to each question and add up your scores at
the end:
1. Do you believe that sexuality is:
a) black and white – you're either gay or straight;
b) changeable – there are no clear boundaries;
c) completely dependent on the gender of your current partner?

2. Do you feel that women are:
a) more likely to be able to please you sexually than men;
b) can be as attractive and sensual as men, but not really a
   turn-on sexually;
c) designed to appeal to men only?

3. Would you let a woman know that you found her attractive
   by:
a) paying her a straightforward compliment, as you would
   anyone;
b) being very attentive and indirectly flattering her;
c) using eye contact and flirting with her?

4. If you were to sleep with a woman would it be:
a) due to sexual curiosity;
b) to fulfil a deeply held sexual desire;
c) because you are occupying her partner's side of the bed
   for the night?

5. Would you suppress your feelings for a heterosexual
   woman because:
a) you would assume that your feelings were fleeting and you
   wouldn't take them seriously;
b) you couldn't trust yourself not to go too far;
c) you wouldn't have them in the first place?

6. When you fantasise during sex or masturbation are your
   fantasies:

a) sometimes about men and sometimes about women:
b) always about men and straight sex;
c) specifically about women?

7. With the woman that you have been closest to, have you:
a) been sexually intimate with her;
b) had an enduring platonic friendship with her;
c) sometimes wondered if you fancied her?

8. An old female friend comes out as a lesbian. Do you:
a) cut off all links with her;
b) not really understand and try to avoid the subject;
c) talk to her about your bisexual fantasies?

9. Your mother makes a disparaging comment about homo-sexuality. Do you:
a) agree that it's disgusting;
b) disagree and say that everyone is different;
c) feel guilty and keep quiet?

10. In a discussion about bisexuality you are most likely to express:
a) indifference;
b) disgust;
c) curiosity?

11. You and your friends end up in a club with a mixed gay/straight crowd. A woman asks you to dance. Do you:
a) feel thrilled and flattered, and agree to dance;
b) refuse and feel embarrassed;
c) feel very insulted and angry?

12. Your best female friend confesses to having sexual thoughts about you. Are you:
a) horrified;
b) upset and confused;

c) unsure about whether to confess the same?

13. If you wanted to try something different sexually would it:
a) always be something to do with the opposite sex;
b) be with another woman;
c) be with either sex?

14. If you could have sex with a very attractive man or a very attractive woman, would you:
a) choose the man immediately;
b) hesitate, then choose the man;
c) have a genuine dilemma about whom to choose?

15. After a drunken night you remember kissing a female friend. Are you:
a) mortified – you must have done it for a joke;
b) amused – you and your friend can have a good laugh about it;
c) intrigued and excited?

16. Your boyfriend finds you reading an erotic story about a lesbian encounter. Do you:
a) say that you hope that sort of thing doesn't turn him on because it certainly doesn't turn you on;
b) fantasise about the story when you make love with him;
c) admit that you find it exciting?

17. You see two women kissing each other in the street. Do you feel:
a) disgusted at the sight of lesbian behaviour in public;
b) that sort of thing should be done in private;
c) good for them?

18. If a lesbian started to work in the same office as you, would you:
a) be totally indifferent to her sexuality;

b) feel uneasy;
c) want to ask her lots of questions about her sexuality?

19. You've just read an article on women who pay female
    prostitutes for sex. Do you:
a) think it's an interesting idea;
b) think it's a horrible idea;
c) pick up the phone?

20. Your friends are recalling the female school teachers they
    had crushes on. Do you:
a) wonder how they could have ever fancied a female teacher;
b) feel nostalgic as you remember the crush you had on one
   of your own teachers;
c) laugh at the silly phases teenagers go through?

How did you score?

1.	a) 2;	b) 4;	c) 5
2.	a) 5;	b) 3;	c) 2
3.	a) 3;	b) 4;	c) 5
4.	a) 4;	b) 5;	c) 3
5.	a) 4;	b) 5;	c) 3
6.	a) 4;	b) 3;	c) 5
7.	a) 5;	b) 3;	c) 4
8.	a) 1;	b) 2;	c) 4
9.	a) 1;	b) 3;	c) 4
10.	a) 3;	b) 1;	c) 4
11.	a) 4;	b) 3;	c) 1
12.	a) 1;	b) 2;	c) 4
13.	a) 2;	b) 5;	c) 4
14.	a) 2;	b) 4;	c) 5
15.	a) 2;	b) 3;	c) 4
16.	a) 2;	b) 5;	c) 4
17.	a) 1;	b) 2;	c) 3
18.	a) 3;	b) 2;	c) 4
19.	a) 4;	b) 1;	c) 5
20.	a) 1;	b) 4;	c) 2

If you scored between 35 and 52:
Bisexuality is certainly off your sexual menu. Not only that, but you may be intolerant of people who are bisexual or homosexual. Perhaps you have inherited rigid sexual codes from your parents, or you grew up in an aggressively heterosexual environment? Whatever the reason, it is worth asking why you feel so hostile. Try to accept that although you've chosen to place yourself on the 'straight' end of the spectrum it would be a dull old world if we were all identical.

If you scored between 53 and 71:
You are content with your sexuality and don't see any reason to question it. You are tolerant and try not to judge other people's behaviour, although if you are forced to confront the issue of bisexuality, it's possible that you may become embarrassed, reticent or a little unsure of yourself. Perhaps, privately, you are curious about bisexuality and would like to know more? Alternatively, you may be completely at home with bisexuality: you would kiss another woman for a dare or a laugh, but it really wouldn't be anything more deeply rooted than that – you know that your sexual allegiances are most definitely with men.

If you scored between 72 and 80:
You are sexually open to both men and women, if not in practice then in theory. Bisexuality has different meanings for different women. For some, it's a way of life: you can sleep with either sex with equal pleasure. For others, it is an aspect of their sexuality that only surfaces occasionally: you may have had one or several sexual experiences with women, but you still define yourself as heterosexual. For others, bisexuality is an intriguing thought: you have never had an experience with a woman but you think you would like to. For others still, same-sex experiences are something to be fantasised about but not acted upon: erotic thoughts about lesbianism can prove exciting – perhaps you share them with your partner – but you cannot imagine actually sleeping with a woman.

Further Reading

Here are some of the books that might give you further knowledge and pleasure:

Adultery by Annette Lawson
A Woman's Guide to Adultery by Carol Clulow
Emotional Intelligence by Daniel Goleman
Families and How to Survive Them by John Cleese and Robyn Skinner
Friendship by Steve Duck
Jane Eyre by Charlotte Brontë
Love in the Time of the Cholera by Gabriel Garcia Marquez
Men, An Investigation into the Emotional Male by Phillip Hodson
New Joy of Sex by Alex Comfort
New Passages by Gail Sheehy
Nothing Natural by Jenni Diski
Persuasion by Jane Austen
Sex in the Forbidden Zone by Peter Rutter
Sexual Intimacy by Anne Hooper
The Age of Innocence by Edith Wharton
The Midnight Partner by Bart Davis
Wuthering Heights by Emily Brontë